THE
CINEMA
OF
SATYAJIT RAY

Bhaskar Chattopadhyay is an author, translator and screenwriter who lives and works in Bangalore, India. His translations include *14: Stories That Inspired Satyajit Ray* (HarperCollins, 2014) and Bibhutibhushan Bandyopadhyay's *Aranyak* (Penguin Random House, 2022). He has novelised Satyajit Ray's seminal film *Nayak* (HarperCollins, 2018). His own works include the novels *Patang* (Hachette, 2016), *Here Falls the Shadow* (Hachette, 2017) and *The Disappearance of Sally Sequeira* (Hachette, 2018).

Praise for *The Cinema of Satyajit Ray*

'Its first part contains short narrations with his [Bhaskar Chattopadhyay's] informed opinions on all of Ray's films—feature, short feature and documentary—arranged chronologically. This would delight the new readers and work as a handy companion to the viewers of Ray's cinema. But, the second part of the book, appropriately titled "Meditations on Ray, His Films, His Film-Making"—all in the form of intelligent question-answer pieces, would interest even those cineastes fairly acquainted with his ouevre.'
Amitabha Bhattacharya, *The Book Review*

'[A] good addition to the ever-growing library of works on the film maker. It will provide a very good frame of reference for further research on the cinema of Satyajit Ray.'
Shoma A. Chatterji, *Hindustan Times*

'This work in English could be characterised as a Satyajit Ray dictionary.'
G. Pramod, *Manorama*, in Malayalam

THE CINEMA OF SATYAJIT RAY

BHASKAR CHATTOPADHYAY

WESTLAND
NON-FICTION

First published by Westland Non-Fiction, an imprint of Westland Publications Private Limited, in 2021

Published by Westland Non-Fiction, an imprint of Westland Books, a division of Nasadiya Technologies Private Limited, in 2023

No. 269/2B, First Floor, 'Irai Arul', Vimalraj Street, Nethaji Nagar, Allappakkam Main Road, Maduravoyal, Chennai 600095

Westland, the Westland logo, Westland Non-Fiction and the Westland Non-Fiction logo are the trademarks of Nasadiya Technologies Private Limited, or its affiliates.

All interior photographs courtesy: Society for the Preservation of Satyajit Ray Archives.

Bhaskar Chattopadhyay asserts the moral right to be identified as the author of this work.

ISBN: 9789357761369

10 9 8 7 6 5 4 3 2 1

Typeset by R. Ajith Kumar
Printed at Nutech Print Services-India

CONTENTS

Introduction   ix

Part I: The Films of Satyajit Ray

Pather Panchali: A Song of the Little Road (1955)   3

Aparajito: The Unvanquished (1956)   9

Parash Pathar: The Philosopher's Stone (1958)   14

Jalsaghar: The Music Room (1958)   18

Apur Sansar: The World of Apu (1959)   23

Devi: The Goddess (1960)   28

Postmaster (1961)   34

Monihara: The Lost Jewels (1961)   38

Samapti: The Conclusion (1961)   42

Rabindranath Tagore (1961)   47

Kanchenjungha (1962)   52

Abhijan: The Expedition (1962)   57

Mahanagar: The Big City (1963)   62

Charulata: The Lonely Wife (1964)   67

Two (1964)   72

Kapurush: The Coward (1965)   76

Mahapurush: The Holy Man (1965)   80

Nayak: The Hero (1966)   85

Chiriyakhana: The Zoo (1967)   90

Goopy Gyne Bagha Byne: The Adventures of Goopy
     and Bagha (1969)   94

Aranyer Din Ratri: Days and Nights of the Forest (1969)   99
Pratidwandi: The Adversary (1970)   104
Seemabaddha: Company Limited (1971)   109
Sikkim (1971)   114
The Inner Eye (1972)   118
Ashani Sanket: The Distant Thunder (1973)   122
Sonar Kella: The Golden Fortress (1974)   126
Jana Aranya: The Middleman (1975)   130
Bala (1976)   134
Shatranj Ke Khilari: The Chess Players (1977)   138
Joy Baba Felunath: The Elephant God (1979)   143
Hirak Rajar Deshe: The Kingdom of Diamonds (1980)   147
Pikoo (1980)   151
Sadgati: Deliverance (1981)   155
Ghare Baire: The Home and the World (1984)   159
Sukumar Ray (1987)   163
Ganashatru: An Enemy of the People (1990)   167
Shakha Proshakha: Branches of a Tree (1990)   171
Agantuk: The Stranger (1992)   175

Part II: Meditations on Ray, His Films, His Film-Making

Aparna Sen: 'Ray's greatest strength was his power of
    suggestion'   183

Barun Chanda: '*Seemabaddha* is an accurate depiction of the
    rat race in the corporate world'   194

Chandak Sengoopta: 'Ray is profoundly out of fashion
    in academic circles'   203

Dhritiman Chaterji: 'Satyajit Ray did not believe in god'   214

Jai Arjun Singh: 'Many of the more mainstream Indian
    filmmakers felt a bit intimidated by Ray'   222

M.K. Raghavendra: 'Ray himself was a very good critic,
   though he didn't write much criticism'   227

Madhabi Mukherjee: 'In his films, Satyajit Ray has never
   shown any ugliness'   232

Mamata Shankar: '*Agantuk* was the culmination of one of
   the most illustrious careers in cinema history'   239

Neeraj Ghaywan: 'Ray never compromised his narrative
   for the sake of his politics'   249

Oliver Craske: 'Satyajit Ray was a polymath talent, but the flip
   side of that is being a bit of a control freak'   256

Pradip Mukherjee: 'Even on the first day of the shoot, every
   single person in the unit knew that the whole film had
   already been made in his head'   266

Sharmila Tagore: 'Whenever I travel abroad, wherever there
   is good cinema, people know me because of *Devi*'   272

Shyam Benegal: 'If Satyajit Ray would have made a film today,
   the state wouldn't dare to interfere with it in any way'   278

Siddhartha Chatterjee: 'Not a single Bengali parent in the 1980s
   or the 1990s named their child "Topshe"'   285

Srijit Mukherji: 'To someone like me, Satyajit Ray is like a
   multistorey library'   295

Tinnu Anand: 'Tinnu, I don't want you to feel like an
   outsider!'   302

Vikramaditya Motwane: 'Satyajit Ray was India's greatest
   complete filmmaker'   309

Acknowledgements   316

INTRODUCTION

I WAS INTRODUCED TO THE CINEMA OF SATYAJIT RAY BY MY FATHER, when I must have been about nine or ten years old. My father had a government job in a small town in Assam and my parents were keen that I learn the Bengali language, despite it not being taught as a subject in school. Very early on in my childhood, therefore, my mother introduced me to the language, starting with abridged editions of Indian mythological epics, then moving on to comics and finally to other literature. I am not quite sure, but as far as I can remember, I think I may have read Ray's literature before I was introduced to his cinema. But what I do remember was that like any other child from a Bengali household, the first Ray film I ever watched was *Goopy Gyne Bagha Byne* (The Adventures of Goopy and Bagha). I remember it was love at first sight. My parents were regular visitors to the cinema and I would often go with them. But never had I watched anything like this before. Here was a film that did not exhibit that extremely annoying trait of assuming that just because I was a child, I was childish, that I had to be spoken to in a sing-song voice or that I did not know the ways of the world. I was as hooked to the screen as my parents were. For the first time, I was being treated as an equal.

The more I grew up, the more I realised that simplicity was the hallmark of a Ray film. This simplicity came from a rare trait that any filmmaker in the world can hope to possess—the confidence that his or her audience is intelligent. This is not very difficult to understand if you think about it. We respect those who respect us, don't we? If someone talks down to us or tries to show off, we get put off instantly. The same happens in the arts. Every artist in the world has a way of saying things. Although there are many other connotations to the word, in simple terms, this can be called the artist's 'voice'. Ray's voice had a unique trait: it liked to say only so much—just enough to express his thoughts. No more, no less. The Roman poet Horace once asked, 'If you can realistically render a cypress tree, would you include one when commissioned to paint a sailor in the midst of a shipwreck?' A rather pertinent question. Just because you have the knowledge and the ability to say a lot on a subject, doesn't mean you need to. Art is as much about what not to say than about what to.

Nor are Ray's films esoteric, by any stretch of the imagination. He always made films that could be easily understood by everyone. This fascination for effective communication is often reflected in Ray's literature too, in which, time and again, he expresses his dislike for art that can be understood and appreciated only by a small group of people. His films, therefore, were never solely for the purpose of making a deep and grave philosophical statement; nor were they merely a form of light entertainment and escape. The fact that he was able to strike a fine balance between the two is what made someone like me fall in love with his cinema.

In writing this book too, I have tried to follow the teachings of Ray. If there is anything this book is *not*, it's a textbook. It is not intended to be a deep, analytical study of his films, nor of his filmmaking. This book is primarily meant to take the films of Ray to a larger audience, to tell them that Ray's films are accessible, that they can be easily understood and that even in all their simplicity, they give us beautiful messages without ever trying to be preachy. They tell us stories that we can all understand and relate to, derive joy from and marvel at. If anything, this book is my humble but sincere attempt to break down the invisible, unwritten and omnipresent class system in film appreciation—the very notion that one person's understanding of a film is any better or worse than that of another.

The book, as you will see, has been divided into two sections. The first carries essays—one each for the thirty-nine films that Ray made in his career. These essays were first published in a weekly column I had written for the web portal *Firstpost*, from 2017 to 2018. Those who had followed the column had repeatedly asked me to publish these essays in the form of a book, and although the suggestion had merit, the only reason I kept postponing the idea was because I felt there would be something missing in such a book, if indeed it were to come out. But for the life of me, I was not being able to pinpoint what lacuna that would be. In the spring of 2021, while soaking in the sun on the terrace of a beautiful holiday home in the verdant hills of the Nilgiris, it suddenly struck me that to truly understand the films of Ray, one would have to understand Ray the filmmaker as well. That is when the idea of the interviews came to me. Since I had myself never had the good fortune of meeting Ray, I decided to speak to those who had worked closely with him, studied his life and works, and/or had been influenced by his cinema. All for one purpose— to try and understand the man behind the films. If the first part of this book is about the art, you will find that the second is about the artist.

Since this book is not a textbook, I do not have any advice for you to read it in any specific manner. Please feel free to read it in any way that suits you. I do have two requests to make, though—I feel these will help you understand the text better. Since Ray mostly made films in the Bengali language and worked with cast and crew from Bengal, some of the essays and interviews might have terms and honorifics that are quintessentially Bengali. For instance, Ray has often been referred to in this book as 'Manik-da', 'Manik Kaku' and 'Manik Jethu'. 'Manik' (the Bengali word for gem, no less!) was Ray's pet name. The term 'da' respectfully refers to an elder brother, just as the words 'kaku' and 'jethu' mean uncle, depending on whether the gentleman being referred to is younger to or older than the speaker's own father. You may find other such words in the text as well. Wherever possible, a translation has been provided. But as with even the best translations in the world, some part of the essence of the message or the emotion may have been lost. This is a loss that I can only hope to minimise but not eradicate. My first request, therefore, is to trust me when I say that I have tried my best to capture the spirit of the original in my translation. And the second would be to watch the films that I have discussed in this book. I will consider this book a success only if it has created an urge in you to witness, appreciate, criticise and analyse the cinema of Satyajit Ray.

Bhaskar Chattopadhyay
Bangalore, 2021

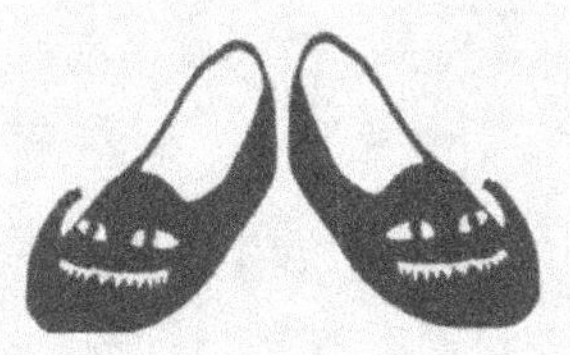

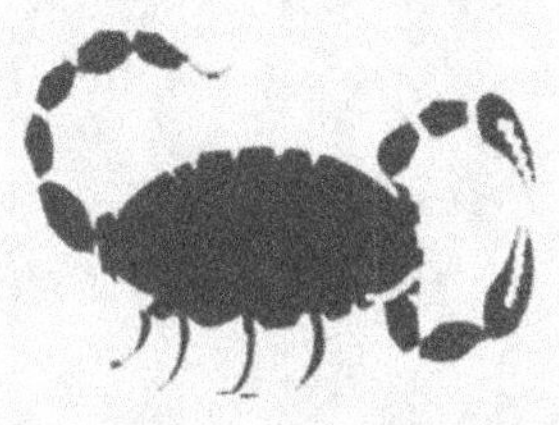

PART I

THE FILMS OF SATYAJIT RAY

Pather Panchali

A Song of the Little Road (1955)

During my six-month-long stay in London, I watched ninety-nine films. My first travel outside the country would thus be etched in my memory forever, for all the beautiful films I watched. But the one film that truly had an impact on my mind was Vittorio De Sica's Bicycle Thieves. The appeal of the film cannot be described in mere words. But what appealed to me, even more, was the fact that whatever I had ever wanted to do in my films, De Sica had done exactly the same, and quite successfully at that. Who said inexperienced people cannot be made to act? Who said one can't shoot in the middle of the rains? Who said make-up is mandatory? If my mind was looking for a sanction for everything radical that I had wanted to do if I ever made a film, I had found it in that one film by De Sica. I stayed in the continent for one more month, touring Paris, Venice, Lucerne and Salzburg. Then I returned to London and boarded a ship to return home. It was on this voyage back home that I wrote the first draft of Pather Panchali.

THESE ARE THE WORDS OF SATYAJIT RAY. IT IS NOW A WIDELY KNOWN fact that his debut film, *Pather Panchali*, took Indian cinema to a whole

Apu and Durga symbolise childlike innocence in the face of abject poverty.

new level. It made the world sit up and take notice of our cinema, which, before the film came along, was looked upon merely as a means of escape from reality. The fact that cinema can be used as a medium to tell real human stories and that it has a space independent of other performing arts such as the opera or the theatre, was largely unknown, and certainly not practised. But the history of Indian cinema dates back to as early as the end of the nineteenth century. We had been making films for decades before Ray made his debut in 1955. Why is it, then, that his film suddenly brought a new wave of thought in our cinema? What is so special about *Pather Panchali* that even today, it stands out, strong and tall, as the beacon of Indian cinema in the world? Before we try and answer that question, a few quick words about the film itself.

Pather Panchali is based on Bibhutibhushan Bandyopadhyay's novel of the same name. Bandyopadhyay was Ray's favourite novelist, because, according to Ray, no one described the joyous beauty of nature and its impact on the human mind as elegantly as Bandyopadhyay did. *Pather Panchali*—the film—does not have a story in the conventional sense of the term. It describes the harsh life of a poor Brahmin family in a village of Bengal. The father—Harihar—an educated priest, is an optimist, and pursues his literary ambitions without caring where the family's next meal is going to come from. His wife, Sarbajaya, has a firmer grip on the household and hence comes across as a strict and ill-tempered woman. She is perpetually worried about the future of her children—Apu and Durga—and resents the fact that her husband has to feed and shelter his sister, the eighty-year-old widow, Indir Thakrun. The film largely follows the lives of the two children, who, despite their poverty, find great joy in the pure beauty of their village and its surroundings.

Pather Panchali has been critically acclaimed for its humanism, but that's only one of the many reasons it is considered a great film. It is not like Western audiences had not seen humanism on screen before. A significant influence on Ray, Jean Renoir's 1945 film *The Southerner* is a classic example. But if you take a closer look at *Pather Panchali*, you'll realise that Ray's mastery over the medium of film is derived from the same source as Bandyopadhyay's skill with the written word—and it lies in the very *manner* a scene is depicted. Consider, for instance, the scene in which a sweetmeat vendor passes by Apu and Durga's house. The two children are poor, they do not have money to buy sweets, but why should that stop them from following the man along as he makes his way through the muddy roads of the village? And why shouldn't a street dog follow them too? The image of the vendor, carrying a basket of joy on his shoulder, followed by a pre-teen Durga, followed by her brother Apu and finally a dog—reflected in the tranquil waters of the village pond—makes for such a magnificent juxtaposition of poverty, innocence and the simple pleasures of life. There are thousands of ways this scene could have been depicted, but like a true master who knows his craft, Ray chose this one—and stole our hearts.

The film is filled with such beautiful palettes. Every frame is a painting in itself—a beautiful depiction of village life or a fascinating study of human nature. Watch as the frail old Indir Thakrun gets thrown out of the house by a heavily pregnant Sarbajaya, but an excited Durga brings her back a few days later for a glimpse of the newborn Apu. The simplicity of the scene is far more precious than the years of experience professional actors could have brought in. When the same Indir Thakrun is found lying dead in the middle of a bamboo grove by Apu and Durga, the tall bamboo trees creaking gently in the breeze as the two children witness death for the first time, we realise that no amount of production budget and technical wizardry can achieve what the simple and sincere habit of observation can. A seasoned artist, Ray had the watchful eye of a painter, and an open mind that was willing to accept and absorb the various shades of life. This is evident in the famous scene in which Apu and Durga wander out in search of a calf and see a train for the first time in their lives—a massive beast whose angry roars they had only heard from their village. As the iron serpent rumbles its way through a field full of white catkins, it leaves a trail of dark smoke against the cloudless sky.

Is it only the aesthetics, then, that make *Pather Panchali* the film it is today? Most decisively not. Because the film makes brilliant statements too—about human life, poverty, the very notion of happiness. Harihar is an aspiring playwright—everyone respects him because he is a learned Brahmin, and yet, there is no tangible value to either his literary genius or his lineage. Sarbajaya knows that her resentment towards her aged sister-in-law is wrong, but every time she feels the pangs of conscience, she summons the memories of the old hag stealing from her kitchen, if only to justify her own cruel actions. Poverty is shown as a strange thing—one that promptly breaks down all conventional norms of right and wrong. Indir Thakrun is aware that she has no place to go, and she feels the hurt and the angst when her brother's wife insults her, but her love for the family is far stronger, and she keeps turning up like a bad penny. Durga, the firstborn, is close to her aunt, and steals guavas from a neighbour's orchard to bring to the old lady. Watch her witness a girlfriend's wedding with longing in her eyes, knowing very well that her parents will probably never find a good bridegroom for her. And then, there's Apu—the pampered son, taken care of by everyone in the family. At the end of the film, when tragedy strikes, and neither his mother nor his sister is around to take care of him, he takes a dip in the village pond all by himself, combs his hair, puts on a dhoti and a *chadar*, and steps out of the house with an umbrella in his hand that is almost as big as himself. It is that one moment—that moment of realisation in Apu that he has grown up, and that there is now a void in his life left behind by dear ones—that the rest of the film culminates in. And it is a moment that will take your breath away.

One can go on and on about the many marvels of the film: the soul-stirring music by Ravi Shankar, for instance, or the beautiful camerawork by Subrata Mitra, who—believe it or not—had never so much as looked down a film camera before in his life, or the remarkable art direction of Bansi Chandragupta. Shot entirely on location, on a shoestring budget, mostly with actors who were facing the camera for the first time, and technicians with virtually no experience of filmmaking whatsoever, Ray accomplished what seasoned filmmakers with sound financial support could not in decades—neither before *Pather Panchali*, nor after it. For as long as the medium of film exists, and as long as people watch cinema, *Pather Panchali* will remain one of the greatest films ever made and a reminder that one may need money to make a good film, but one needs a deep and respectful understanding of human nature to make a great one.

Aparajito
The Unvanquished (1956)

AFTER THE UNPRECEDENTED POPULARITY OF HIS DEBUT FILM *Pather Panchali*, the idea of filming a sequel began to emerge in Satyajit Ray's mind. The fact that Bibhutibhushan Bandyopadhyay's novel of the same name (on which Ray had made his first film) had a sequel, and that it told the story of Apu in a new setting and explored the relationship between a widowed mother and her adolescent son, appealed to Ray as a fascinating subject for cinema. In 1956, a year after the release of *Pather Panchali*, Ray made *Aparajito*.

A few years have passed since Durga's death. Harihar has finally realised that there's nothing left for him and his family in the village of Nishchindipur. The family has moved to Kashi (Varanasi), where its situation is shown to have improved considerably. The shadows of the hand-to-mouth existence that Sarbajaya had become so used to living under have now been lifted. Harihar works as a priest on the ghats by the holy river and earns enough for the household. Apu has found new friends in Kashi. But tragedy strikes the family again with the untimely death of Harihar. As would have happened in any ordinary male-centric middle-class household in India in those days, the death of the bread earner thrusts Sarbajaya and her son into poverty once again. She takes up the job of a cook in a rich household of Kashi, but decides to give

As he begins to discover a new world, young Apu grows distant from his widowed mother.

it up when her uncle comes visiting and asks her to come with him to his village in Bengal.

In the village, young Apu decides to go to school. He is a keen learner and soon secures a scholarship that promises to pay for his college fees. Young, intelligent and ambitious, Apu soon leaves for Calcutta (now Kolkata). Sarbajaya is left all alone in the village. As Apu relishes his new-found freedom and basks in the warmth of a new life with new friends and experiences, Sarbajaya worries about her son and pines for a glimpse of him—for he is all she is left with now. Her health deteriorates and she begins to wither away. When Apu comes home during the holidays, he learns that his mother has passed away. As Apu laments the death of his mother, he realises that he is left all alone in the world now, having lost everyone—his old aunt, his sister and his parents.

The film deals with a subject that is universal—the relationship between a parent and a child, at a tender time when the parent is ageing and the child is growing up. Talking about the film, noted film critic Roger Ebert said, 'The relationship between Apu and his mother observes truths that must exist in all cultures: how the parent makes sacrifices for years, only to see the child turn aside and move thoughtlessly away into adulthood.'*

Among all of Ray's commentaries on the new versus the old, *Aparajito* is the purest, the most timeless and the most important one. It crystallises the thoughts that go through every parent's mind as he or she watches, in mute acceptance, the child discovering new wings to fly away into another world—a world in which the parent has no place. But what is even more important to note is that the film also deals with the duelling emotions that run through the mind of the child as he passes through this difficult phase of metamorphosis—his ambitions and his desire for a better life perpetually at war with the very roots that prevent him from flying high. This is depicted beautifully in a scene from the film. Apu has come home to visit his mother, but his heart lies in the city and

---

* Roger Ebert, *The Great Movies*, Crown, 2003.

its many attractions. He soon realises that the life he has left behind in the city is now his true life and is hence in a hurry to return, refusing to stay for even one more day. His mother is saddened to see this, but Apu doesn't seem to care. It seems he has not even noticed his mother's grief as he leaves to catch a train back to the city. At the station, after having purchased a ticket, as Apu is waiting for the train, we can see that his mind is not at rest. And we know then that we had been wrong about him all along, and that he is neither unaware of nor indifferent to his mother's pain. The train pulls into the station, but in the very next shot, Apu is seen coming back home. As a shocked Sarbajaya hugs her son and asks him why he has returned, a smiling Apu simply says, 'I missed the train.'

It is this unstated love and sacrifice for each other—blossoming amid a simmering tension of breaking old shackles to embrace a new world—that makes *Aparajito* a great film and a timeless classic. Karuna Banerjee is perfect as Sarbajaya—the woman who has seen more dead bodies than days of happiness. Even when her household's financial situation improves briefly, her woes hardly cease to exist, as she keeps fighting off a debauched neighbour who lusts after her. Banerjee brings a certain hopelessness to her character, as opposed to her husband's undying optimism. When she loses everything, she is content with her son staying with her in the village and earning his bread through priesthood. But the mind of the son, played beautifully by Smaran Ghoshal, has already been ignited by the new world. Priesthood is too archaic an idea for him now, as he learns about the amazing stories of the Aurora Borealis, the Eskimos, the adventures of Dr Livingstone and the lives of famous scientists such as Galileo, Newton and Faraday. He now wants to know more, explore further, and refuses to remain rooted to a place. Unwilling to make the same mistake he saw his father make, and haunted by the memories of the repercussions that followed, he promptly packs his bags and leaves for the city, almost in a hurry.

Technically speaking, *Aparajito* is nothing short of a marvel. It is now a widely known fact that cinematographer Subrata Mitra invented the concept of 'bounce lighting' for the film—and this idea went on to be practised by filmmakers all over the world. To film the scenes of the inner courtyard of Harihar's house in Kashi, art director Bansi Chandragupta built the set of the entire courtyard in a studio in Calcutta. But no matter how much he tried, he could not get the diffused daylight that is often seen to pour in through the open top of such a courtyard during the morning hours. Mitra solved this problem by covering the top of the set with a white painter's cloth and then bouncing studio lights off the white cloth to give the impression of daylight seeping into the courtyard from the top. If you watch the scenes on screen, there is no way you will be able to tell that the courtyard is, in fact, a set, or that there's a fake sky above the actors' heads!

Aparajito deserves special mention for the haunting background score by Ravi Shankar. The film also marks the beginning of Ray's fascination with recording ambient sounds and using them to highlight the mood of a scene—a practice he continued until his last film, made thirty-six years later. The train returns as a connecting motif. As Sarbajaya sits in her backyard and looks out at the fields, she can see the train chugging along against the horizon, much like Apu and Durga had in a field full of white catkins in *Pather Panchali*.

Aparajito did not find success at the box office but was critically acclaimed all over the world. It won many awards and is now considered a timeless classic. It is a worthy successor to *Pather Panchali* and beautifully paves the way for Ray's 1959 film, *Apur Sansar*. Together, these three films constitute what is now known as the Apu trilogy.

Parash Pathar

The Philosopher's Stone (1958)

IN 1958, AFTER MAKING TWO 'SERIOUS' FILMS, NAMELY *PATHER Panchali* and *Aparajito*, both of which were critically acclaimed but commercially unsuccessful, Satyajit Ray wanted to make something light-hearted, something with which he could connect with the average cine-goer in Bengal. There were two choices that appealed to his sensibilities—either a film with song and dance or a film with humour. With this end in mind, Ray set out to make *Jalsaghar*, which was to have elaborate song-and-dance sequences in it. But one thing led to another, and he had to make and release another film first—one that he adapted from a comic short story written by veteran Bengali author Rajshekhar Bose, also known by his pen name Parashuram. This film was titled *Parash Pathar* (The Philosopher's Stone), and it is perhaps the most criminally underrated film that the veteran filmmaker ever directed in his career spanning thirty-seven years.

The story of the film is simple. By and large, Ray did not deviate too much from the original short story while adapting it for the screen. A middle-aged, middle-class Bengali bank clerk named Paresh Dutta is stuck in the rain while returning from office one evening. He takes shelter in a park, where he stumbles upon a small, shiny pebble. He picks it up and brings it home without giving it much thought, but it soon turns out

Even after stumbling upon the fabled philosopher's stone, Paresh Chandra Dutta realises that his troubles are far from over.

that the pebble is the mythical Philosopher's Stone, which can magically turn any base metal it comes in contact with into pure gold. Paresh's fortune takes a sudden and drastic turn for the better and he becomes a rich man. But he soon realises that not only is keeping wealth far more difficult than earning it, but also that all the gold in the world cannot buy some of the most basic things in life.

Essentially a comedy, the film is perhaps the only one in Ray's filmography that is rather Chaplinesque in nature—in that it always presents its humour with an underlying layer of pathos. For instance, in the film's opening scene, the narrator rues the misfortune of the middle-class, office-going clerks of Bengal, whose fortunes turn according to the whims and fancies of their British bosses. In another brilliant scene towards the middle of the film, Paresh's wife, Giribala, laments that although she now has everything she could wish for, she misses her old neighbours from the seedy by-lane where she used to live. Just as the humour is never in your face, the tragedy, too, is invariably subtle. Little details, such as the fact that the Duttas never let go of their old and faithful servant or that they are always generous in their donations, endear them to the audience, which feels for them when the tragedy strikes.

Despite the financial constraints under which Ray had to work early on in his career, the film was technically brilliant. For one, it had some clever use of light, especially in a brilliantly shot scene at a cocktail party to which Paresh is invited, and in which, despite all his wealth, he struggles to find social acceptance. In another side-scrolling scene, juxtaposing common pedestrians with the lavish Governor's House in Calcutta, Paresh is seen hastily walking back home after a charity football match, knowing well that his tattered umbrella will not protect him from the impending thunderstorm. In yet another scene, the poor clerk decides to throw the magical stone away, out of sheer fear of god's wrath, but changes his mind when he accidentally finds himself in the middle of an industrial dump yard, with mound after mound of metal scrap spread out as far as his eyes can see, the possibilities now slowly beginning to emerge in his head. With these scenes, Ray successfully connects with the fears and insecurities of the common man. These scenes illustrate that Ray's genius was anything but a one- or two-film wonder. Also, consider this. The film's lead role is played by a gentleman named Tulsi Chakarabarti—a veteran Bengali character actor—of whom Ray had once said that without him, no comic scene in Bengali cinema would be complete. And yet, Ray uses him to depict the tragedy in the delusion of contentment that wealth has to offer. Only a skilful director, ably supported by a master actor, can achieve something like that.

Humour, as we all know, is a difficult thing to execute and achieve. Among others, the one tricky aspect about humour is that it works best in the context of its own milieu, and this is even more true when it is presented on screen, when it plays out in front of one's eyes. *Parash Pathar* is an apt example of this. Lauded more in Bengal than anywhere outside of it, and failing almost outright with foreign audiences, the film never got its due, which is why it hardly features in any discussion of Ray's cinema. But make no mistake, it is one of the finest films that Ray has made. While its humour may not have had universal reach, the message of the film is no less far-reaching. The humanism that Ray is known for—both in the Occident and closer home—is very much part of the film. Its unmistakeable presence is vouched for by the fact that in *Parash Pathar*, Ray shows, with admirable dexterity and without being preachy in even a single shot, that true magic lies inside a man's heart, and that even a simple act of kindness can turn any base emotion into pure gold.

Jalsaghar

The Music Room (1958)

AFTER THE BOX-OFFICE FAILURE OF *APARAJITO*—THE SECOND FILM
in the Apu trilogy—Satyajit Ray was in desperate need to make a hit
film. It was then that he decided to study the mind of the average Bengali
middle-class cine-goer to understand what they usually looked for in a
film. Song and dance, he figured, and a dash of comedy. He made up
his mind and decided to cater to both these demands of the audience.
In 1958, he made two films—the excellent comedy *Parash Pathar* (The
Philosopher's Stone) and *Jalsaghar* (The Music Room), a film richly
filled with songs and dances.

Jalsaghar is one of Ray's many commentaries on the subject of old
versus new. While in some of his later films—especially the City trilogy—
he shows the new in poor light and endorses age-old values and belief
systems, in his earlier films such as *Jalsaghar* and *Devi*, he describes what
happens when we are either unable or unwilling to let go of old, archaic
and rotting rules and norms to make room for the new.

Jalsaghar is based on a popular long short story written by
Tarashankar Bandyopadhyay. Aged zamindar Bishwambhar Roy spends
his days in his dilapidated palace on the banks of a river. His days of
glory are over, thanks to the river, which is slowly swallowing his land
and closing in on his mansion, and which has also claimed the lives of

Bishwambhar Roy settles down for an evening of music, dance and wine.

his beloved wife and son in a boating accident on a stormy monsoon night. When he was a young man, the irrepressible Bishwambhar Roy used to roll in materialistic pleasures. Night after night, he used to drown himself in wine, attending music and dance recitals that he set up in the majestic music room of his palace. Some of the best artistes in the country performed for him, earning their *inaam,* or reward, from a true connoisseur of the arts. But his passion for music and dance was only surpassed by his pride, dangerously bordering on vanity. The fact that he was the raja of the land was something he had always held dear and never missed an opportunity to remind others of. As the land around him kept getting washed away by the advancing river, his coffers began to dry up. Unfazed, he continued to sell off ornaments and other items of his family heirloom, just so he could keep up his stately lifestyle. After the death of his wife and son, the music room remains shut for four years, but when a young, self-made businessman organises a musical soiree in his own house in the village, Bishwambhar Roy's pride is hurt—his blue blood begins to boil and he spends whatever little he has in his treasury to arrange one final recital in his palace's *jalsaghar,* all in a bid to satisfy his vanity.

A tragedy of epic proportions, the film is a haunting tale of moral erosion, more than anything else—not too different from the erosion of the landlord's land by the steady but sure advance of the river. The erstwhile zamindar knows very well that his days are over, that the privy council has decided to take control of his properties, abolishing the practice of zamindari forever. But he is never fully able to come to terms with this bitter fact. Instead of consolidating his property to make the right investment decisions to secure his future, he squanders whatever little remains on a passion he cannot give up. Riddled with the guilt of rolling in the pleasures of music while his family's boat capsized, he stays away from music and dance for several years. But soon enough, his ego gets the better of him and he returns to the music room to prove a point—a point utterly trivial in the context of things happening around him.

Veteran Bengali actor Chhabi Biswas plays the role of Bishwambhar Roy with such regal charm that it is almost impossible to imagine anyone else in that role. With his performance, Biswas is able to pull off the unthinkable—he can make us feel sorry for him, even when we know that what he is doing is sheer foolishness. It's not an easy task to do—the role could easily have become a caricature, half-baked and unconvincing. But Biswas is the perfect anti-hero—a sick mind riddled with addiction and narcissism. And yet, we love him for what he is. He is vain but not cruel. He opens the doors of his palace so that the entire village can take shelter from the wrath of the river. He loves his family and is extremely fond of his stately rides—the stallion Toofan and the majestic elephant Moti. In a heart-wrenching scene in the second half of the film, when a young and upstart moneylender comes to invite him to his house-warming ceremony, he politely refuses to go. While the businessman is allowed to finish drinking his sherbet before leaving, the camera slowly moves towards Bishwambhar Roy's face. There he sits! The pipe of his hookah in hand, like a true king, keeping up the image, face proud, head held high, although knowing fully well that he is finished forever. It is in that moment that our heart weeps for him. Would this have been possible had this role been played by anyone other than Biswas? We don't think so. Nor did Ray. In an interview he gave many years later, Ray confessed that he had stopped making films with such regal characters simply because Biswas had passed away.

Jalsaghar boasts some of the most beautiful song-and-dance sequences ever shot on film, by such artistes as Begum Akhtar, Salamat Ali Khan, Roshan Kumari, Ustad Waheed Khan and Ustad Bismillah Khan. Rich in the finery of thumri, Malhaar and Kathak, the film is one of the most shining examples of the use of song and dance in Indian cinema. In the final scene of the film, as an inebriated, exhausted and paupered Bishwambhar Roy finds the lights of his music room going out one by one, Ray does what only a mind as fertile in imagination as his can do. He provides eerie background music to the scene by playing a composition of Finnish composer Johan Julius Sibelius in reverse and combining it with the soul-stirring music of Ustad Vilayat Khan. The resulting score, along with the visuals of a frightened Chhabi Biswas running around madly in his music room, is a treat for the audience and perfectly captures the mood of decline and death.

Apur Sansar

The World of Apu (1959)

SATYAJIT RAY'S FASCINATION WITH BIBHUTIBHUSHAN
Bandyopadhyay's immortal creation, Apu, lasted across three films,
known in the world of cinema as the Apu trilogy. For the final film
in the trilogy, Ray focused on the life and experiences of a grown-up
Apu. In it, through the journey of the young man, he portrayed the
cyclical nature of human existence and such universal emotions as
happiness and grief, love and loss and denial and acceptance, as they
keep shaping our lives. This film, which Ray made in 1959 after two
attempts at making 'popular' cinema in between, was *Apur Sansar* (The
World of Apu).

When the film begins, we meet Apu, a handsome young man with
dreamy eyes and empty pockets. He doesn't have money to pay his rent,
so he knocks on the doors of every prospective employer in Calcutta
but fails to secure a job. Yet, Apu doesn't lose hope. On the contrary, he
has literary ambitions and plans to write a novel someday but is too lazy
and careless to pursue this dream. His laid-back existence is financed by
the private tuitions he takes, but with not enough money coming in, he
knows he needs to look for a full-time job. This bothers him, because
he either finds himself overqualified for available jobs or underqualified
for the jobs he wants. Under such circumstances, one day, his old friend

Apu finally reconciles with his son, bringing the trilogy to a beautiful end.

Pulu visits him to invite him to his cousin Aparna's wedding in a village in Khulna.

On the day of the wedding, however, the bride's family realises, much to their horror, that the groom has a serious mental disorder and that he often turns violent. While Aparna's father still wants to marry his daughter off to the groom, it is her mother who puts her foot down and calls off the alliance. A shroud of gloom descends upon the village, since in accordance to the traditional beliefs of those days, Aparna is about to miss the announced auspicious hour of the wedding and will thus be cursed for life. To avoid such a tragedy, Pulu begs Apu to accept his cousin's hand in marriage. Apu flatly refuses at first, but on realising that the entire village's hopes are pinned on him, he agrees to marry the girl he hasn't even seen.

Apu brings Aparna home to Calcutta, and despite being raised in an affluent household, Aparna takes to a life of modest means and domesticity quite easily. Apu is worried because he has no job, but like a true companion for life, Aparna assures him that everything will be all right, without ever saying so in as many words. She is the perfect wife that a man can hope to be blessed with, and to her, her husband's happiness and well-being are of paramount importance. Apu leads a content life of domestic bliss with Aparna, and she soon gets pregnant. The couple are happy beyond measure, but this happiness doesn't last for long. While delivering her child, Aparna passes away.

Apu is broken and shattered. Unable to accept the death of Aparna, he leaves the city and wanders through the length and breadth of the country. Back in the village, his son, Kajol, is growing up almost like an orphan, but Apu refuses to return to the village, because in his mind, he blames his son for the death of his wife, whom he loved so much. In the end, however, weary and exhausted, he returns to the village, and on seeing his son for the first time, he realises his mistake. He accepts his son with open arms and finds peace and closure. The father and son walk away to a new beginning.

While its predecessors, *Pather Panchali* and *Aparajito*, were praised for their rich aesthetics and deep humanism, *Apur Sansar* has been lauded the world over for its fascinating study of love and loss. Two scenes in the film, both involving Apu, highlight these two emotions in two contrasting manners, and yet both of them are so natural and visually stunning that they might well be considered among the best scenes ever written and shot by Ray. The first is a scene from the morning after Apu has brought Aparna home. The night has passed, and unable to show lovemaking between the couple to a largely traditional family audience, Ray shows the romance between Apu and Aparna through a series of shots subtly suggestive of what has passed. As the beautiful Aparna—the vermilion dot on her forehead now slightly smudged—tries to leave the bed, she finds the free end of her sari tied in a knot to Apu's dhoti. As Aparna frees herself, slaps her husband's back as reprimand for such mischief and begins her morning chores, Apu watches her from bed, stumbling upon one of her hairpins under his pillow. His face is filled with the fond remembrance of the previous night, and with a content smile on his face, he opens a packet of cigarettes to find a small handwritten note inside, which says, 'Only one. After meals. You promised.' No amount of depiction of sex or lovemaking could have created such a beautiful suggestion of romance as this one sequence does.

The second scene shows Apu returning from work one day, reading his wife's letter from the village on the way, only to reach home and find her brother waiting for him with news of her death. In a state of indescribable grief, disbelief, shock and sheer rage, the otherwise mild-mannered and sensitive Apu clenches his teeth and punches the bearer of the news across the face—a sudden surge of uncontrollable emotion so beautifully understood by Ray and portrayed by his leading man, Soumitra Chattopadhyay, that it aches one's heart just to think about it. It is moments such as these that make *Apur Sansar* the film we all know. And the entire length of the film is full of such moments. Watch out for the expression on the face of Aparna's mother when she threatens to kill herself if her daughter is forced to marry a madman. Or the fleeting moment of sadness on Apu's face when Aparna's mother blesses him with long life—a moment when he perhaps remembers his mother. Or the look on Apu's face as he describes the plot of his novel to his friend, and Ravi Shankar's haunting flute theme from *Pather Panchali* slowly rises in the background as we begin to realise that Apu's novel is more autobiographical than he is himself willing to admit.

But perhaps the best scene in the film comes towards the end, when Apu meets his son Kajol for the first time. In an instant, his misgivings towards the child are wiped out, washed away in his tears, as he asks himself how something so beautiful and innocent can be the cause of his beloved's death. He embraces his son and hoists him up on his shoulders, and for the first time since the beginning of the film, we see a twinkle of joy in Apu's eyes—the same twinkle that we had seen when he was a child in *Pather Panchali*.

Apur Sansar marks the debut of both Soumitra Chattopadhyay and Sharmila Tagore, as Apu and Aparna, respectively, both of whom went on to appear in a number of films by Ray, and both of whom, outside the filmography of Ray, went on to make their mark in the Bengali and Hindi film industries respectively. Their first film performance together, however, was perhaps their individual career bests.

With *Apur Sansar*, Ray brought his Apu trilogy to an end. Several critics around the world consider it among his best films. It is also the film that sealed his position as a filmmaker who, despite his fresh and ground-breaking ideas of cinema, had a steady finger on the pulse of his audience.

Devi

The Goddess (1960)

DURING THE BENGAL RENAISSANCE, WHICH IS SAID TO HAVE BEGUN with Raja Ram Mohan Roy (1772–1833) and ended with Rabindranath Tagore (1861–1941), there had been several prominent luminaries and enlightened individuals who spoke out against a number of social, cultural and religious evils that were widely accepted as prevalent norms until then. Tagore, for instance, had strong views against the rampant religious zealotry that was seen among several sections of people practising the Hindu religion in eighteenth- and nineteenth-century Bengal. But since Tagore himself was a practitioner of the Brahmo religion, he consciously refrained from making a comment on the subject and, instead, asked one of his contemporaries, Prabhat Kumar Mukhopadhyay, who was a Hindu Brahmin and a free-thinking individual at the same time, to write a story about a young girl who found herself a victim of religious superstition in an orthodox zamindar family in rural Bengal. As a direct outcome of this request, Mukhopadhyay wrote a short story titled 'Devi' (The Goddess), which was adapted for the screen by Satyajit Ray many years later, in 1960.

Devi is one of Ray's most tragic films. It tells the story of Dayamoyee, the sixteen-year-old wife of Umaprasad, who is the younger son of Kalikinkar Chaudhuri, an extremely erudite and highly revered zamindar

Dayamoyee is stunned to muteness as devotees begin to worship her as the goddess incarnate.

in an unnamed riverside village of undivided Bengal. Kalikinkar has been a devout worshipper of the goddess Kali all his life, and his devotion towards the deity is exemplary. Now that he has aged, he has given the responsibility of the zamindari to his elder son, Taraprasad, and spends his days in the service of the goddess. He is extremely fond of Dayamoyee, who is the perfect daughter-in-law. Dayamoyee makes all arrangements for his morning and evening prayers, never forgets to bring him his medicine and is always at his beck and call. And she does all this without uttering a single word—as was considered the desired characteristic of an ideal daughter-in-law in those days. Despite the fact that her husband, Umaprasad, lives in the city, young Dayamoyee hardly seems to find any time for herself, because when she is not taking care of her aged father-in-law, she is busy looking after Khoka, the five-year-old son of Taraprasad and his wife who refuses to eat, bathe or sleep unless his favourite aunt has pampered him enough.

One night, Kalikinkar has a dream, in which he sees the face of the dynasty's deity merging with the face of Dayamoyee. The old zamindar gets it into his head that his younger daughter-in-law is an incarnation of Kali. He immediately falls at her feet, 'instals' her in the family's temple and then begins a heart-wrenching show of religious superstition. The helpless young girl becomes the object of everyone's veneration and is subjected to hours and hours of ceremonial procedures and worship every day. Everyone thinks she is the goddess herself, and those who do not have no option but to remain silent for fear of earning the wrath of the zamindar. Things take a turn for the worse when the old village beggar brings his ailing grandson to Dayamoyee and begs her to spare his life. When the dying boy is made to drink the *charanamrita*—the holy water used to wash Dayamoyee's feet—the boy survives, further strenghening everyone's belief that she is the goddess herself. Back in the city, when Umaprasad learns that his wife is being worshipped as an idol in his village, he rushes back and accuses his father of torturing her. But Dayamoyee refuses to run away with him, fearing that some harm may come upon her husband if he goes against the will of the deity and earns Her wrath. Finally, when Khoka falls sick, Kalikinkar begs Dayamoyee to revive him. Dayamoyee cradles the febrile Khoka in her arms all through the night, just like she used to, but before the sun rises, the ailing boy dies. It is then that everyone blames Dayamoyee for the boy's death. No one worships her any more, no one brings gifts and flowers to her that morning. And not being able to recover from the shocking death of the dear boy she loved so much, Dayamoyee loses her mind and runs away towards the river, presumably to be consumed by its waters—just as the idol of a goddess gets lost in the depths of a river at the end of annual festivities.

As expected, Ray faced severe criticism for having made the film. Ray himself was a Brahmo and was accused of showing the Hindu religion in poor light without understanding the teachings of the religion too well. Nothing could be farther from the truth. First, Ray's deep knowledge of the Hindu religion was far stronger than that of some of the fanatics who were up in arms against him, and this is quite evident in the film itself. It manifests in the intricate rules and religious customs of the Hindu Brahmin's way of worship and prayer depicted in the film. Secondly, and more importantly, not once in the film does Ray say anything against the Hindu religion per se. For instance, in the very opening scene of the film, the entire family is shown happily celebrating the festival of the goddess Durga and the fireworks that follow. There is devotion and contentment on everyone's faces—a sense of satisfaction that comes from having fulfilled one's spiritual duties. What Ray opposes, and sends a strong message against, are the man-made, self-imposed superstitions that flout all logic and cause harm to human life and everything that humanity stands for. The film makes a strong commentary against all such blind beliefs and says that no religion in the world is greater than logic and reason.

On both technical and creative counts, *Devi* scores high on the scale of aesthetic parameters. Consider, for example, a scene between Kalikinkar and Umaprasad, in which the son accuses his father of having lost his mind. The aged patriarch has a fleeting moment of self-doubt but quickly cuts through it by reciting line after line from an entire section of Kalidas's *Raghuvamsa* in a bid to prove to his son that he has not turned senile. Through veteran actor Chhabi Biswas's soaring recitation of the lines, Ray gives his audience a simple, yet crucial message—that in the matters of religion, even the most knowledgeable man can succumb to irrational behaviour and that education does not necessarily lead to enlightenment. That he does this in a single, uncut, three-minute-long shot only goes to show the film's technical brilliance, not to mention the prowess of the actors involved. In another scene, Khoka is hiding behind the door of Dayamoyee's bedroom, and just as she enters, Khoka jumps out and scares her. When his favourite aunt asks him what would have happened if she would have died of the scare, the little boy replies nonchalantly, 'That would have been fun!' Through this scene, Ray once again proves his deep understanding of the mind of a child. That the little boy does not even understand the concept of death becomes all the more tragic when he himself dies a dismal death—without proper treatment, without the necessary medicines,bit by bit, in the arms of the same aunt whom he had scared to death once.

Through *Devi*, Ray speaks about the selfish opportunism and the dynamics of power that lie at the bedrock of organised religion. Everything in false devotion is a transaction, he explains—a crude give-and-take donning the seemingly pristine garb of spirituality. This is why there is pride in Kalikinkar's voice when he claims to have devoted his whole life to the goddess—pride, mind you, not bliss. This is why everyone falls at Dayamoyee's feet as long as she is the giver of blessings (the name 'Dayamoyee' itself translates to 'one who offers infinite mercy'). And this is also why, when she fails to save the dying boy, everyone crassly abandons her without any hesitation whatsoever. In a brief but meaningful scene, the family priest, who has assisted Kalikinkar in his prayers over the years, is seen hanging his head in woeful shame when the much-revered zamindar grovels at his daughter-in-law's feet.

These shifts of power are evident not just in the periphery of the family's temple, but in the corridors and bedchambers of the zamindar's mansion too. The elder daughter-in-law, Harasundari, Taraprasad's wife, knows that the much younger Dayamoyee is now at the centre of everyone's attention and cannot help but feel, albeit briefly, the pangs of envy. When her husband detects these feelings haunting Harasundari's mind, he makes a mockery of it all by falling at her feet and claiming that *she*, and not Dayamoyee, is the real goddess and the object of (at least) his veneration. Harasundari is, of course, not amused by this, and the fact that her son Khoka pines for his aunt more than he does for his own mother does not help allay her insecurities either. In fact, with Khoka gone, and her alcoholic and clearly inept husband making a fool of himself on every given occasion, Harasundari finds herself very lonely in a mansion teeming with people.

Devi also shows the plight of women in nineteenth-century rural Bengal. On one hand, there is Dayamoyee, who has no choice but to silently bear the atrocities inflicted upon her day after day in the name of faith and devotion; and on the other, there is Harasundari, who knows that she is all but a pawn in the great game of male entitlement and privileged upper-caste patriarchy. Speaking about the film, actress Sharmila Tagore, who brought so much to the role of Dayamoyee, once said,

Even today, like Dayamoyee, scores of women continue to suffer injustice in the name of family, tradition, culture and honour. After so many years of independence from British rule, India still remains largely a patriarchal society with dark pockets of ignorance and superstition where excessive religious orthodoxy continues to victimize women. Till such time religion is used to perpetuate ignorance and superstition, till such time the true, tolerant, progressive nature of religion continues to elude mankind, Satyajit Ray's *Devi* will remain extremely relevant and a must-see for anyone who loves meaningful cinema.[*]

---

[*] Bhaskar Chattopadhyay, *14 Stories That Inspired Satyajit Ray*, HarperCollins, 2014.

Postmaster (1961)

IN 1961, SATYAJIT RAY DIRECTED *TEEN KANYA* (THREE DAUGHTERS), an anthology of three films adapted from three short stories written by Rabindranath Tagore, as a tribute to the great man on the occasion of his birth centenary. Each film in the anthology tells the story of a girl or a woman. In the segment titled *Postmaster*, Ray tells the beautiful and heart-wrenching story of a twelve-year-old orphan servant girl named Ratan.

The story of *Postmaster* is simple. When a new postmaster arrives in the village, he finds it extremely difficult to leave his usual urban life behind and overcome the many day-to-day hindrances of rural existence. His evenings are lonely, with the post office rather secluded and surrounded by large trees and wild bushes. Amid the sinister yelps of foxes and the continuous rantings of the village loony, he finds it impossible to have a good night's sleep. His only solace is his servant—a young girl named Ratan—who gives him company and keeps him engaged in conversation, distracting him from his fears and worries. Although the postmaster distrusts her at first, the orphan girl soon wins his trust. The good-natured postmaster treats her with love and respect—something she is not accustomed to, thanks to the ill treatment and physical abuse she has received from her previous masters. She soon finds a deep emotional connect with the 'Notun Babu', her 'new master'. Eager to learn, her bond with her master is strengthened further when he begins to teach

The postmaster's detached affection is mistaken for genuine care and concern by Ratan, the young girl.

her how to read and write. And before you know it, she makes the mistake of assuming that she is an integral and inseparable part of her master's life. When the postmaster is attacked by a nasty bout of malaria, Ratan nurses him back to health. But little does she know that her master has already made up his mind to quit his job and return to the city, leaving her behind. Devastated to learn the truth, Ratan breaks down at first, but soon picks up the pieces and is seen serving her 'Notun Babu'—yet another new postmaster of the village, because that is her barren destiny, something that a brief shower of love is not going to change.

As with all his films set in a rural backdrop, Ray's depiction of the village of Ulapur in Bengal is incomparable. As is his portrayal of the villagers. The camera lingers lovingly along the muddy village path surrounded by wild outgrowths of vines and shrubs. There is a pond nearby, and the postmaster's initial enthusiasm of taking a dip in the cool waters is soon crushed when he stumbles upon a snakeskin lying on its banks. The village madman is a ragged, unkempt old man, complete with a fishing rod under his armpit and an angler's cap on his head, who marches in military style on entirely wrong beats. The relatively sane and more educated villagers gather at the post office to see the wonder that the new postmaster is—a man who has the habit of writing poetry and reading English novels of Scott, among others. In a bid to impress the all-important man, they even invite him to an evening of music recitals, which turns out to be a rather amateurish, cacophonic and unintentionally comic affair. And amid all this is Ratan.

In the beginning, the postmaster treats Ratan with harmless neglect. In a heart-warming scene, Ratan points to a family photograph of the postmaster and asks who the young girl in the picture is. On learning that she is her master's sister and a good singer too, she seems to feel a sudden pang of envy, and quickly breaks into a song herself. Beautifully shot, the scene shows the postmaster's face, his eyes shut in inattention as we hear the soulful voice of the young Ratan, until even the postmaster cannot neglect her ungroomed, untrained and yet extremely admirable sense of music.

In adapting *Postmaster* for the screen, Ray made several changes to the story by Tagore, adding quite a few comic elements. But the one big change he made was the ending. In the original story, Ratan is shown to fall at her master's feet, begging him to take her along with him to the city, whereas in the film, she simply walks past her old master, wiping her tears, even as he tries to stop her to give her a few annas in tip. In an interview, Ray was asked why he had made this change, to which the filmmaker simply said that he felt that the original would have looked rather 'Victorian' on screen, going on to add that the audience accepted the change with open arms, as was evident from the success of the film.

Anil Chatterjee plays the well-meaning postmaster with remarkable dexterity. He is loving and caring, and yet, not once does it occur to him that young Ratan has become emotionally dependent on him. And when the realisation does dawn upon him, he lacks the courage to walk back to the post office and take Ratan along with him. Chandana Banerjee plays the young Ratan with such simplicity and natural flair that it's impossible to take one's eyes off her. It would perhaps not be incorrect to say that she was one of the best child actors Ray ever worked with—she tugged at our heartstrings with every smile, every twitch of her expressive eyes and every teardrop she shed. In what is perhaps the most beautiful scene of the film, the postmaster asks the twelve-year-old Ratan about her mother, to which she simply says, 'She died,' then, adding moments later, 'when I was a child'.

Monihara

The Lost Jewels (1961)

IT IS WELL KNOWN THAT APART FROM BEING ONE OF THE GREATEST filmmakers in the world, Satyajit Ray was also a prolific author of children's literature. Among his writings were several horror stories, but in his film career spanning four decades, he made only one horror film—and that too was not based on one of his own works. In 1961, on the occasion of Rabindranath Tagore's birth centenary, Ray made an anthology of films based on the short stories of Tagore. The anthology, titled *Teen Kanya* (Three Daughters), comprised of three films with female protagonists. The second film in the anthology was based on a ghost story written by Tagore, titled *Monihara* (The Lost Jewels).

The story of *Monihara* begins as dusk falls, when a village schoolmaster walks through the compound of an abandoned and derelict mansion and sits on the banks of a river. There, he meets a stranger and tells him that he has been writing the strange and rather tragic history of the former owners of the mansion—the rich businessman Phanibhushan and his young wife, the beautiful Monimalika. Happy to have finally found an audience, the schoolmaster narrates to the stranger the story of Monimalika, who seemed to have had an abnormal obsession with jewels and ornaments. Her caring and somewhat timid husband showered all his love and attention on her, and yet didn't seem to be able to win her

Phanibhushan doesn't seem to be able to win his wife
Monimalika's heart.

heart. She was sad because even after ten years of marriage, she couldn't bear a child. She also had a piercing suspicion in her mind that all her relatives and in-laws spoke ill of her behind her back. The only thing that made her happy was her ever-growing collection of jewels and ornaments, which she guarded with her life. When a devastating fire destroyed Phanibhushan's jute factory, he found himself in dire financial straits. He told his wife that he would need to raise money urgently, to pay off his debtors. Monimalika suspected that her husband would try and sell off all her jewels to get the money. Phanibhushan had no such intentions. He went to the city, and was not only successful in raising money to pay off his debt but also managed to buy a gold necklace for his wife. Meanwhile, while he was gone, the paranoid Monimalika summoned a distant cousin of hers and sought his help to go back to her parents' house with all her jewels. The shrewd cousin agreed, and presumably murdered her on the way and ran away with her jewels. When Phanibhushan returned, Monimalika was nowhere to be found. Devastated, he lamented her loss, only to realise that his wife's ghost had come back to claim the gold necklace he had bought for her.

The most unsettling part of *Monihara* is its atmosphere. A large mansion next to the Ganga, the full moon shining on the waters of the river, the beautiful and yet psychologically unwell Monimalika singing in her soulful voice, the yelping of the foxes and the hooting of the owls, the wind howling through the vast corridors of the mansion, the marble fairies standing in the garden in mute observation, the thin veil of fog over the abundant lawns, the sound of a late-night village opera floating in the air—all help build the perfect setting for a ghost story. In the climax, when Monimalika's shadowy, silhouetted form walks into Phanibhushan's bedchamber and shakes her head 'no' to her husband's jubilant 'Moni, you've come back?', you cannot help but get goosebumps at the hint of her beautiful yet scary eyes watching from the darkness. In the final twist in the film, when the schoolmaster finishes his story and the stranger says that he has liked it a lot but the story has several factual errors, the old teacher asks the stranger how he could be so sure. To this, the stranger simply reveals that he is none other than Phanibhushan himself, bids him farewell and vanishes into thin air, making the audience realise that Phanibhushan must have himself died of shock on seeing his wife's ghost. Ray carries the element of shock and horror right to the end of the film, leaving us with a disturbing doubt in our minds—were the events of the story true? Did they really happen? Or were they merely the old schoolmaster's imagination, culminating in a hallucination induced by the regular consumption of opium?

The performances by the film's lead characters are extremely commendable. Kali Banerjee, as the easy-going, all-forgiving and romantic husband, injects life into an otherwise feeble Phanibhushan. His love for his wife comes before everything else, and it is this unconditional, blind love that spells his doom. Kanika Majumdar plays Monimalika with haunting charm. As she sits on her bed, looks out at the river and sings a soulful song, you cannot help but feel sad for her. But moments later, on witnessing the lust for a new jewel shining in her eyes, you realise you have been wrong all along. Her love, if one could call it that, is purely material. She is the epitome of greed for everything that glitters. And it is in her insatiable thirst for gold and jewels that we find a sick mind—perpetually scared, doubting and full of distrust for everyone. She doesn't have an iota of regret for leaving her husband—her only regret is that she couldn't get the necklace he had promised her. Cold, loveless and devoid of any sympathy whatsoever, she ventures out on to a dark path, only to meet her inevitable end. *Monihara* is the perfect example of what a horror film should induce in its audience—hopelessness. For there is no greater horror in the world than hopelessness.

Samapti

The Conclusion (1961)

THERE HAVE BEEN SEVERAL PEOPLE WHO HAVE HAD A profound impact on Satyajit Ray's creative career. Bibhutibhushan Bandyopadhyay's keen observations on nature, his own teacher Benode Behari Mukherjee's approach to positivity and an unshakeable dedication to his art, and French anthropologist Claude Lévi-Strauss's deep insights into the true meaning of civilisation—all of these found a place in Ray's work and life in some form or the other, time and again. Among these great minds, however, there was one that injected the very notion of freethinking into his veins—a notion that, as we all know today, was a pillar of Ray's success as one of the champions of meaningful cinema in India. That individual, whose teachings— in Ray's own words—set his mind on fire, was none other than Rabindranath Tagore. In 1961, on Tagore's birth centenary, Ray paid tribute to the great man with an anthology of three films based on three short stories by Tagore. In this essay, we will discuss one of these films—*Samapti* (The Conclusion).

At its very core, *Samapti* is a love story, which shows the rather painful journey of its lead character, Mrinmoyi (played with great compassion by a magnificent Aparna Sen), from being an unruly and carefree young girl to a loving wife. A young graduate named Amulya has just finished his

Mrinmoyi cannot come to terms with her marriage.

exams and returned to his riverside village in Bengal with an assumed air of urban supremacy. While alighting from the boat on the muddy banks of the river, he slips and falls, setting a free-spirited tomboyish girl named Mrinmoyi into an uncontrollable bout of laughter. Not at all amused by this insult, Amulya is rather furious with the girl, who soon scoots from the spot. When his mother asks him to get married before going back to the city to study further, Amulya insists on taking Mrinmoyi as his bride, because, by now, after another close encounter with the girl, he has fallen in love with her. Mrinmoyi, however, is severely opposed to the very notion of marriage, because she believes it will inevitably bind her to domestic life, putting an end to her wayward and happy-go-lucky days of climbing trees to pick fruits, swinging from the branch of a tree by the river and playing with her pet squirrel. But as was the practice in those days, she doesn't have a say in the matter and is promptly married off to Amulya. On the night of the wedding, Amulya realises that his wife has been forced into the marriage. Not willing to win her by force, Amulya goes back to the city, leaving Mrinmoyi behind. And it is then that Mrinmoyi begins to realise, much to her surprise, that she is actually beginning to miss the man she had refused to accept as her husband.

With a few necessary changes to the original story to keep the events confined to the village itself, Ray ensured that he stuck to the essence of Tagore's message. He deals with the character of Mrinmoyi with great compassion, making us realise, time and again, that she is someone with merely the body of a woman but the mind of a little girl. Her whims, her fancies, her obstinacy, nothing comes in the way of the fact that in her heart of hearts, her point of view is rather simple—she loves her freedom. And Ray maintains this note throughout the film. When her husband leaves her behind in the village and goes away to the city, causing much disgrace to her family, she begins to recall his comforting words of support and realises that she has made the grave mistake of misunderstanding him and that her ideas about marital life need not necessarily be true. And when her husband comes back to the village and looks for her through a raging storm, she realises, perhaps for the first time, how much he loves her. That someone can do this much for her—a poor, madcap, loony girl, who everyone has always reprimanded and rebuked—is enough to make her fall in love.

Ray uses comedy to tackle the first half of the film, with Amulya finding it difficult to adjust to village life after his long stay in the city. But in the second half, the film dives headlong into the tragedy of an unwilling young girl losing her independence to marriage. Amulya's character is beautifully portrayed by Ray's go-to man, Soumitra Chattopadhyay. He is the kind of man who likes to reason with his wife to reach a point of marital harmony and does not believe in curbing her freedom. Although his initial approach to Mrinmoyi is one of a conqueror, he soon realises that he genuinely loves the girl who had once laughed at him. To keep peace with a mother he loves and cares for, and not wanting to force his newly wed wife into submission at the same time, he goes away from it all, considering the failure of the marriage his own fault.

As with his previous films, Ray's portrayal of rural life in Bengal is absolutely marvellous in this film as well, with pretty sailboats plying up and down a free-flowing river by the side of the village, an abandoned chariot of Lord Jagannath at the base of a massive tree, ample trees and plants all around, and post-monsoon pathways full of the worst possible slush and mud that one can imagine. The thunderstorms, the cocks crowing to announce the rising of the sun, the white sheet of smog hanging just over the fields in the evenings, the ponds, the orchards—everything is captured meticulously by the camera. Ray's detailing and wit also deserve special mention, for instance, in a scene where Amulya places a framed photograph of his hero, Napoleon Bonaparte, on the shelf of his room, and hours later, on realising that he will not be able to win the love of Mrinmoyi so easily, pushes it right towards the back of the shelf in a dark corner. Or in another scene, when he and his mother are quarrelling over his choice of bride, an equally shrill and cacophonic piece from Indian classical music plays full blast on an old gramophone in the room.

But perhaps the most beautiful scene in the film comes towards the end, when Mrinmoyi is lying on her bed in her mother's house and thinking about her husband, and one of her friends walks into the room to inform her that her pet squirrel has died. As the dead rodent hangs in front of her face, she feels sad for a moment, but soon gets over it and goes back to the loving daydreams of her estranged husband. We realise that with the death of the squirrel, a symbol of her childhood, Mrinmoyi has shed her old skin too, and although it did take some time, she has now finally stopped being a girl and matured into a woman.

Rabindranath Tagore (1961)

RABINDRANATH TAGORE'S WORK AND PHILOSOPHY HAD A STRONG influence on Satyajit Ray's life and work. Ray made as many as five films based on short stories, novellas and novels written by Tagore—that's the most number of times he has ever adapted any writer's work. It was at Tagore's Shantiniketan that Ray learnt how to draw and paint. In later years, Ray's drawings, sketches, illustrations and designs inspired thousands of artists and art enthusiasts all over the world. Like Tagore, Ray's music has been deeply inspired by elements of both Western classical and raga-based Indian classical music. Ray's philosophy—on matters such as religion, science, social structure, education, revolution, civilisation and humanity—has had vivid reflections of Tagore's way of thinking. Although he never spoke about it in as many words, it would perhaps be safe to assume that Ray's mind was ignited by the fire that Tagore stoked. It was fitting, then, that in 1961, on the occasion of the birth centenary of Tagore, Ray was asked to make a documentary on the life and teachings of Tagore. Talking about the documentary in Andrew Robinson's biography of him, titled *Satyajit Ray: The Inner Eye*, the filmmaker says, 'ten or twelve minutes of it are among the most moving and powerful things that I have produced.'*

---

* Andrew Robinson, *Satyajit Ray: The Inner Eye*, IB Tauris, revised and updated edition, January 1989.

*An illustration
of Tagore by
Satyajit Ray.*

The fifty-two-minute film begins with an astonishingly large congregation of mourners flocking the streets of Calcutta, trying to catch one last glimpse of Tagore's corpse being taken through a funeral procession. Ray's narration states how, despite the poet's mortal remains having perished, he has left behind a heritage of words, music and poetry—of ideas and ideals—and how it has the power to move and inspire us—now, and for days to come. The film then briefly talks about the city of Calcutta, where Tagore was born, quickly moving on to describe a genealogical table that details Tagore's lineage, going all the way back to the eighth century, when a group of learned Brahmins migrated from Kannauj in Uttar Pradesh to settle down in Bengal. It is in this family tree that young 'Rabi', as he was fondly called, was born.

The film then talks about Rabi's childhood and how he was deeply influenced by the teachings and traditions of the father of the Indian Renaissance—Raja Ram Mohan Roy—a tradition that his father Maharshi Debendranath Tagore had imbibed and passed on to his children. Young Rabi was a thinking child, a dreamer, and was never quite able to adjust to the formal environment of a classroom. After he moved from one school to another over several years and hated them all, it was finally decided that Rabi would be schooled at home.

The film then goes on to describe his travels with his father, the publication of his first book of verse at the age of thirteen, his journey to London at the age of seventeen and his voluntary abandoning of higher studies at the University of London. With a mind keen to explore the arts and the written word, Tagore continued to be fascinated by Western classical music and world literature, but he refused to remain confined within the walls of a classroom. At the age of twenty-two, after his wedding, he was asked by his father to take over the reins of the family estate, for which he had to go and live in the heart of rural Bengal, right on the banks of the River Padma. It is the influence of his contact with nature and the poor peasants of his estate that we see in his later works. It was almost as if a whole new world had opened up for him—a world far removed from the abundances of the Western world, and yet, in many ways, similar.

Worried about the education of his children and plagued by his own nightmarish childhood experiences with conventional practices of education, Tagore decided to set up an experimental school at a property named Shantiniketan, which his father had acquired a few years ago. It was to be a school set up on the lines of Upanishadic education, similar to the forest hermitages of classical India. To arrange the money to set up the school, Tagore had to sell, among other things, the copyright of his books. His wife pitched in by selling some of her wedding ornaments.

In the years that followed, Tagore participated in a series of protests against the political upheavals in the province of Bengal. In a bid to crush the possibilities of a united front against the British government, Lord Curzon, then the Viceroy of India, had decided to divide the state of Bengal into two—each with its own religious majority. But in doing so, he severely underestimated the nationalist sentiments of the people of Bengal, who rose in peaceful protest, singing the soul-stirring songs of revolution written by Tagore himself. Tagore participated in these processions in person. But the Swadeshi movement quickly took on a character that Rabindranath could not condone—one of armed rebellion, bordering on terrorism. For the rest of his life, Tagore continued to stress on the necessity of peace and tolerance, and explained how the path to freedom was to be paved on the foundation of these two virtues alone. In 1919, in response to the Jallianwala Bagh massacre in Amritsar, Tagore renounced the knighthood that the Queen's government had bestowed upon him.

In his later years, while still inspiring many to continue the freedom movement in India, Tagore turned his attention to much broader themes, choosing to focus on the meaning of humanity and civilisation itself. It is during these times that the masses in the Occident came in contact with his teachings and thoughts, and Tagore was soon hailed as a progressive and influential world figure.

In 1941, at the height of the Second World War, Tagore wrote a speech on the occasion of his eightieth birthday. This speech, titled 'Crisis in

Civilisation', was to be his last message to the world. Ray closes his film with a few words from this very speech. He says,

> *I had at one time believed that the springs of civilisation would issue out of the heart of Europe. But today when I am about to quit the world, that faith has gone bankrupt altogether. As I look around, I see the crumbling ruins of a proud civilisation strewn like a vast heap of futility. And yet I shall not commit the grievous sin of losing faith in Man. I would rather look forward to the opening of a new chapter in his history after the cataclysm is over and the atmosphere rendered clean with the spirit of service and sacrifice. Perhaps that dawn will come from this horizon, from the East where the sun rises. A day will come when unvanquished Man will retrace his path of conquest, despite all barriers, to win back his lost human heritage.*

Viewing the film well into the twenty-first century, we realise that the words are as relevant today as they were all those years ago. Such was the foresight of the great poet.

Owing to his dislike for the English translation of Tagore's poetry, Ray decided not to use such translations in his film at all. He felt that it would create a wrong impression of the great poet's work in the minds of Western audiences. Despite this complete absence of Tagore's poetry in his film, Ray's film was able to capture the true essence of the poet's teachings and philosophy, and remains one of the greatest documentaries on the life and work of Tagore.

Kanchenjungha (1962)

IN HIS LONG FILMMAKING CAREER, SATYAJIT RAY MOSTLY ADAPTED the literary works of others. In other words, for most of his career, he interpreted the works of other writers. It was not until 1962 that Ray plunged headlong into his first act of pure creation, for which he wrote an original screenplay right from scratch and went on to make it into a film. The background to the writing of this screenplay is an interesting one. Ray was initially toying with the idea of a film in which a family goes on a picnic. He had thought of the beginning of the film and the ending—both revolving around a family photograph, but with different interpretations, as revealed through the events and interactions in the body of the film. When this idea did not materialise for logistical reasons, Ray converted the seed of the idea into another story set in the hill station of Darjeeling, where a large family comes together for a holiday. That film, which went on to become perhaps a unique film in Ray's career, was *Kanchenjungha*.

The events of the film span out in real time, over a late afternoon, near the Observatory Hill road of Darjeeling. Rai Bahadur Indranath Roy Chaudhuri's family has come to the Himalayan hill station for a holiday, and the members are all supposed to head back to Calcutta the next day. Indranath himself is a highly successful and affluent man—he is the chairman of as many as five companies. But he is not without his faults. He is vain, brash, a British-sympathiser, and tends to look down

Monisha is wooed by her suitor.

upon people and seal their fates with his judgements, decisions and proclamations. His wife, Labanya, is a docile and submissive woman, quite aware of her husband's nature and yet unable to voice her protests. The elderly couple have three children. The eldest is Anil—a hopeless and incorrigible womaniser who talks too much and thinks too little. Then there's the elder daughter, Anima, who is married to a reticent man named Shankar. The couple is going through a failed marriage and the two are barely holding on to it for the sake of their daughter. The youngest of Indranath's children is the beautiful Monisha—a young woman of independent spirit and thought. Also in the family is Jagadish, Labanya's widower brother and an ornithologist by passion. Other than the family, three other people converge at the misty hill station. There's a young, affluent and eligible bachelor named Banerjee—a suitor for Monisha, armed with the blessings of her autocratic father. Then there's an old man, who used to be Anil's private tutor several years ago. And finally, there's the old man's nephew—a young, unemployed man named Ashoke. As the film progresses, the paths of all these characters cross, and through their interactions and conversations, the fragmented narrative moves forward.

Quite early on in the film, we realise that Banerjee is about to propose marriage to Monisha and that the patriarch of the family is viewing this 'arrangement' as a matter of great social and financial benefit to himself. We also realise that Monisha, who has seen the outcome of such loveless marriages in as many as two instances right there in her own family (one of her mother, the other of her elder sister), is hesitant to accept the impending proposal. In fact, she takes refuge in the company of Ashoke, whom she knows is poor and timid, just to escape from the barrage of hints that her suitor keeps dropping throughout the afternoon. Anima, in turn, is torn between her lover and the husband she does not love. Shankar has recently found out about his wife's affair and is calmly transactional and perfectly willing to discuss an amicable divorce. Labanya has remained voiceless in the face of her husband's fury all her life, but after she sees her elder daughter's home crumbling in front of her eyes, she is understandably worried about the fate of her younger one. Unable to voice her opinion, she seeks support from her brother Jagadish, who promises to help her. Ashoke finds himself in a decidedly uncomfortable position in all this. He knows that the Rai Bahadur can get him that coveted job that has been eluding him for months. But his self-esteem does not allow him to suck up to the vain old man, who wears his love for the British on his sleeve and does not hesitate to discount the contributions of India's freedom fighters.

Kanchenjungha is a film that is far ahead of its time. For one, it is an experiment in filmmaking within the limited confines of both time and space. Secondly, it is a film in which the 'mood' changes with the change in weather. The film begins when the sun is shining brightly upon Darjeeling—everything seems in its proper place, everyone seems happy and calm. Then come the clouds, and ugly secrets tumble out of the proverbial closet one after the other. Finally, the mist rolls in, covering the quaint little town, and we begin to witness unmistakeable hints of doubt in every character's mind. Finally, when the mist clears, those doubts turn into decisions of various kinds, which finally culminate into a happy ending as the sun begins to shine brightly once again—this time revealing the majestic Kanchenjungha before our eyes.

It is almost impossible to believe that Ray wrote the screenplay of *Kanchenjungha* in ten days, and even more so that he wrapped up the shooting of the film (his first colour film, no less) in as few as twenty-four days. A master of thrift—both in the making of the film and in its contents—Ray created a motion picture whose technical brilliance, layered messages and superlative performances had no match anywhere in the world. One wonders how he did that, and perhaps the answer lies partially in his creative genius and partially in what he saw as the core source of his inspiration—the Himalayas. For it was the terrace of the Windermere in Darjeeling where he wrote the screenplay of *Kanchenjungha*, and although he makes one of the characters in the film say the following words, we know, by a fair estimate, that it is, in fact, Ray describing how he came around to pulling off the greatest creative stunt of his career:

> *Maybe it is this place that has got something to do with it ... I have never seen anything like this before. The majestic Himalayas, these silent pine trees, this strange play of sunlight, clouds and mist. It's so unreal, almost like a dream state. My head was in a whirl, and everything seemed to change before my eyes. As if I wasn't myself any more, as if I was someone special. A hero! A giant! As if I was full of courage ... careless ... undaunted. And as if no one could stop me any more.*

Abhijan

The Expedition (1962)

IN 1962, WHILE HE WAS BUSY WITH POST-PRODUCTION WORK ON his film *Kanchenjungha*, Satyajit Ray was approached by his producer friend Bijoy Chattopadhyay to consult on a film that the latter was about to direct. The film was to be an adaptation of veteran Bengali author Tarashankar Bandopadhyay's 1946 novel, *Abhijan* (The Expedition). Since Ray had already adapted Bandopadhyay's *Jalsaghar* (The Music Room) in 1958, Chattopadhyay felt that his involvement in the project would be of immense value. Ray, of course, agreed to help his friend. While scouting for a location, Ray fell so deeply in love with the wind-swept locales of the Birbhum district of Bengal that he offered to direct the entire film himself. This came as a relief to his friend, who was getting cold feet even before the shooting had begun. That very year, *Abhijan* was released, and despite being one of Ray's lesser-known films, it went on to become one of his biggest box-office successes.

The film tells the story of Narsingh, a young Rajput taxi driver living and working in Bengal. Narsingh owns a 1930 Chrysler sedan, which he uses to ferry passengers between two villages. His passion for the car is equalled—and perhaps surpassed—by that of his assistant-cum-handyman Rama, who protects the car with his heart, soul and spirit. Narsingh is going through a bad phase in life, as his wife has run away

Taxi driver Narsingh tries to learn the English language, while his handyman Rama washes the Chrysler in the background.

with another man. A Kshatriya by caste and a descendant of the bloodline of none other than Maharana Pratap, he cannot tolerate indignity, insult or defeat of any kind. To add to his woes, an impulsive bout of rash driving leaves him in the bad books of the district's traffic inspector, who has not only cancelled his licence but insulted him and thrown him out of his office. Disillusioned and dejected, Narsingh decides to return to his hometown in the neighbouring district, but on the way back, he picks up a stranded middle-aged Marwari businessman named Sukhanram and his companion—a young woman named Gulabi. When Sukhanram offers to help Narsingh set up a taxi service in his village, the Rajput thinks he can find a way to reclaim his lost respect. Little does he know that Sukhanram has plans to use his car for smuggling opium, or that the rustic and comely widow Gulabi is being sold into the flesh trade by the businessman. Also appearing in the story is a Christian man named Joseph, who used to be a family friend; his young and educated sister Neeli, whom Narsingh finds himself drawn to; and her crippled lover. In the end, Narsingh finds himself standing at the crossroads, where a single decision can lead him either to a life of dignity or to one of prosperity.

Although *Abhijan* is one of Ray's more 'commercially inclined' films, there are some aspects of its craft that deserve high critical commendation. For one, *Abhijan* has perhaps some of the best editing work ever seen in a Satyajit Ray film. The cutting is top-notch, especially in the first half of the film. The setting up of the shots, the blocking, the camerawork—everything pulls you right into the scenes. Consider the iconic opening shot of the film, for instance, where Narsingh and the owner of a local garage are having a drink at a hooch store. The camera stays on a mechanic, dwelling on the pleasure he derives in taking a dig at Narsingh's bruised pride. In a broken mirror on the wall behind him, we see half of Narsingh's face—sullen, gloomy and shattered like the mirror itself. He sulks at all of womanhood, curses his luck and, yet, has the guts to refuse an offer of partnership with the opportunistic mechanic. To him, the most important thing is the blood flowing in his veins, and with the two-and-a-half-minute-long single-shot scene, Ray successfully convinces us of this simple fact, beautifully setting up the mood for the rest of the film.

In another scene, when Gulabi (beautifully played—or should we say, downplayed—by Waheeda Rehman) pleads with Narsingh to save her from an inebriated Sukhanram by letting her stay in his room for the night, the ill-tempered driver barks at her and asks her to 'go sit in that corner'. Gulabi mistakes Narsingh's misogyny and apathy for his virtue, for here is a man who, for the first time in her life, hasn't lusted after her. It is this brief moment of respite in an otherwise miserable life of sexual and emotional abuse that is reason enough for her to find heaven in the company of a man who does not even like her, and to promptly decide that she would give anything to spend the rest of her life with him. The scene is devastatingly tragic and beautiful at the same time, and Ray handles it with great sensitivity and a deep understanding of a woman's heart.

The film also marks the beginning of Ray's long-term association with actor Rabi Ghosh, who went on to act in several of Ray's films, including his final one, *Agantuk* (The Stranger). Ghosh is spot-on as Narsingh's handyman Rama, hitting all the right notes with his impeccable comic timing, beautiful expressions and perfect body language, which most actors can only dream of mastering. His allegiance to his employer is unshakeable, but in a beautiful scene in which Narsingh announces that he has decided to sell the Chrysler, Rama shows, with breathtakingly beautiful flair, that his love for the car, which he has nurtured and cared for with great love and affection over the years, is even greater than his loyalty to his master.

Soumitra Chattopadhyay once again excels as the proud, foul-mouthed, hot-tempered, blue-blooded taxi driver struggling to find his place in a world where honour and dignity stand for nothing. His bruised ego, his constant desire to be respected and his deep-seated insecurities lead him to take a few wrong turns in life, but the warrior within him knows how to find his way back. It has been said that long-time Ray admirer, director Martin Scorsese took inspiration from Chatterjee's Narsingh to create the iconic character of Travis Bickle in his 1976 film *Taxi Driver*. While there may or may not be some truth to that claim, Chatterjee infuses the character with a never-ending conflict of emotions, a vast range of shades, effortlessly making it his own. Consider, for example, his hatred for women—which is totally absent in his attitude towards Neeli, whom he sees as an educated woman, one to be respected and revered. Or the conflict between his fierce desire to remain independent and the urge to earn dignity through financial stability. Chatterjee pulls off these clashes of emotion with great skill and makes us root for him. We want him to take Rama under his wing again. We want him to rescue Gulabi from the clutches of her oppressors. We want him to win, but not through shortcuts. But more than anything else, we want him to find peace. And that's exactly what he does in the film's climax. In *Abhijan*, then, Ray shows us that the greatest expedition that we can ever hope to embark upon is the one we are in the middle of right now, right this moment.

Mahanagar

The Big City (1963)

THE YEAR WAS 1963. SATYAJIT RAY, ALREADY ESTABLISHED BY THEN as one of the best filmmakers India had ever produced, had just come out of making two of his weakest and least popular films, which had received unprecedented criticism and were commercial failures. He had, in his own words, learnt the bitter lesson of what happens when commerce starts interfering with the art of filmmaking. Under such unfavourable circumstances, Ray made a film that silenced all his critics in a single sweep—a film that once again exposed the hypocrisies of middle-class Bengali society when it came to empowering its women. That film, which Ray adapted from a short story by Bengali author Narendranath Mitra, was *Mahanagar* (The Big City).

Arati is the quintessential middle-class Bengali homemaker—a perfect wife to her loving husband Subrata, a caring mother to her eight-year-old son Pintu, and an obedient, dutiful and deeply respectful daughter-in-law to her husband's parents, Priyagopal and Sarojini. Although not quite hand to mouth, the family does live under significant financial strain, especially after retired schoolmaster Priyagopal decides to leave his village and come and live with his son in the big city. Subrata is the sole earning member of the family and has as many as six mouths to feed, including a school-going sister. Outside of work, he takes private

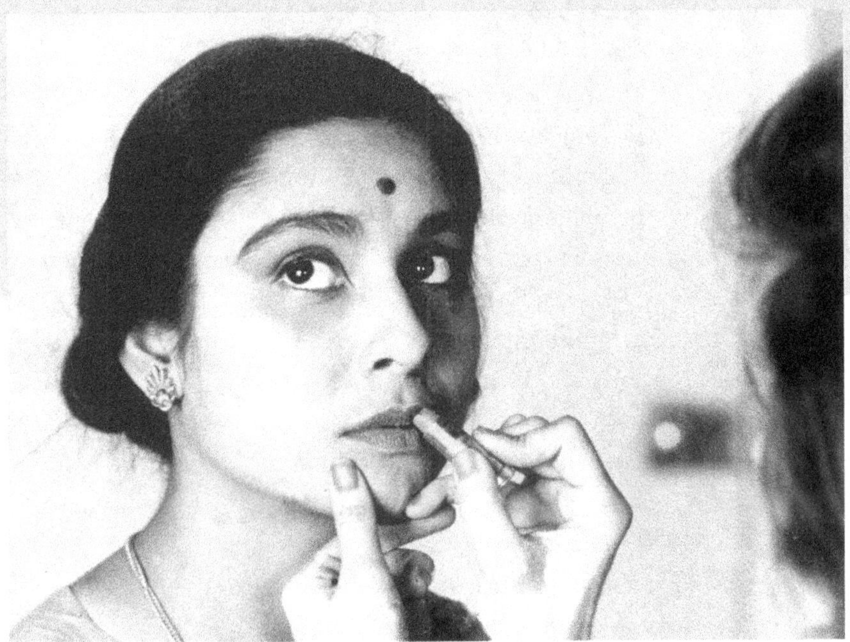

Edith applies lipstick on her friend and colleague Arati.

tuitions for a few students, but even then, his income seems to fall short. Arati manages the household without any complaints and performs her duties with grace and elegance. One day, when she learns that a family acquaintance's wife has taken up a job, she wonders why she, too, can't do the same to ease the burden on her husband. Subrata supports his wife, but her in-laws don't. Arati soon secures the job of a salesgirl in a firm selling knitting machines, and money begins to flow in. Thanks to the hard work that comes so naturally to her as a housewife, Arati's income soon begins to exceed that of her husband, and this makes Subrata rather insecure. He asks Arati to give up her job and resume her role as the perfect homemaker once again. Arati agrees, because to her, domestic amity is far more important than money. But on the very day that she is supposed to submit her resignation, her husband loses his job, which forces her to continue to play the role of the bread earner of the family, even amid grave personal turmoil at her workplace.

Ray's usual technical brilliance, economy of dialogue, appropriately paced narrative and mind-boggling detailing aside, what sets *Mahanagar* apart is the social relevance of the subject. Anyone who has either experienced or studied the life of a typical middle-class household in India will be able to identify with the many obstacles that the woman of the house has to negotiate day in and day out. While some of these problems are financial—for instance, when her husband asks her about the condition of her coffers at the end of the month, Arati says with an assuring smile on her face, 'We have enough for three more days'—there are some others that have to do with the mindset of the people around her—for instance, her father-in-law refuses to accept her first month's salary when she offers it to him as a respectful gift. 'The place of a woman is at home'—this was the unwritten rule of all such households until not very long ago, and perhaps is even today. Suffering under severe financial burdens and yet not allowing a smart, educated and perfectly capable woman to bring home money—this has been a common practice. And this does not even begin to take into account the other consideration of the entire issue—a woman's financial independence, her individuality, separate from that of her role as a wife, a mother or a daughter-in-law. Ray strikes, and strikes hard, at the heart of this prejudice—and shows us, in a very gentle way, how flawed the logic against working women is.

One of the most fascinating things about *Mahanagar* is its deep character study, without even once showing a single individual in a negative or poor light. Take the patriarch of the family, for instance. An aged and mentally anguished retired schoolteacher, who laments the cursed luck of meagre-salaried teachers in this country, Priyagopal goes around the city visiting his former students—all of them now established and successful individuals in their own right—and vents his misgivings about his own son. In a beautifully written scene early on in the film, he goes to one such ex-student, who is now a famous ophthalmologist, and tells him with great hesitation that he needs eyeglasses but cannot afford them. When his student tells him with great reverence that he would be more than happy to offer a pair of eyeglasses to him as a *gurudakshina*, the old man seems to find great peace, not because he would have glasses but because of that specific word that his student chose to use.

Subrata's character has been beautifully portrayed as well. Towards the beginning, despite feeling helpless amid his financial constraints, he takes it all with great maturity and composure—for instance, when he remarks jokingly, 'People are becoming millionaires simply by manufacturing beedis, and a BA-pass bank employee is losing his hair worrying about where his next meal is going to come from.' When his wife decides to take up a job, he is enthusiastically supportive of her—in fact, he finds the idea rather useful for the family. But in the face of domestic dissension, further fuelled by his own rapidly diminishing stature as the sole earning member of the family, he feels threatened and coldly withdraws his support—inadvertently distancing himself from his wife. He does come back to his wife, though, that, too, in the face of great tragedy, standing up for her in heartfelt, unconditional support this time, showing that his natural maturity and sense of right and wrong hasn't been shrouded by the veils of prejudice.

But the biggest and brightest star of the film is undoubtedly its leading lady, Madhabi Mukherjee. In the role of Arati, she gives one of the best performances of her career. She goes from the all-seeing, ever-smiling, perfect housewife at the beginning of the film to a fiercely independent, strong, confident and ethically upright young woman, who knows how to stand up against injustice by the end of the story. She is a loving mother in one instance and a skilful salesgirl in another. A good friend in one scene and a dutiful wife in another. She doesn't have any qualms about playing second fiddle to her man, simply because she doesn't believe that thwarts her stature in any way. And at the same time, she doesn't hesitate to protest against racial prejudice at her workplace. And in doing so, she shows us that be it a homemaker behind the closed doors of a household or a bright employee of a reputed merchant firm in the big bad world, there is one thing that is common to all women—an indomitable spirit.

Charulata

The Lonely Wife (1964)

WHEN ASKED BY INTERVIEWERS WHICH WAS HIS PERSONAL favourite among all the films he had made in his forty-year-long career, Satyajit Ray always said it was the film that had the least number of defects, and therefore, the one film that he would make in exactly the same way if asked to remake it—*Charulata* (The Lonely Wife). Today, this film—along with the Apu trilogy—acts as representative of his entire body of work.

The film is an adaptation of a novella titled *Nashtanirh* (The Broken Nest), written by Rabindranath Tagore. Set in the late nineteenth century, it tells the story of a young, intelligent, educated and beautiful woman named Charulata. She is the wife of an affluent, upper-class Bengali gentleman named Bhupati. A product of the Bengal Renaissance, Bhupati is an out-and-out liberal and runs an English-language newspaper named *The Sentinel*, aimed at criticising the unfair practices of the British government in India. Bhupati and Charu's marriage is a childless one, and the man has very little time for his wife. But he loves his wife dearly, encouraging her inherent artistic talents to flourish. Charu spends her days reading and supervising domestic chores. In such a situation arrives Bhupati's cousin Amal—a jovial, free-spirited young man, fresh out of college, with no ambition in life other than the pursuit of his

The iconic close-up shot from the film.

literary ambitions. Bhupati entrusts his cousin with the responsibility of nurturing Charu's artistic talents. Amal and Charu, both of the same age, and more friends than relatives, begin to spend time together. But as the days go by, Charu begins to fall in love with Amal. Sensing this, and unwilling to betray his brother's trust, Amal distances himself from Charu and leaves the city. Charu is shocked and dejected, and seeing her lament the void that Amal has left in her life, Bhupati realises the truth. The man and his wife are now left behind to reconcile—to pick up the pieces and rebuild their broken nest.

It is virtually impossible to place one's finger on one thing that makes *Charulata* one of Ray's finest films. With so many elements coming together to elevate the film to the height it has achieved today, one can only say that it is a miracle, along with the sublime acumen of a visionary director such as Ray, that created such a fine piece of cinema. Consider the visual storytelling, for instance. In the opening scene of the film, Ray establishes two important facts of the story with admirable finesse and a remarkable understatement. We see Charu moving from one room of the house to the other, watching passers-by on the street below from the windows. And then she wanders around in a room, meandering through a maze of furniture with a book in hand, her fingers gently caressing the edge of a table, as she absent-mindedly hums a tune to herself. We instantly know two things about her. First, that she is a woman confined to the interiors of her house, much like the mynah in the cage seen later in the film. And second, that she is bored—reading the same books over and over again, wandering around in her own home, not knowing where to go. Not a single word of dialogue is spoken—there's no narration—and yet, with such elegance, Ray sets up the mood for the rest of the story.

The rest of the film is filled with such marvellous examples of visual storytelling. Charu is standing at the doorway of her bedroom and Bhupati passes by without so much as noticing her, and she immediately raises her opera glasses to her eyes in a symbolic bid to bring her husband closer to herself. Charu swaying gently on a swing in the garden as Amal lies on a mat under a tree, soaking in the play of light and shade—a moment of liberation for both of them, beautifully poised to turn into a moment of coming together. The attraction here is not sexual in nature, although the sexual tension does exist in the latter half of the film. But here, it is just the freeing of the spirit, under the open skies.

If the moving images are not enough, consider the brilliance of Ray's background music. Understated to the extent that it almost becomes an integral part of the image on screen, Ray uses a mix of Tagore's songs and his own compositions to gently hover around the setting, giving the scenes a magical, dream-like quality. Coupled with the beautiful and well-researched set design by his art director Bansi Chandragupta and an excellent sound design, these scenes transport one to the inner world of a late-nineteenth-century upper-class household.

And then, of course, there are the performances. That the three central characters of the film give the best performances of their careers in the same film speaks volumes about this aspect of the film. Sailen Mukherjee, a veteran actor of the stage, accepts the tutelage of his director and plays each scene assigned to him with perfection. His Bhupati is so consumed by the ideas of liberalism that he cannot see the plight of his wife even when she is in his arms. When he finds out the true feelings of his wife, he is shattered, and wanders aimlessly through the streets of the city, weeping silently. The ebullient Amal, played beautifully by Soumitra Chattopadhyay, steals your heart right from the scene in which he enters the household unannounced and unexpected in the middle of a typical Bengal *kalboishakhi* (the violent Nor'westers), reciting the lines from Bankim Chandra Chattopadhyay's novel at the top of his voice. Notice the ease with which he walks into his brother's office, offers him a quick pranam and casually points to the desk, asking, 'Who's that tea for?', gulping it down in an instant the very next moment. His scenes with his *bouthaan* (sister-in-law) are elegant and the camaraderie is visible as they look at each other with affection and admiration.

From the opening scene all the way to the last, though, the film is completely owned by Madhabi Mukherjee, who *becomes* Charulata— blood, bone and vein. Bored beyond redemption and languishing in the company of a rustic sister-in-law, with whom she cannot have a single meaningful conversation, she is much like the mynah she herself cages. Mukherjee plays Charu with a deep understanding of the character and a visible sense of empathy for her. It has often been seen that while lending shades of grey to the protagonist of a film, an actor tends to bring in a semblance of justification, which tends to simmer just under the surface of the character she or he is playing, thus forcing the character to just fall short of being real. But Madhabi Mukherjee is too intelligent an actress to make that mistake. She brings to Charu an alarming degree of envy, an unrestrained attraction towards a man she knows she cannot desire and an almost invisible suspension of her loyalty towards her husband, making Charulata one of the finest female characters ever assayed on the Indian screen.

Two (1964)

AN UNQUENCHABLE THIRST FOR VARIETY IS THE HALLMARK OF A great artist. Having directed several feature films and one documentary, Ray made a short film in 1964—a twelve-minute film under the banner of 'Esso World Theatre', a cultural programme telecast by the non-profit government-funded television programming distributor in America named the PBS (Public Broadcasting Service) and sponsored by the American oil company Esso. In a bid to showcase the world outside their own to their viewers, and yet to make them understand what was being shown on screen, the producers had requested Ray to make the film in a Bengali setting but in the English language. The combination didn't quite appeal to Ray, who decided to solve the problem by doing away with the spoken word altogether in his film, seeing this as an opportunity to pay tribute to the golden era of silent films. The film he thus made was called *Two*, and it depended solely on sound and music. Although it is perhaps the least watched of Ray's works, critics and experts around the world consider it one of the best films ever made by him.

Ray called *Two* a 'film fable', one which showed two boys, both six–seven years old, duelling with each other, each showing off his toys in a bid to outdo the other, in the middle of a lonely and breezy summer afternoon. The first boy comes from an affluent family. The film opens with a shot (which was later used in another short film by Ray titled

The rich boy has everything, and yet, by the end of the film, he realises he is not free.

Pikoo) of his parents leaving him alone at his palatial home with a large collection of toys. The boy, wearing a Mickey Mouse cap, wanders from room to room, bursting balloons from the night before, which happened to be his birthday. He plays with his toys, especially with a robot he has been gifted and a toy tower that he has been building all morning. Despite all the toys around him, he soon gets bored and is wondering what to do to pass time, when, suddenly, on hearing the sound of a flute, he rushes to his window to find a young boy of the same age as he, living in a shanty dwelling in the grassland behind his house, playing his flute happily. In a bid to draw the poor boy's attention, the rich boy brings his own expensive electronic trumpet to the window and bellows with it. And soon, before you know it, the two boys begin showing off their toys and masks to each other—the rich kid's expensive ones, and the poor boy's cheap, handmade ones. Very soon, the poor boy realises that his prized possessions are no match for the rich boy's, and decides to give up and engage himself in flying his kite instead. The rich boy is clearly not happy with this decision, because he is confined to the house and his competitor is out there in the open. In a fit of childish envy, he shoots the poor boy's kite down with his toy airgun. Realising that the rich boy is way too powerful and will not let him play in peace, the poor boy sadly retires behind his hut and resumes playing his flute. The rich boy, now victorious but left all alone, sits and thinks about what he has done, even as he tries to drown out the sound of the flute in the cacophony of his toys. In the final scene of the film, his toy robot, now left unattended and unguided, walks into the tall tower he has built with painstaking efforts, making it crash to the ground.

The film is inarguably the most allegorical of Ray's entire body of work. Despite being a simple tale involving two young boys, it deals with such complex subjects as loneliness, the human capital, the socio-economic divide, the philosophy of happiness and contentment, the evils of consumerism, the futility of war, mankind's resistance to oppression and the true meaning of freedom. Ray himself considered *Two* one of his most profound works and, in a letter he wrote to his biographer

Marie Seton, described it as 'a film that packs quite a punch in its ten minutes'. Ray had been deeply moved by the Vietnam War; in later years, he made several veiled as well as direct commentaries (such as *Goopy Gyne Bagha Byne* and *Pratidwandi,* respectively) on the war, and about the extraordinary resilience shown by the ordinary people, mostly the peasants of Vietnam, in the face of death brought upon them by a superpower such as America. But many years before these films, he made a silent protest against the war in *Two.* Through the poor boy, he shows the infallible capacity of the human spirit to pick up the pieces after a great loss and move on, to find a quiet, undisturbed corner of the world to resume life. As a stark contrast, through the rich boy, he shows the hollow rewards of a victory earned through vile means, especially in a battle that shouldn't have taken place in the first place. In *Two,* Ray also shows his deep understanding of the mind of a child. Impressionable and prone to mimic what it sees around itself—both good and bad—a child's mind can be as pretty as it can be perilous. In *Two,* for instance, while one boy turns a moment of loneliness into one of joyous music, the other sees it as an opportunity for destruction.

Two is the sort of film that stays with you for days, even after you have stopped thinking about it in your conscious mind. Because it is not one message that it sends your way. The film is a hard-hitting basket of messages and meanings—all densely packed in a twelve-minute film. And such a feat is possible only by a filmmaker such as Ray.

Kapurush

The Coward (1965)

The women in Satyajit Ray's films have always been exceptionally strong characters. This could perhaps be attributed to his personal experiences with the two women in his life—his mother, who, widowed at a very young age, showed exemplary courage and grit to raise him single-handedly, and his wife, who stood by him and lent her wholehearted support to his creative pursuits, even when things weren't going well for him. In his 1965 film *Kapurush* (The Coward) too, Ray chooses to portray the silent courage of a strong-willed woman, by juxtaposing her against the film's protagonist, who is timid, irresolute and unsure of himself.

The film's story is quite straightforward and simple. Amitabha Roy is a young screenwriter living and working in Calcutta, who is stranded in a small and remote town in the foothills of the Himalayas when his car breaks down in the middle of the night. A local tea planter named Bimal Gupta offers to shelter him for the night in his bungalow in a nearby tea estate, somewhat out of his own desire for company in such a lonely and godforsaken place. With no alternative for spending the night, Amitabha accepts, only to find that the planter's wife is a woman named Karuna, whom he was in love with several years ago. In the rest of the film, it is revealed that Amitabha and Karuna used to be in the

Over the course of the film, Karuna proves to
Amitabha, time and again, that he is a coward.

same college and were in love with each other. When Karuna's uncle had decided to marry her off to someone else, she had left everything behind and come to Amitabha to start a new life with him. But the jobless and insecure Amitabha had lacked the courage to take such a bold step and had broken Karuna's heart by letting her down and sending her back to her family. Amitabha had gone his own way and Karuna had ended up marrying Bimal Gupta instead.

As the film progresses, we find Amitabha's bruised ego not being able to cope with the fact that Karuna has quietly adjusted to her new life, and he keeps insisting that she is not happy—until he realises that it is he, not her, who lacks the strength to bear the tragedy of the break-up. In the film's beautiful climax, Amitabha is presented with another opportunity to get back with the love of his life after all these years, and is faced with a dilemma that will turn out to be the litmus test of his character.

The film, released in 1965, is an adaptation of a short story written by veteran Bengali author Premendra Mitra, and other than the geographical backdrop and a few other details, primarily those around the planter gentleman and his rather simplistic view of life, Ray pretty much sticks to the original story. As with all his other films from those marvellous years of his career, Ray infuses his screenplay with a breezy quality, going back and forth in time to help the story move forward. The flashbacks move in reverse order of chronology, helping the viewers truly understand the hopeless deterioration of the states of mind of the young lovers. We see the glow on the young couple's faces fade away as their relationship slowly yet surely seems to fail the test of time. While the man's spirit only weakens as their love faces seemingly unsurmountable hurdles, the woman's firmness only goes from strength to strength—until they find themselves standing too far apart from each other for any meaningful association any more. This realisation comes in a scene that has very little dialogue—and all that Ray uses to portray the emotions of the two characters involved are their expressions and gestures. Like the rest of the film, the film's background score is minimalistic in its essence, with most of the themes playing only during the transition between the two timelines.

It is not easy to portray a grey character convincingly, especially when the character requires a certain complexity, almost bordering on an unshakeable conviction that every single action of his is a justifiable one. Soumitra Chattopadhyay plays the young and hesitant Amitabha with admirable charm. He is a sight for sore eyes in one instant and a despairing mess in another. We can easily see that he is hurting to find his old flame playing the perfect wife to another man, but with admirable dexterity, he also ensures that he doesn't get our compassion. Only an actor of the highest order can achieve something like that.

Haradhan Bandopadhyay is excellent as the lonely and burnt-out tea planter, who is bored to death 'growing this blasted tea, and drinking whisky' to drown his loneliness. He laughs out loud at the slightest of pretexts, perhaps only to suffocate the voice of his inner conscience. His views of life are without any complexities and his loquaciousness is a perfect antidote to his wife's natural reticence.

But the real star of the film is Karuna, played brilliantly by veteran actress Madhabi Mukherjee. She emotes with her eyes throughout the film, exhibiting a complete spectrum of feelings—right from those of a teenage college girl embarrassed to discover on board a moving bus that she has forgotten her purse back home, all the way to the calm confidence of a jilted woman who has made peace with her life and who will never trust any man again. Her biggest strength is her power to forgive and forget. And it is through her eyes that we witness the cowardice of the film's protagonist. In the end, the essence of Ray's *Kapurush* can perhaps best be summed up in a simple scene early on in the film, where the young Amitabha pleads with Karuna to give him some time to settle down before taking the big leap of marriage, at which Karuna turns towards him with subtle contempt in her eyes and says, 'It is not time that you lack, it is something else.'

Mahapurush
The Holy Man (1965)

THE SUBJECT OF FRAUDULENT HOLY MEN HAS RETURNED TO Satyajit Ray's works as themes on several occasions and in several forms. In many of his short stories, novellas and novels, and a sixty-five-minute film titled *Mahapurush* (The Holy Man), Ray tried to address the issue and managed to show with great acumen the dangers involved in being patrons of such self-professed saints and voices of god in the name of religious piousness and devotion. In *Mahapurush*, Ray's treatment of the subject is through comedy—a far cry from two of his other films that presented serious and all-out criticisms of blind faith (*Devi* and *Ganashatru*).

Adapted from a hilarious short story written by eminent Bengali author and humourist Rajshekhar Basu (more popularly known by his pen name Parashuram), *Mahapurush* tells the story of Birinchi Baba, a holy man who claims to have seen the founding of the city of Varanasi more than two thousand years ago, and to have had arguments with Jesus Christ on the subject of wealth, and to have been friends with Plato, and to have taught the theory of relativity to a young fellow named Einstein, among several other such tall and outrageous claims. Birinchi Baba meets an affluent old advocate, who has recently lost his wife, and has a profound impact on the widower's already bruised mind. The advocate

The 'gang' that busts the godman's myth.

invites Birinchi Baba and his assistant to his home in Calcutta, and the Baba makes a 'semi-permanent settlement' in the old man's house, giving sermons and offering spiritual advice. In a matter of days, several devotees begin to throng the old man's house to meet the Baba and take his blessings—most of these people quite rich and affluent themselves, and capable of bribing their way to the front row for greater proximity to the saint. When the advocate asks his daughter to become a disciple of the Baba, the young girl's lover, a young man named Satya, turns to his gang of friends for help, and the four men devise a plan to expose Birinchi Baba.

One of the most fascinating things about Ray was that when tackling a social evil, religious fanaticism or superstition of any kind, he always studied the subject very carefully to fully understand it before criticising it. In this film too, Ray knew the importance of understanding exactly why a conman in a saffron robe is able to make a fool of so many seemingly educated and intelligent men and women. And this led to making his antagonist seem like a worthy opponent, which is why he decided to spend more than half the film in exhibiting the many skills of Birinchi Baba—those that enable him to rule the hearts of his devotees with such finesse. As the leader of the gang trying to plan the exposé himself admits, Birinchi Baba has many admirable qualities. For instance, he is an actor of the highest order, extremely well read, one who has a very good understanding of mass psychology, has a photographic memory and an astonishingly fertile imagination, commands a remarkable presence of mind, and, above all, has the guts to pull off such a charade in front of so many people day after day. In his speeches, Birinchi Baba tells one lie after another, but he tells them with such flair, with so much imagination, that they don't seem like fabrications anymore, certainly not to the uninitiated or the poorly informed. He is a smooth talker often saying the same things in many different ways, but not once making it seem like he's repeating himself. In his free time, he reads. As a man, he has an extremely pleasing personality, and despite being malicious in intent, is careful not to be excessively greedy.

Having spent enough time painting his antagonist's character well, Ray lay considerable emphasis on describing the gang that plans and executes the exposé as well. The leader of the group is Nibaran Chakraborty, a professor in a college in the city. He is a man of few words, reads a wide variety of subjects (from *Madame Bovary* to Shakespeare), loves chess, is a free thinker and despises hypocrites. Paramartha Chatterjee is a young insurance agent, who also tries his hand at hatha yoga in his free time. And the third member of the gang is a middle-aged man named Nitai-da, a poor ledger-keeper in a local merchant office, who is fed up of his routine existence and an incessantly nagging wife. What this ragtag group of individuals have in common, though, is an unquenchable thirst to do something interesting and meaningful in their lives from time to time. When Satya brings the news of Birinchi Baba to them, they come together to help him send the holy man packing and win his lady-love's heart in the process.

The film itself was part of a double feature, screened along with Ray's *Kapurush* (The Coward). As with several other comedies of Ray, *Mahapurush*, too, wasn't as well received by Western audiences as some of his serious films. This is perhaps because it is difficult to absorb the nuances of a comic story outside of its milieu, unless the comedy is presented in more 'physical' forms, such as slapstick or tomfoolery. *Mahapurush* was neither, and was primarily a dialogue-based comedy.

And that brings us to another remarkable aspect of Ray's approach to cinema. Despite knowing that a large portion of his audience was from outside the country, Ray never tried to target his films at them. As he himself claimed, his primary audience was always the average Bengali man and woman. It is for them that he made his films. In consciously choosing to do so, he showed exceptional creative maturity, because working in Bengal—with Bengali actors and a Bengali crew—to make a film for an audience far removed from the Bengali way of life would be a perfect recipe for artistic disaster. Ray knew this and was willing to sacrifice foreign critical acclaim on some of his subjects, only to be showered with praise for many others. For him, the art and its execution always took precedence over what followed by way of reception—and that always showed in his films, without exception. In *Mahapurush* too, this is evident, and the film was extremely well received by its target audience.

Nayak

The Hero (1966)

Satyajit Ray often used to say that he did not like making grand films and that he would rather tell the story of the ordinary man, the man on the street. Like his films, his short stories, too, mirrored this preference—most of them describing the lives of ordinary men, all of whom were, without exception, very lonely. Why, then, did Ray decide to make *Nayak* (The Hero), a film on the life of an immensely popular matinee idol—a brash, haughty young superstar riding the waves of popularity and enjoying it to the hilt? The answer is hidden in the many layers of the film itself—a film that is so rich, so deep and yet, told in such simple language that perhaps it would not be a mistake to claim that it featured among the best works of Ray's illustrious career.

Arindam Mukherjee is the indomitable superstar in the Bengali film industry and has been riding high on the popularity charts, thanks to a seemingly never-ending string of box-office hits. He is invited to Delhi to receive a prestigious award, and not being able to secure a flight seat, he boards a train instead, planning to 'sleep it off' until he reaches his destination. Travelling with him in the same train are myriad characters from various walks of life, each with his or her own story. The most interesting of these, however, is Aditi—a young journalist for a women's magazine titled *Adhunika* (the Modern Woman). Aditi abhors the glitz

Arindam refuses to help his old friend Biresh.

and glamour of meaningless commercial cinema and harbours nothing but mute disdain for the superstar travelling with her. However, in a bid to increase the sales of her magazine, she requests Arindam Mukherjee for an interview, and the bored star agrees in good humour. Unwilling to answer her questions honestly at first, he begins to frustrate the novice journalist. But soon enough, owing to a subconscious need to speak to someone, Arindam begins to wander down the dark lanes and by-lanes of his memories—both good and bad—and begins to describe various incidents in his life. As Aditi tries to get to the man behind the star layer by layer, she begins to discover a haunting truth—that despite all the fandom, popularity and success, Arindam Mukherjee is an inherently lonely man who needs a friend, more than anything else. His insecurities, guilt, grief and hatred towards himself—everything comes bare as he inadvertently opens his heart to this woman. On the other hand, Aditi, who has got the 'scoop' of her life, realises that she has scratched one surface too many and that Arindam Mukherjee is no different than anyone else riding on that train. And it is in this realisation that her hatred for the superstar ceases to exist. As the train pulls into Delhi station, she decides not to publish the interview, leaving the hero surrounded by his fans, and disappears from his life forever.

The film is one of only three feature films in Ray's body of work that are not adaptations and are original screenplays written by Ray himself. Told in free style, punctuated with occasional humour and smart wit, running back and forth, thanks to flashbacks and dream sequences, and taking its time to denude the protagonist of his external garb of casual indifference, *Nayak* is perhaps the best example of one of Ray's many cinematic skills—his mastery over the narrative. It is not easy to handle multiple storylines intersecting with each other. But Ray does it with admirable flair and with such simplicity that not one transition looks jarring. What's even more astonishing and awe-inspiring is that each of the passengers travelling in the train somehow seems to be connected with the protagonist, in how the void in their lives is not unlike that in the life of a superstar. And it is in that sense that Arindam Mukherjee is reduced to just another passenger in the train, journeying through life, from one point to another.

The film boasts some terrific performances—in fact, there are far too many of them to simply gloss over. Yet, there are two that deserve special mention. Sharmila Tagore plays Aditi with grace, elegance and intelligence, exuding a calm confidence that catches the star's attention, because he is normally used to seeing the obliged faces of fans and sycophants crowding around him. When she comes out of her shell and reaches out to the man behind the superstar, you can see that her concern is genuine—and that it does not depend on box-office figures or the desire to secure an autograph. She reaches out to Arindam Mukherjee as a woman would reach out to a man who needs someone to talk to. There is a scene in the film in which she chides him in a stern voice, and for a fleeting moment, we see her bare *her* heart to the man, for a change. In one of the most poignant scenes of the film, one that is studied by film enthusiasts all over the world today, when the train is about to reach its final destination, Aditi walks up to Arindam Mukherjee to say goodbye and tears up the sheets of paper in which she had recorded her interview with him. When Arindam Mukherjee asks her why she did that and if she knew the interview by heart, she replies by saying, 'I'll … keep it in my heart.'

And then there is Uttam Kumar. Bengal's greatest superstar plays Bengal's greatest superstar in Ray's *Nayak*. If that is not one of the greatest casting coups in the history of Indian cinema, I don't know what is. Kumar, at the height of his popularity then, played a matinee idol whose insecurities and guilt were to be stripped bare in the film. Not an easy decision to take, if you think about it. But Kumar shows that he is not considered the star of the millennium without reason. In a long career of fantastic performances, his work in *Nayak* is, by far, his best. He smiles and cries; he is frightened and begs for his life; he is vindictive and ruthless; he is a king and a wretch; ambitious in the beginning and hopeless when he has achieved it all; he is a romantic at heart in one scene, and repentant and frustrated in another—all within the span of one film. Ray was exceedingly impressed with Kumar's acting skills. When Kumar passed away, Ray wrote in his obituary that appeared in *Sunday* in August 1980, 'I hardly recall any discussion with Uttam on a serious analytical level on the character he was playing. And yet he constantly surprised and delighted me with unexpected little details of action and behaviour which came from him and not from me, which were always in character and always enhanced a scene. They were so spontaneous that it seemed he produced these out of his sleeve. If there was any cogitation involved, he never spoke about it.'

With a touching story, a collection of fantastic performances and a great captain at the helm of it all, *Nayak* is easily one of Ray's most incisive and detailed studies of human nature. Ray goes to the heart of the question—who is truly happy?—turning it on its head and asking instead: What, in fact, is true happiness? Which of those passengers in the train are truly happy and content? A careful watching of the film and a little reflection would make us realise that perhaps the most inconsequential characters of the film are the ones who are truly happy, which could, in turn, probably make us wonder: have we been looking for happiness in all the wrong places all this while?

Chiriyakhana

The Zoo (1967)

IT IS A WIDELY KNOWN FACT THAT FILMMAKER SATYAJIT RAY WAS also the creator of one of the most popular detectives in Bengali literature—private investigator Prodosh Chandra Mitra, or Feluda—and that he went on to make two films based on Feluda's adventures. Those unfamiliar with Ray's filmography may probably not know that Ray had also made a film on an adventure of the other popular sleuth of Bengal—detective Byomkesh Bakshi. That film, made in 1967 and starring the legendary Uttam Kumar, was *Chiriyakhana* (The Zoo). While all the ingredients seemed to be in place—a fascinating story, a popular detective, the greatest matinee idol of Bengali cinema playing the said detective and the master of the craft himself directing him in that role—*Chiriyakhana* has since earned the dubious reputation of being considered by Ray himself as the weakest film in his body of work.

A retired judge named Nishanath Sen approaches Byomkesh Bakshi on a rainy day. He tells Byomkesh that he has a nursery and a dairy farm in the suburbs of the city and that several 'inmates' live in his colony and work for him. These inmates are not ordinary people—each of them has either some sort of physical deformity or a dark past. Nishanath tasks Byomkesh with finding more information on a certain song from an old Bengali film, because he suspects that the actress who sang it might

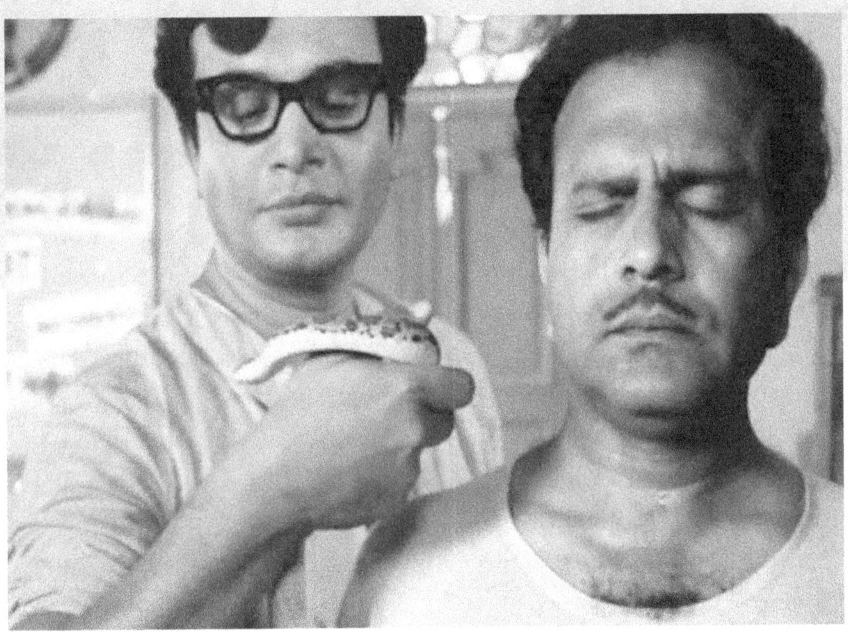

Byomkesh having a bit of fun with his 'spineless' friend. And, of course, with Ajit.

be hiding in his colony under an assumed identity. Nishanath also tells Byomkesh that of late, someone has been sending various motor parts to his office, although the objective of such a strange exercise was a complete mystery to him. Byomkesh and his friend Ajit visit Nishanath's colony and meet the strange and suspicious characters inhabiting it, but before they can investigate further, Nishanath is murdered. It then falls upon Byomkesh to find out who the killer is and how the man is related to the song or to the mysterious motor parts.

Veteran crime writer Sharadindu Bandyopadhyay's story serves as a wonderful setting for Uttam Kumar to work his magic as Byomkesh Bakshi, which he does with commendable flair. But Ray's lack of attention to detail and the generally rushed flow of the film are for every film fan to see. The scenes hardly 'hold' together. The background music is in shambles. The audio is of very poor quality, and the dubbing is worse. There are issues with continuity. And despite some genuine efforts, the characters sometimes descend into caricature. The screenplay is not even remotely close to the high standards of Ray's usual work, and some of the scenes, such as a sequence in which Byomkesh shadows one of the inmates of the colony to a seedy Anglo-Indian neighbourhood in Calcutta, are, frankly, childish. The film does have some good camerawork in some scenes, though—for instance, the one in which Byomkesh interrogates the deceased judge's wife. And although Kumar brings just the right mix of sharp wit and carefree spirit to the character of the sleuth, he alone cannot save the film from being a disaster.

A bit of background might help one understand why some of these errors might have crept into the film. Right from the inception of the film, *Chiriyakhana* had been riddled with one problem after another—ranging from Ray's usual financiers backing out at the last moment, and problems with schedules and dates when Kumar bagged a role in a Hindi film in Bombay (now Mumbai), to problems with crowd management during outdoor shoots and coffers running dry while the film was being made. And, finally, there was the unexpectedly impossible task of finding distributors once the film was somehow completed. Ray kept his patience and stuck with the film, going to the extent of improvising with the film's background music when he ran out of money. It is said that he locked himself in a hotel room with nothing but a tape recorder and whatever musical instruments he could find lying around in his house. When he stepped out of the room the next day, the film's background score was ready.

Of course, objectively speaking, these are not reasons enough to justify the poor quality of the film, because Ray had faced much greater hardships and far worse obstacles in making the absolutely marvellous film we all know him for—*Pather Panchali*. But every creative artist has to have one black spot on his otherwise impressive résumé. For Ray, that turned out to be *Chiriyakhana*. There is no doubt that it is a poor film, by all standards. But what is remarkably strange to note is what happened after it was released in theatres. In a scene early on in the film, Nishanath Sen asks Byomkesh Bakshi, 'Do you watch Bengali films?' To which Byomkesh immediately responds in the negative without a trace of hesitation, reflecting Ray's own strongly critical views on the quality of Bengali films being made in those days, and their audience. It is perhaps a strange twist of irony, then, that the same audience made his film *Chiriyakhana*—which was, by his own admittance, the worst he ever made—into a box-office success!

Goopy Gyne Bagha Byne
The Adventures of Goopy and Bagha (1969)

WHEN SATYAJIT RAY'S THIRTEEN-YEAR-OLD SON COMPLAINED TO him one day that he only made films for adults, Ray decided to make a fun-filled adventure fantasy film for children. Finding the right story was the least of his problems, because Ray came from a family of illustrious writers of children's literature. Of the abundant treasure trove of such stories that his ancestors—both male and female—had left behind as legacy, Ray chose one written by his grandfather, Upendrakishore Ray Chowdhury, who was one of the pioneers of the cultural renaissance of Bengal. This story, a fantasy of sorts, spoke about the amazing adventures of two simpletons from two neighbouring villages—Goopy, who liked to sing, and Bagha, who liked to play the dhol. But as luck would have it, despite their keen interest in singing and playing the dhol, nature had not bestowed either of them with the gift of music. When Goopy and Bagha rile the king with their tone-deaf cacophony, they are exiled from their respective villages and happen to meet in the middle of a dense forest, where they stumble upon the King of Ghosts, who gives them three magic boons. The first allows them to ask for any food or dress whenever they like. The second gives them each a pair of magic

*Goopy and Bagha find out that they have
been blessed by the King of Ghosts.*

shoes so they can travel wherever they like in the blink of an eye. And in the third, and most important boon, they are given the gift of music, so much so that they are able to hold anyone in their magical thrall with their music. Armed with these three magic boons, they reach the kingdom of Shundi, only to learn that the king of Halla has declared war against his brother, the peace-loving king of Shundi. Goopy and Bagha take great risks to visit Halla as spies, and stop the war in the nick of time.

As discussed before, the story was the least of Ray's problems—it was always there, within his reach. But right from the outset, Ray knew that unlike the films he had made so far, this one would cost a great deal of money to make. His regular financiers backed out and Ray spent the better half of the year looking for producers, finally finding one but on the condition that he would have to make the entire film in black and white to save costs. Not one to give up easily, Ray did make the film, and it went on to become one of the biggest commercial successes not only of his career but of the Bengali film industry as well. Because, like his forefathers, Ray, too, knew that a good children's story is not enjoyed only by children, but by adults as well.

In *Goopy Gyne Bagha Byne*, Ray introduced certain subtle themes and messages, which made the film more than just a fantasy tale—it became a strong sociopolitical commentary on the notion of war and peace. For instance, when the evil prime minister of Halla sends his spy to find out what preparations the people of Shundi had made for the eventuality of war, the spy comes back to report that they had made none. On being asked what they *did* have instead, the spy reports in a dreamy voice, 'They have fruits and flowers in the trees, they have crops in their fields, birds singing on the branches, people living happily …' Then again, when Goopy and Bagha are captured in Halla and thrown into prison, their magic shoes not with them anymore, they feel powerless and face death behind bars. But music? How does one cage music? In the middle of the night, Goopy sings a soulful number, his voice soaring like a free bird over the palace, finally reaching the ears of the king of Halla with a simple message, 'If only once he would come down from his throne and enjoy the cool breeze in the fields, he would find his peace, he would find his peace, he would find his peace.'

One of the most fascinating things about this film is the recurring theme of simplicity. On meeting the King of Ghosts, for instance, when Goopy and Bagha could have asked for all the wealth in the world, they merely ask that their basic needs be fulfilled instead, because being village simpletons, even the little that they have is good enough for them. Technically, too, the film is brilliant, with an epic six-and-a-half-minute dance of the ghosts that Goopy and Bagha witness in the middle of the forest. The piece is a combination of Indian classical dances, with four categories of ghosts—the warriors, the sahibs, the priests and the common man—warring among themselves, finally killing each other off. Ray makes a strong social commentary based on the caste system and shows us that even the most powerful certainty in the world—death itself—is futile in the face of the insatiable hunger for war.

The film's casting was also rather interesting. Ray decided to cast Jahar Roy, a leading comedian in Bengali cinema, as the principal antagonist—the evil prime minister of Halla. Casting Santosh Dutta, another popular comedian, as both the king of Shundi and the king of Halla, and making several actors play multiple roles in the film are also interesting casting decisions—perhaps taken to save costs. While it was lauded widely in Bengal, and met with great critical and commercial acclaim outside India as well (particularly in Rome), one of the foreign criticisms of the film was that with a running time of 132 minutes, it was too long for a children's film. There may be some truth in that.

Tapen Chatterjee played Goopy, bringing to the role the endearing simplicity of a village bumpkin. In contrast to him in both physical stature and mannerisms was Rabi Ghosh as the much shorter Bagha, who, despite his street-smart ways, gelled well with his partner simply because of his good nature. Goopy may have been slow on the uptake, but he was no fool. Similarly, Bagha may have known what's best for him, but he was not one to further his own cause at the cost of someone else's.

In the duo, Ray gave us a lasting legacy of two immortal characters that have since formed an inseparable part of the Bengali lifestyle. Goopy and Bagha—two happy-go-lucky friends who love to sing, eat and travel to their heart's content. Isn't that the dream we all have?

But no discussion on *Goopy Gyne Bagha Byne* is complete without saying a few words about its music. Ray had always been known to use Indian music, instruments, leitmotifs and themes in his films. But never before had he used music so effectively to portray the mood of a story. The music of the film is light, joyous and gives a sense of cheerfulness without even once being loud or lurid. Like the story, the music, too, is simple, stripped to its bare minimum, and dwelling only on happy notes, bearing a sense of hope and love and everything that's beautiful. It is, if you were to listen to it carefully, exactly the sort of music that a father would compose for his child.

Aranyer Din Ratri

Days and Nights of the Forest (1969)

THERE ARE MANY WHO CONSIDER *ARANYER DIN RATRI* (DAYS AND Nights of the Forest) the best film of Satyajit Ray's post-Apu trilogy career. And why wouldn't they? High on subtlety, technically brilliant and hauntingly scored, it is a magnificent study of the urban youth, who have been conditioned to exist in a heightened state of callousness towards the rural poor, set against the serene and yet ruthless backdrop of the great leveller—the forest.

Four young men, city-bred and brimming with confidence, travel to the forests of Bihar to escape the daily grind of urban life, where each of them goes through a series of experiences that changes them in one way or the other. While the vain Asim (played by Soumitra Chattopadhyay) meets a beautiful and educated young lady named Aparna (Sharmila Tagore), who crushes his pride with ruthless subtlety, the easy-going and good-natured Sanjay (Subhendu Chatterjee) is faced with a moral dilemma that makes him question his own beliefs. The shy sportsman Hari (Samit Bhanja) is enamoured by the brimming sexuality of a young tribal girl, and good old Shekhar (Rabi Ghosh, in one of the best performances of his film career) finds himself helping all his friends, despite being fondly considered to be the buffoon of the gang. At the end

Aparna's calm maturity hurts Ashim's fragile ego.

of the film, as they leave the forest behind and go back to their day-to-day lives in the city, each of the friends realises that the forest has held up a mirror to his face and that he is now a changed man, although none of them dares to divulge the same to the others.

The film is an adaptation of legendary Bengali author Sunil Gangopadhyay's novel of the same name, but it is also true that Ray made several changes to the story to make it suitable for the screen. It is a widely known fact that the author was not happy with these changes. But for the film medium, the outcome worked exceedingly well. The humour is apt and subtle, for instance, in the scene where the four city-bred men are enjoying a refreshing bath with the ice-cold water of a well just outside the forest bungalow, and two young ladies they met the previous day show up at the bungalow right then, causing the men immense embarrassment. Or in the scene in which Shekhar tries to bribe the forest ranger with a cigarette and requests him to let them stay at the bungalow without reservation, but the man leaves without promising anything, prompting Sanjay to comment, 'There goes your Gold Flake.'

One of the most common mistakes in studying *Aranyer Din Ratri* is the assumption that it is a film about four men. Nothing could be farther from the truth. Consider the character of Jaya (played by Kaberi Bose), for instance, who has lost her husband to suicide—probably because of a failed extramarital affair. In one of the most tragic scenes in the film, the young Jaya propositions the bright and handsome Sanjay, but when Sanjay hesitates, she giggles nervously and asks, 'Why are you so frightened? You look like you've seen a ghost!', only to turn grave and sad the next moment, adding, 'A ghost indeed! What else do you call a woman when her husband dies?' Ray exposes the hypocrisy and double standards of society when it comes to the natural state of being a woman. In another scene, the brash and confident Asim tries to talk his way out of a nasty incident when the conservator of the forest catches them staying at the forest bungalow without proper permission. When he fails, and is almost about to be kicked out, it is Aparna who turns out to be the conservator's acquaintance and who manages the situation with her natural grace and composed presence of mind. The fact that this has hurt Asim's masculine pride does not escape Aparna's attention and she once again dissolves the tension elegantly by letting Asim win in a game they play during a picnic. But perhaps the most beautiful, least discussed and most overlooked scene of the film comes at a Santhal village fair, where the chivalrous Asim insists on paying for everything that Aparna buys. Aparna quietly lets him go ahead and pay. At the end of the day, when Asim asks for her phone number, she writes her number on a currency note and hands it to Asim, saying, 'I couldn't find any other scrap of paper.' One of the most influential film critics in the US, Pauline Keele, while writing for the *New Yorker*, said, 'No artist has done more than Ray to make us re-evaluate the commonplace'—and this one scene from *Aranyer Din Ratri* illustrates that comment beautifully.

A word or two needs to be said about the film's technical brilliance. The opening credits of the film are done beautifully. Among other things, Ray was a skilled calligrapher himself, and an adman too, and he used both skills to create the opening of the film, in which the scene of a dense forest rushing by, witnessed from inside a moving car, is inlaid into the title of the film. But the most famous talked-about technical wizardry in the film is Ray's handling of the camera during the famous 'memory game' scene. The four friends and the two women are sitting in a circle, and each has to take turns to say the name of a famous personality, adding on to the names that have been said before his or her turn, thus forming a long chain of names to test one's memory. Ray shot the scene by placing the camera right at the centre of the circle and turning the camera in sharp 'swivels' to focus on each person's face as they played the game. What's surprising is that he did the entire thing with nothing but his bare hands, with no additional mechanical contraption built for the scene—*none whatsoever*! The film was shot in 1970, but even today, that one scene is studied in film schools all over the world as an example of simplicity and economy in the craft of cinema.

There is no doubt that *Aranyer Din Ratri* is a landmark film, not only in the filmography of Ray, but in the history of world cinema as well. A keen observer, Ray is known for the intrinsic humanism in his films—and this film, in particular, offers a beautiful study of man, nature and the very nature of man.

Pratidwandi

The Adversary (1970)

IT IS SAID THAT ONE OF THE RESPONSIBILITIES OF AN ARTIST IS TO reflect the times he lives in, to paint an accurate picture of what he sees around him. In the beginning of the turbulent 1970s, on witnessing the moral decadence of the world he found himself in and the complete breakdown of the very fabric of society, along with the painful dilemma of seeing the slow death of the city he so loved in the face of his staunch unwillingness to abandon it, Satyajit Ray did what he did best—he made a film about it. The film was to go on to become the first of a trilogy of his observations on the myth of urban life. The other two films in his now famous 'Calcutta trilogy' are *Seemabaddha* (Company Limited) and *Jana Aranya* (The Middleman)—but the film that set it all off, way back in 1970, is *Pratidwandi* (The Adversary).

Ray adapted *Pratidwandi* from a novel of the same name by veteran Bengali writer Sunil Gangopadhyay. Siddhartha Chaudhuri is a twenty-five-year-old man living in Calcutta who has had to give up his medical studies after the unexpected death of his father. He now lives with his widowed mother and two younger siblings. Siddhartha's daily routine comprises of walking the city's streets looking for a job, appearing in interviews and hanging out with two of his friends who are continuing their studies. After roaming around the city with the cruel sun beating

A frustrated and seething Siddhartha battling with the city.

down on him all day, he returns home at night, only to face the usual middle-class-household problems. His sister is the only earning member of the family, and although Siddhartha is fiercely protective of her, he knows that she has secured her job not because of her merit but thanks to her stunning looks. There are rumours of an affair between her and her boss—a married and rather affluent man working for a private firm— and although Siddhartha does not believe in the rumours, he suspects that the man in question might be taking advantage of his sister. Also in the family is Siddhartha's younger brother, who is actively involved in student politics. Despite being a brilliant student, the young boy is a revolutionary in spirit, and Siddhartha is worried for his safety. But neither of his siblings pay much attention to what Siddhartha has to say to them, and this adds to his steadily growing frustration. Despite his initial resistance to the idea, by the end of the film, Siddhartha is forced to leave the city and take up a job outside Calcutta.

Several things make *Pratidwandi* a great film. But perhaps chief among them is the way Ray handles the character of his protagonist. Frustrated beyond measure but still keeping his sanity, ethics and decorum intact, Siddhartha is a man caught between a family that he cares about but cannot relate to anymore, a girl who is romantically interested in him but cannot commit to him because of her own problems, and a city that seems hell-bent upon shoving him down to the ground every time he tries to stand up on his feet.

Take his two siblings, for example. They represent two opposite ends of the spectrum. While his sister has realised that it is all right to use one's physical charm to survive in this brutal and materialistic world, where every single interaction is a transaction in one form or the other, his brother still believes in a dream state of equality for all and is willing to achieve it through armed rebellion, if necessary. What's really interesting is that in their own ways, they both think their elder brother has changed beyond recognition since the death of their father. While his sister feels that Siddhartha doesn't have the necessary shrewdness to make a living for himself in the jungle out there, his brother detests his quest for a life of servitude and generally thinks of him as too weak to protest any injustice towards him. Both are right, as a matter of fact, and the more Siddhartha comes to realise this, the more his angst towards the city grows. One can see the exasperation simmering inside him as he sees his friends having a good time, his brother and sister going about their lives in their own ways, and the city striking him over and over again with its corruption, its lack of ethics and its complete apathy towards his condition. In a beautiful scene towards the beginning of the film, as he finds a bit of shade in a park folly and sits down for a moment of relaxation—exhausted and defeated from one more unsuccessful job interview—a bunch of hippies reaches the spot, dancing and swaying under the influence of drugs and alcohol, having a good time, admiring the holy cows of India and the green trees, and generally saying things that make no sense at all. Siddhartha watches them for some time, wondering what a happily oblivious state they were living in and how their apparently silly behaviour could be justified only by the peace in their minds. Perplexing as it is, he seems to find this peace in the minds of everyone around him—as if everyone is happily going about their own lives, and here he is, running from pillar to post, unable to find acceptance anywhere.

Without a shred of doubt, the two greatest characters in *Pratidwandi* are the two adversaries—Siddhartha and the city of Calcutta. Dhritiman Chaterji plays the calm, reserved, reticent young man who is barely holding it together, and he does it with such finesse that you can feel the tension building with each passing scene. The way Chaterji holds a frame is stuff younger actors of our generation can only dream of. His body language, his slight stoop, his impeccable diction, his expressions, everything brings Siddhartha alive on screen. In one of his essays titled 'An Indian New Wave?', Ray proposed his own definition of a film star, 'A star is a person on the screen who continues to be expressive and interesting even after he or she has stopped doing anything.'* And he went on to name Dhritiman Chaterji as an example of a true film star.

---

* Satyajit Ray, *Our Films, Their Films*, Orient Blackswan, 2001.

And you can see what he meant when you see Siddhartha Chaudhuri in *Pratidwandi*. Throughout the film, even as he tirelessly battles the situation he is in, even with all the rejections he faces and despite the bitter sense of insecurity looming large, Siddhartha can't help but remember the call of an unknown bird he had heard when he was a child. What an absolutely beautiful thought!

But at the end of the war between a vast city and a puny foot soldier, the inevitable happens. It is Siddhartha who finally accepts defeat. He crumbles under pressure and his patience gives way. He is forced to leave the city and take up a job in a small town. In one of the most beautiful concluding scenes ever captured on film, Siddhartha finally finds peace in the most unexpected way and accepts his fate.

Seemabaddha

Company Limited (1971)

IT IS NOW A WELL-KNOWN FACT THAT BEFORE HE BECAME A filmmaker, Satyajit Ray had had a brief professional career with the British advertising agency named DJ Keymer & Co. in the 1940s, working as a junior visualiser for the firm. Ray's stint with the company was hardly a happy one, and it was perhaps drawing on his experience of the futility of rat race in such corporate firms that he decided to adapt to the screen a novel on the same subject by renowned Bengali writer Mani Shankar Mukherjee. In 1971, Ray made *Seemabaddha* (Company Limited), which went on to win the National Film Award for Best Feature Film that year.

Shyamalendu Chatterjee is a sales and marketing manager in Hindustan Peters, a British-run electric fans and lights manufacturing company, heading its fan division. He is a promising young man, extremely ambitious, and is quite popular within the company. He is due for a promotion to the level of director, but vying for the same position is his colleague and rival—the sales and marketing manager of the lights division. The company pays him an exceedingly handsome salary and has given him a sprawling apartment in a posh neighbourhood of Calcutta, where he lives with his wife. His seven-year-old son studies in a boarding school in Darjeeling, and owing to a company policy, his parents live

Shyamalendu hatches a plan to save his career.

in a separate apartment in the other part of town. Shyamalendu has had modest beginnings—and at the beginning of his career, he was an idealistic teacher. But the glitter and glamour of the corporate world corrupted him and he is now a smart and shrewd man with his eye on a place among the board of directors of the company.

When Shyamalendu's sister-in-law comes to visit them from Patna, he takes an instant liking to her. For the first time since he met her many years ago, he notices young Tutul as a woman rather than as a little girl. Tutul, too, is extremely fond of her brother-in-law and is secretly envious of her sister's luck. She looks up to Shyamalendu, who used to be her father's favourite student and a principled young man with a taste for the more refined aspects of life. But now things have changed. Tutul accompanies her sister and brother-in-law as they show her around the city, dining at fancy restaurants and clubs, betting on horses at the racecourse and shopping at upmarket stores. This stark change in her sister's lifestyle startles her but she takes it all in good spirit, enjoying all of it without once letting go of her small-town sensibilities. And through the days that pass, she can't help but admire her brother-in-law all over again, this time in a new light—as a hard-working, intelligent and successful man. Little does she know that to earn his promotion, her brother-in-law can stoop to unthinkable lows. When she does find out, she is shattered, and Shyamalendu, despite having secured the much-sought-after promotion, is left ashamed, dissatisfied and disillusioned, having lost the respect of the young woman who once thought the world of him.

In *Seemabaddha*, Ray highlights the unbridled greed that often tends to creep into the lives of successful corporate executives. It is also a comment on being too ambitious. In a rather poignant scene from the film, an old and wise Tamil gentleman, who is soon to retire from Hindustan Peter's salary division after several decades of service, quotes Joseph Conrad to warn Shyamalendu, 'All ambitions are lawful except those which climb upward on the miseries or credulities of mankind.' Ray is careful to present Shyamalendu as an extremely deserving candidate for the promotion he seeks, but, at the same time, shows him as weak and afraid at the crossroads of life when a moral and ethical dilemma challenges his character. As Shyamalendu himself admits, most of the things he has to do in his life 'are like geography', a subject he hated in school, but one that he was forced to study, since it was in the syllabus. Not once does Ray show his protagonist as a villainous character. It is almost as if he is forced to do the things he does to reach the top. It is another matter, of course, that his love for the summit makes him so blind that he fails to see what he has become in the end.

Like a masterful captain in complete command of his craft, Ray extracts skilled performances from each of his actors. Sharmila Tagore is fabulous as the small-town girl who almost worships her sister's husband. She delivers a largely muted performance, with just the right hint of feeling out of place in a world that is so alien to her—a world of cocktail parties, fancy salons, lusty corporate bigwigs and cabaret shows, a world where a sudden and unannounced visit by Shyamalendu's old parents in the middle of a party becomes a situation of embarrassment for everyone. In a powerful scene, Tagore's character finds herself in the middle of a party, jumping in shock as a war between the police and a group of Naxalites rages on in the streets outside, with not a single man or woman at the party paying any attention to the sounds of explosion and gunfire, the lively piano music drowning out the sound of death and destruction outside. The contrast portrayed between the haves and the have-nots is stark. In another beautiful scene, as her brother-in-law takes his time to admire her and flirt with her, she calmly walks around the room, gently pulling a book out from a shelf, turning it around and putting it back in its proper position. The scene is a perfect example of 'show, don't tell', describing the decay in the otherwise spic and span and glamorous life of Shyamalendu Chatterjee—who is a post-graduate in English literature, a gold medallist, but who now does not even notice the disarray among his favourite books just ten feet from his eyes.

Barun Chanda's performance as the rising but flawed young executive is nothing short of Ray's other, more celebrated anti-hero—Arindam

Mukherjee of *Nayak*. Chanda injects into the role of Shyamalendu a much-needed human touch, making us like him and loathe him in the same breath. We like him because there are certain undeniably admirable qualities he possesses. Even within the heartless jungle of greed and selfishness, he has managed to keep certain principles alive—for instance, his sympathetic attitude towards the cause of the rebellious young men and women of the city. And at the same time, we abhor his conscious sacrifice of all moral principles and ethics when it comes to the point that he might lose a long-fought battle to his rival. In the end, Chanda's biggest achievement in the film is that in Shyamalendu Chatterjee, he succeeds in making us find a bit of ourselves. Ray's biggest achievement, on the other hand, is to remind us that even after we have achieved everything we have ever desired, we may find ourselves lonely, dejected and discontent.

Sikkim (1971)

Censorship in the arts is not a new thing. It has always existed and will continue to—as long as the powers that be are unable to separate their vested interests from the creative freedom of our artists. Even the most magnificent painters, the most celebrated writers, the finest poets and the greatest filmmakers of all time have had to bear the brunt of this evil menace. And although he was smart enough to make even the most scathing commentary on the sociopolitical situation of his times without ruffling those in power, there is at least one known instance in which even a legend such as Satyajit Ray had to be the victim of state-sponsored censorship. I am talking about Ray's magnificent documentary titled *Sikkim,* which, over a period of almost forty years, was cut, chopped and finally banned by not one but two nations.

Sikkim was not always part of India. It used to be an independent nation, ruled by a *chogyal* (or king). In 1971, in a bid to let the world know about their tiny state, the chogyal Palden Thondup Namgyal, and his *gyalmo* (or queen consort)—an American lady by the name of Hope Cooke—commissioned Ray to make a documentary on their nation state. Ray accepted the assignment and made the film—a beautiful and wholesome depiction of the history, terrain, flora, fauna, art, culture and people of Sikkim. Unfortunately, the chogyal was not happy with the final cut of the film, responding discontentedly to the poverty of the Sikkimese people that Ray had chosen to show in it. Those scenes were

Still from Sikkim. *Photo by Nemai Ghosh.*
Courtesy of Satyaki Ghosh.

cut out of the film. Then came the annexation of Sikkim by the Indian government. Technically speaking, it was not an annexation, though. After India attained independence from the British and went on to become a democracy, a freedom movement began to take shape in Sikkim too, aimed at replacing its monarchy with a democratic government. The chogyal sought help from India to thumb down the movement, and in the ensuing rush to compete with China, India signed a treaty with the chogyal in 1950 to grant Sikkim the status of an Indian protectorate. For two long decades, the ruler of Sikkim staved off India's continuous attempts at formal annexation, until, in 1975, he gave in and opted to make Sikkim a state of the Indian republic. The moment Sikkim became part of India, the Indian government banned Ray's documentary. And it was not until September 2010 that the documentary resurfaced, when the ban was finally lifted by the Ministry of External Affairs. The film was screened at Kolkata International Film Festival later that year, and the large audience gathered to watch the film witnessed what a magnificent work of art Ray had created.

The film opens with Ray explaining the terrain of Sikkim—a speck in the heart of the mighty Himalayas, which, despite their mammoth stature, are nothing but 'young mountains', which have hardly stopped growing. The misty mountains, the melting snow giving birth to mighty waterfalls, the lush valleys, the roaring rivers and the steep hillsides all create a picture of paradise on earth. Ray then goes on to elaborate upon the rich flora of the land—the hundreds of varieties of orchids and rhododendrons that bloom in a wide range of colours. Then come the Sikkimese people, and Ray spends considerable time talking about their origins, religion, occupation and habits. We learn how Sikkim has become a melting pot of cultures, with the Lepchas, the Nepalese, the Bhutias, the Tibetans and even the Indians all huddled together in this idyllic little heaven of a hill state—each continuing to maintain their own identities. Sikkim is shown as a happy state, where education is virtually free for all. Towards the end of the film, Ray chooses to focus on the festivals and celebrations of this idyllic state. One of them is a ceremonial lama dance, in which masked lamas dance in circles to celebrate the warding off of evil spirits. At the end of the Tibetan year, the gates to the royal palace grounds are thrown open and a fun fest takes place, where bouts of gambling, sessions of drinking and playful mirth abound. But amid all this, the disparity in income and well-being is not lost to the discerning eyes of the keen observer.

Soumendu Ray's camera captures the sights of the land with great affection. Consider a white wall of mist and a ropeway car slowly emerging from it, with a worker standing dangerously but sure-footedly on its edge, creating a visual marvel—only to be followed by another, more poetic scene of raindrops sliding down a slanted telegraph wire. Or the giggling faces of children as they walk to school or of peasants as they arrange their wares on a Sunday morning in the middle of the town market in Gangtok, the mighty deity of Kanchenjungha looking down upon them. Witnessing these scenes, there's only one thought that comes to mind: if what remains of the documentary is so visually stunning, how much more beautiful must the whole film have been?

The Inner Eye (1972)

After completing his graduation in economics from Presidency College in Calcutta, Satyajit Ray went to Shantiniketan in 1940 to study painting at the Visva-Bharati university founded by Rabindranath Tagore. It was at Shantiniketan that Ray met the eminent artist Benode Behari Mukherjee, who was a member of the faculty there. Mukherjee was severely myopic in one eye and blind in the other (he became completely blind a few years later, following an unsuccessful cataract operation), but despite his physical handicap, he was an artist par excellence, who continued to produce one remarkable work of art after another. Ray was deeply impacted and inspired by his art, and many years later, as a tribute to his teacher, he made a documentary film on the latter's life and works, aptly titled *The Inner Eye*.

With a running time of twenty minutes, and starring the artist himself, this documentary opens with Mukherjee planning the design of a five-foot-high and sixty-foot-wide wall in a newly developed building in Shantiniketan, with the help of twenty murals. These, in turn, are in the form of coloured tiles manufactured in the district of Purulia. Only a fraction of the daunting task is an enormous and complex jigsaw puzzle, which the artist, now completely blind in both eyes, is seen descending upon with great zest, groping around to locate the pieces and their outlines, and placing them in their proper positions in the puzzle—not once wincing in despair at the daunting task that lies ahead. In his

Ray framing a shot of his teacher Benode Bihari Mukherjee.
Photo by Nemai Ghosh. Courtesy of Satyaki Ghosh.

baritone voice and impeccable diction, Ray goes on to narrate Mukherjee's family background, and how, at a very early age, he showed great promise at sketching and drawing. At the age of twelve, Mukherjee attended Patha Bhavan, a school in Shantiniketan, and at the age of fifteen, shifted to Kala Bhavan as a student of the art wing of Shantiniketan, where he received tutelage under the great artist Nandalal Bose.

Very early on in his learning years, Mukherjee had decided that he had no interest in mythology, which used to be a staple subject of most budding artists of the time. Instead, he turned his attention to his surroundings, drawing the arid and desolate landscapes of the countryside outside the Shantiniketan campus, along with the lives of the Santhals who inhabited them. Ray goes on to explain that although drawing flora was not a problem for Mukherjee, how, thanks to the artist's weak eyesight, drawing small animals and birds was possible only when they were not in a state of motion. Through a series of sketches, drawings and paintings of his early student life, we get a glimpse of the remarkable new talent that had just appeared on the horizon of the Indian art scene.

We further learn from the film that upon his return from a rather rewarding trip to Japan, where he learnt a lot from the works of such great masters of Oriental art as Tawaraya Sotatsu and Toba Sōjō, Mukherjee was assigned to paint a fresco for one of the dormitories of Kala Bhavan. Inspired by an Egyptian fresco he had seen earlier, in which a lovely pond occupied the centre of the artwork, he put a pond at the centre of his fresco too, but went on to pack twenty years of his loving and unhurried observations of the countryside, all depicted around that very pond. Needless to say, the resulting work of art was a telling study of the rural way of life in Bengal.

Ray goes on to talk about some of the other works of Mukherjee in the years that followed, including a fresco on the wall of China Bhavan in Shantiniketan, where a more austere composition of life on campus replaces the free-flowing lyricism of the pond fresco. In yet another fresco—which Ray goes on to describe as 'the only example of a truly epic conception in twentieth-century Indian art'—the artist plans, researches and executes an elaborate depiction of the lives of the saints and mystics of medieval India, covering three walls of a large hall. With shades of influences from various disparate art forms from all over the world, and yet all of them coming together as a synthesised, cohesive and organic whole, it is virtually impossible to believe that the entire fresco was painted directly on the walls, without any preliminary tracing whatsoever—a feat that only reveals the remarkable confidence that an artist has in his capabilities. While talking to Ray about the masterpiece, Mukherjee says, in his trademark wit, 'I've taken only those elements which seemed pre-Renaissance to me. And whether it's Byzantine, or Jain, or *Pot*, or *Paata*, a historian may differentiate between these forms, but how does it matter to an artist like you or me, tell me? If you put a folk figure next to a Jain one, whose daddy is going to chide you for that?'

In the years that followed, Mukherjee moved around a bit—first to Nepal, where he was offered the job of curatorship for the National Museum in Kathmandu, then to Rajasthan on a teaching assignment and finally to Mussoorie, where he started his own school. It was during this final period that he lost his eyesight forever. However, he continued to paint, draw, sketch, illustrate and create murals for the rest of his life.

Ray's deep reverence for the artist is evident as much from the fact that he set out to make the film with no financial backing whatsoever, as from the tone of his narration. Sparsely does Ray mention Mukherjee's handicap, choosing to show the richness and uniqueness of his art instead. The underlying tone of the film is not one of pity, not even of sympathy. It is one of deep awe and respect. In changing the mood of the film from heavy to witty, the music from light and peppy during the Kathmandu scenes to hopeful and optimistic through the recital of Raga Asavari during the film's final scene, Ray himself paints a beautiful picture of the life of a remarkable man—a devoted artist, a born fighter and, in more ways than one, a great philosopher. All of this is revealed not only through Mukherjee's art but also in the final shot of the film, where Ray signs off with a quote from the man himself, 'Blindness is a new feeling, a new experience, a new state of being.'

Ashani Sanket

The Distant Thunder (1973)

SATYAJIT RAY BEGAN HIS FILM CAREER WITH *PATHER PANCHALI*, an adaptation of a section of the novel of the same name by veteran Bengali writer Bibhutibhushan Bandyopadhyay, whom Ray often described as the perfect novelist, primarily because in adapting the latter's works, Ray had to do very little. Bandyopadhyay's novels were written with such great and immaculate visual detailing that they almost worked as screenplays. Add to this the fact that rarely in the literary horizon of Bengal has an author been able to paint such a beautiful portrait of the relationship between man and nature as he has. After adapting various segments of the author's novels for two more films—*Aparajito and Apur Sansar*—Ray began thinking of going back to Bandyopadhyay, from as early on as 1961. The novel he had in mind was a particularly striking one, and it had moved him immensely. But it was not until 1973 that he actually began working on it. That year, Ray made *Ashani Sanket* (The Distant Thunder), Bandyopadhyay's tragic tale set in the backdrop of the notorious 1943 man-made famine of Bengal that claimed the lives of more than five million men, women and children.

Gangacharan Chakraborty is a Brahmin priest who has recently come to live in a village in Bengal with his beautiful wife Ananga. Gangacharan

Gangacharan consoles his wife Ananga.

also plans to open a school in the village and treat ailing patients to supplement his income. Although his competencies are questionable, there is virtually nobody in the village to question him—he being the only Brahmin in it. Gangacharan is having the time of his life, as a one-eyed man in a village of blind men is expected to have. The villagers worship him, and his food, clothes and other day-to-day necessities are all supplied to him as gifts and tokens of gratitude. Gangacharan is careful not to exploit the villagers, though, because he knows that it is on their reverence that his livelihood depends. Ananga, on the other hand, has an amiable nature and mixes freely with the womenfolk of the village, within the confines of caste rules. There is not a shred of animosity in the system, and the respect the Brahmin couple earns seems completely deserving. Life is idyllic in the tiny village, but not for long.

The war is at its peak—there are warplanes patrolling overhead, children cheering at them and women bathing in the tranquil village pond admiring them. Amid such innocent circumstances, the first glimpse of impending doom is seen in the form of a wizened old Brahmin gentleman (played brilliantly by the veteran character actor Gobindo Chakraborty), who walks in from the neighbouring village with news of scarcity of rice, seeking a hearty meal for himself in turn. Before you know it, the crisis spreads like wildfire and the village grocer announces that he does not have supply of rice. Prices of all other food items soar in no time, until they become unaffordable. And bit by bit, the innocence of the village slowly begins to crumble before Gangacharan and Ananga's eyes. The men worry at first and then stoop to looting and rioting. The women are forced to hunt for snails from the pond and eat them, or walk miles into a dense forest to dig up wild potatoes. The age-old adage of *homo homini lupus* (man is wolf to man) comes true once again, and while hoarders try to take advantage of the hunger of the poor villagers, some women are forced to sell more than their souls to lusting men in return for a meal. Gangacharan now realises that people's reverence takes a backseat in the face of insatiable hunger, and that he himself has been reduced to a commoner, hunting for a fistful of rice.

Soumitra Chattopadhyay plays the role of the unsuspecting Brahmin priest Gangacharan, who, despite being cautious in holding his fort in the village, fails to see the catastrophe racing towards him. He is mildly vain at first, thankful for his privilege as well, but towards the end of the film, he is shown his place, until he becomes one with everyone else in the village in the final scene. Bangladeshi actress Babita is stunning as Ananga, whose charm almost costs her her life. She is the epitome of domesticity, and although she is bound by the rules of the caste system prevalent in the society she inhabits, she is neither unkind nor inhuman to those around her. Veteran Bengali actress Sandhya Mukherjee plays the role of Chutki, the bubbly, proud, fiery village belle, who is ultimately forced by dire circumstances to sell her body to a local brickyard manager in exchange for food. Every single character in the film plays his or her role perfectly and in beautiful harmony.

The most striking aspect of *Ashani Sanket* is the role nature plays in the film. There, in that scenic village, nature continues to remain as beautiful as ever, with serene ponds, pretty butterflies frolicking in the mud, ants and dragonflies going about their business, lovely flowers blooming, thus highlighting the fact that the tragedy brought upon the village has not been unleashed by the fury of nature and that it is entirely artificial and man-made. Another salient feature of the film is that except in its final scene, not even once does Ray make any sort of reference—veiled or otherwise—to the poverty of the villagers. The village is shown as a happy place before the onslaught of the crisis, but as soon as the famine arrives, people begin to lose all sense of proportion—and understandably so. It is this realisation—that such a sudden, radical and unthinkable decline of human values *can* actually happen in the face of decimation—that truly sets *Ashani Sanket* apart as a study of the great famine of Bengal, and of the vulnerability of the human spirit.

Sonar Kella

The Golden Fortress (1974)

SATYAJIT RAY ONCE REMARKED THAT HE NEVER EARNED NEARLY enough money from his work as a filmmaker and that it was his income from his books that allowed him to run his day-to-day household expenses. Ray's popularity as a writer of young adult literature may not have been as widespread as his popularity as a filmmaker, but within the state of Bengal, his stature as an author is no less important. Ray wrote several independent Bengali short stories, a series of science fiction adventures with a protagonist named Professor Shonku, and another series of short stories depicting the fantastic adventures of an old man named Tarini Khuro (or Tarini Uncle), who, during his youth, had had several remarkable and often supernatural experiences in various parts of India. But the one body of work that made Ray a shining star in the literary scene of Bengal through the 1970s and the 1980s was the series of mystery adventures of his immortal creation—detective Prodosh Chandra Mitra, more popularly known to the young and the old simply as Feluda. The adventures of Feluda became so popular that Ray decided to make not one but two films based on two of his most famous Feluda novels. In this essay, we are going to talk about one of these films—*Sonar Kella* (The Golden Fortress), which won Ray two National Awards.

Feluda has a train to catch.

Mukul Dhar, a seven-year-old boy living in north Calcutta, can remember events and scenes from his past life, when he used to live in Rajasthan hundreds of years ago. He talks about a fortress made of gold, and of precious gems and stones buried in the ground of his house. When two seasoned criminals learn about Mukul from the local papers, they try to kidnap him, hoping that the boy will be able to pinpoint the location of the buried treasure to them. But they soon find out that they have kidnapped the wrong boy, and that the real Mukul has gone off to Rajasthan in search of the golden fortress with renowned parapsychologist Dr Hemanga Mohan Hazra, who is researching reincarnations. When Mukul's father learns of the kidnapping, he seeks the help of detective Feluda. And then Feluda and his cousin Topshe embark on a cross-country chase of the two criminals in a bid to nab them before they get to Mukul.

Although Ray liked the story of *Sonar Kella* as a possible subject for a film, he was not too keen on making a whodunit. He believed that, in general, whodunits did not make for suitable cinematic subjects, thanks to the long speech at the end of the story in which the detective reveals all and explains how the crime was committed and how he managed to catch the culprits. How was he to make *Sonar Kella*, then? Ray had a solution for that. He changed the story a little while writing the screenplay and revealed the identity of the two criminals right at the beginning of the film. The rest of the film, thus, became a purely Hitchcockian affair, with the audience knowing what the detective doesn't, making it more of a suspense adventure film than a whodunit. But the taking away of the mystery element from the story did not, by any means, diminish the beauty of the film. In fact, for the cinematic medium, it worked out wonderfully, because the audience could now stop worrying about the identity of the culprits and focus on the splendours of Rajasthan, the keen intelligence of the protagonist and the comic relief brought in by Feluda and Topshe's co-passenger, a popular but bumbling thriller writer named Lal Mohan Ganguli, who wrote under the pen name 'Jatayu'.

As expected, *Sonar Kella* was one of Ray's most commercially successful films, because fans of Feluda were now seeing him on screen, that, too, played by one of their most beloved actors—and Ray's go-to man—Soumitra Chattopadhyay. Ably supported by the young Topshe (Siddhartha Chatterjee) and Lal Mohan Babu (veteran Bengali comic actor Santosh Dutta, after whose death Ray announced that he would never make another Feluda film again, because 'Jatayu was no more'), Feluda goes on a bumpy ride through Rajasthan in pursuit of the criminals. In what is widely considered the most iconic scene of the film, the trio go on a high-speed, breathtaking camel ride through the Thar desert to catch a train that would take them to Jaisalmer, where a fortress made of yellow limestone had been revealed to be the golden fortress of Mukul's past life.

Full of witty and intelligent dialogues, the film is a treat for those who are interested in puns, spoonerism, malapropism and various other forms of wordplay that Ray (and his father before him) were so well known for. In one scene, when Jatayu shows an old Nepali kukri to a man claiming to be a globetrotter, the man responds by asking, 'What's this unsafety razor for?' In another scene, when the same globetrotter flattens the tyres of Feluda's car, Jatayu unwittingly remarks, 'Someone has collected all the broken bottles from all over the world and put them on the road here', to which Feluda calmly responds, 'Which makes it easier to guess who could have done it, right?'

Sonar Kella might just be one of Ray's most entertaining films. It has all the elements of a typical masala potboiler—a case of reincarnation, a smart, intelligent and pistol-toting 'hero', abundant comic relief, beautiful folk music, the thrill of a chase, the scenic backdrop of Rajasthan—and yet, it is not pedestrian at all. It is an intelligent film that can be enjoyed by everyone. Ray strongly believed what great storytellers have always said—that entertainment and intelligence can coexist without negatively affecting each other. Ray's *Sonar Kella* is the perfect example of that belief. It is perhaps one of the most intelligent and entertaining thrillers to have come out of the Bengali film industry.

Jana Aranya
The Middleman (1975)

'I have made both kinds of films—those dealing with contemporary problems, and I have also gone back to the past, to the nineteenth century, and made films on the stories of Tagore and other writers. There, one could think of a noble and heroic character, but no longer today—people have become diminished in stature, I feel.'

THESE ARE THE WORDS OF SATYAJIT RAY, AND THEY PERFECTLY portray his angst and, more importantly, his hopelessness at the rapidly decaying moral fabric of the society he found himself in the late 1960s onwards. It was perhaps this angst that led him to make a social and somewhat political commentary through a string of films in this period, whereas the rest of his filmography otherwise remained largely apolitical. One of the most important films he made during these turbulent times, and by far the most cynical one he made, was *Jana Aranya* (The Middleman). Adapted from a novel by Mani Shankar Mukherjee, more popularly known in Bengali literature simply as Shankar, the film tells the story of a young man named Somnath who graduates from Calcutta University but fails to find a job. After struggling for months, he meets

The soft-spoken and mild-mannered Somnath
slowly matures into a street-smart middleman.

a well-wisher who introduces him to the world of entrepreneurship. Somnath starts a business, acting as a middleman for order supplies, and the money starts flowing in. But he soon realises that no life is easy, and that even in running a successful business one has to turn a blind eye to one's moral code. The film's climax is an out-and-out shocker, in which Somnath is faced with a dilemma of epic proportions, and true to the words of Ray, fails to choose the right path, for he is neither noble, nor a hero.

The one theme running throughout the film is its frustrated cynicism—the feeling that all is lost. Right at the beginning, even as the title credits unfurl, we are shown a typical examination hall from 1970s' Calcutta University—walls covered with leftist political slogans and weak-willed examiners watching helplessly as almost every student openly cheats right in front of their eyes and with complete disregard to their presence. The plight of these teachers spills over to the next scene, where a poor, frustrated, lowly paid teacher fails to read Somnath's answer sheets because the handwriting is quite small and the teacher cannot afford to buy his prescription glasses. A simple, everyday event such as this changes the life of a young man forever, because, for the rest of his life, he will be judged by the marks the teacher must have randomly scribbled on his answer sheets without even bothering to read them.

The cynicism does not end there. As Somnath soon finds out, there are more than one lakh applications for as few as ten job vacancies, and even a back-of-the-envelope calculation tells him that he does not stand a chance. In the interview that he does make it to, he is asked utterly irrelevant questions, such as 'What is the weight of the moon?', giving us another glimpse of the decay in the employment machinery of society.

Jana Aranya is perhaps Ray's most ruthless film, in which he doesn't hold back from dealing one blow after another. In a heart-wrenching scene, Somnath's father asks his sons more about the Naxalite movement, wondering how it is even possible for young men and women to embrace death without any hesitation unless there is a powerful ideal before them. The fact that the old man, himself a freedom fighter, fails to understand the minds of the youth tells us a lot about the state of the nation in those turbulent times. It is not because of a generation gap—it is because, unlike the days of the British Raj, this time, the enemy is within the system.

In another scene, Ray beautifully explores the mind of the average Bengali Brahmin young man when Somnath shows his reluctance to do business, to which an experienced well-wisher (played by Utpal Dutt) remarks that as a Brahmin, he would be comfortable standing and begging for alms in the corner of the street but not be comfortable trading. That's Ray at his cynical best. When Somnath comes home and seeks his father's permission to start a business of his own, his father, a principled old man, hesitates at first, commenting that none of his forefathers had ever done business, but soon follows up with a brilliant realisation, that until about two generations ago, none of them had taken up a job either. Through these scenes, Ray, who himself came from a family of entrepreneurs, strikes at the heart of the deep-rooted irreverence that the Bengali middle-class youth harbours for the very notion of commerce.

But the film's most brutal scenes come when, throughout an eventful night, Somnath is forced to accompany a 'public relations officer' from one part of the city to another, looking for a female escort to satiate the lust of a high-ranking official who could make or break a deal for him. Ray, perhaps for the first time in his filmmaking career, bares his fangs and pokes us in the eye to show us what a strange and hopeless world we live in. Shot beautifully in black and white, with the use of light to symbolically cover only one half of most faces in the night scenes, juxtaposing the ruthless streets and markets against the figure of a loving and caring sister-in-law at home, who supports him no matter what, and once again focusing on the human content more than external glamour, Ray puts Somnath in a world of shocks and surprises, only to make him realise that, right from education and employment to entrepreneurship, this is no country for an honest man.

Bala (1976)

IN HIS FILMMAKING AND LITERARY CAREER SPANNING MORE THAN four decades, there had hardly been an art form that Satyajit Ray had not studied. From a very early age, his mind was truly an open window, letting in the finer sensibilities of life in the form of music, poetry, literature, painting, sculpture and even such performing arts as the trapeze, acrobatics, jugglery and both street and stage illusions. In 1935, when Ray was just fourteen years old, he watched a seventeen-year-old girl on a stage in Calcutta, performing the Bharatanatyam. Ray was mesmerised by the young lady and the art she presented before her audience. He quickly looked up the girl and was fascinated by her remarkable story. In later years, when Ray began making films, he harboured a wish to make a documentary film on her, but it was not before 1976 that he could finally make it. This film, titled *Bala*, was his ode to Tanjore Balasaraswati, one of the greatest classical dancers of our country, and whom Ray considered the greatest Bharatanatyam dancer ever.

The film is a little over thirty minutes long, and quite naturally, almost half of its running time is used to show Bala's dance recitals. During these recitals, Ray takes a backseat, suspending his narration to allow the grace and elegance of the dancer speak for itself. In the first half of the film, though, Ray offers a sort of background to the dance form of Bharatanatyam for the benefit of the uninitiated. In his rich baritone and

Danseuse Balasaraswati in the middle of a
Bharatanatyam recital.

impeccable diction, he describes how the very name of the dance form was derived from the name of sage Bharata, whose seminal work, titled *Natya Shastra*, written in Sanskrit in the fourth century, describes the highly systematised language of mime, dance and music that goes on to constitute the performing art of drama. One of the twenty-seven chapters of the text is devoted to the dance, which formed an inseparable part of classical drama. Although the form of the stage as described in the text is archaic now, some of the dance forms that grew out of classical theatre have survived in different parts of India. Bharatanatyam is one of them. Ray also goes on to explain how the three syllables of the author's name form the initial syllables of the three principal elements of the dance form itself—bhava (or feeling, conveyed through mime), raga (music) and tala (rhythm, through dance). Ray then explains the significance of the mudra, or gesture, in the dance form and how the same gesture can convey a wide range of meanings, depending on the context. Naturally, such an elaborate and intricate arrangement of emotion, music and movement can only be mastered by someone who is highly skilled, deeply devoted, commands exceptional physical energy and has a fine ear for music.

Ray then describes Bala's ancestry and how she was introduced to an audience for the first time in the courtyard of a temple in Kanchipuram, where she gave the first dance recital of her life at the age of seven. She received tutelage under her guru Kandappa Pillai, whose ancestors were musicians in the court of Tanjore, renowned for its patronage of the arts. It was in this very court that a temple dancer named Papammal performed her art more than two hundred years ago, and seven generations later, her bloodline, Balasaraswati, had rightfully taken up dance to carry the family's tradition forward. With the advent of the British in India, the performing arts ceased to receive royal patronage, and temple dancers were relegated to an ostracised segment of society. But Bala's mother, herself a celebrated singer, decided to brave all social norms and set up her daughter's tutelage under Kandappa Pillai.

Several experts then go on to describe Bala's indisputable mastery over Bharatanatyam, her diligence, dedication and the resulting rise to fame, including the impact she had on Western audiences. What follows next is one of the most beautiful pieces in Bala's repertoire—a recital accompanied by the song *Krishna Ni Begane Baaro*, in which a distraught Yashoda implores a child Krishna to return home. The recital by Bala, given on a seashore with the waves of the majestic ocean in the background, was frowned upon by many experts and exponents of the art form, and not without good reason. Criticism ranged from the argument that the rhythm of the waves was a jarring distraction to the rhythm of the piece itself, to the fact that the presence of the ocean in the background was an unnecessary attempt to offer an 'explanation' to the piece—which is the primary responsibility of the dancer, and not the filmmaker.

Irrespective of these criticisms, it is undeniably true that Ray's *Bala* remains, to date, perhaps the most fascinating study of the great dancer, a priceless archive for posterity. Its importance stems not only from the fact that it documents a centuries-old art form and its greatest proponent, but also that it managed to present before us the astonishing range of emotions of a sacred devotee of the art, whose most subtle expressions and most vigorous movements together embrace and encapsulate the rich tradition that is so unique in its beauty and its Indianness. The fact that Ray was able to capture this on film is, in itself, a great feat. Deservedly so, then, the film can be considered a tribute to the greatest dancer of our country by the greatest filmmaker of our times.

Shatranj Ke Khilari

The Chess Players (1977)

WHEN IT CAME TO CINEMA, THROUGH A SERIES OF INTERNATIONALLY acclaimed films in the 1960s and the 1970s, Satyajit Ray secured India's position on the world map—a feat unmatched by anyone before him. And he did so while working in the Bengali film industry, which, along with the industry in Madras (now Chennai), was the proverbial 'younger sibling' of the much bigger, more powerful and significantly more affluent industry of Hindi films centred on Bombay. It is not surprising, then, that time and again, Ray had had to field the one question that everyone in Bombay ended up asking him: when would he make a feature film in Hindi? Like a true film fan, Ray watched Hindi films regularly and enjoyed some of them too. From various books written on the subject and from recently published letters, we get to know that the thought of making a Hindi film did cross Ray's mind several times but that he took his time, for three principal reasons—his rather limited knowledge of the languages of Hindi and Urdu (during those days, dialogue in Bombay's films were in a cocktail of Hindi and Urdu), the fact that his crew members in Bengal depended on his films for their livelihood, and because he hadn't found a suitable subject yet.

Eventually, he did find the subject, in a short story written by Premchand. In 1977, supported by his old crew and a new team of

General James Outram annexes Oudh to Her Majesty's Empire without having to put up so much as a fight against Nawab Wajid Ali Shah. Photo by Nemai Ghosh. Courtesy of Satyaki Ghosh.

translators, Ray took the big leap and made his first Hindi feature film—*Shatranj Ke Khilari* (The Chess Players), which went on to become a landmark film in the history of Hindi cinema.

Ray made significant changes to Premchand's original story, most of these in the form of addition of context. The film begins with a narration (by none other than Amitabh Bachchan), explaining the sociopolitical scenario in Lucknow during the reign of Nawab Wajid Ali Shah, when everyone—rich or poor, young or old—was rolling in the pleasures of living the good life. The ruler of Awadh, Nawab Wajid Ali Shah, was himself a man of refined tastes, more interested in music, poetry and dance than statesmanship. Leaving the affairs of the state to his trusted and loyal prime minister, he drowns himself in the pleasures of life. Under such circumstances, following the orders of Lord Dalhousie, the then governor general of British India, a shrewd military officer named General James Outram plans and executes the annexation of Awadh to the British empire, thus completing a series of politically important acquisitions. This is merely the backdrop, because the real story of the film is about two affluent noblemen of Lucknow, who are so addicted to and engrossed in the game of chess that they completely fail to see that their beloved city is falling prey to the British military forces, and their revered nawab is being taken prisoner. As the film oscillates between these two storylines—both involving a shrewd game of strategy—we find how easily refined tastes tend to become deadly addictions, ultimately leading to one's downfall.

The biggest asset of *Shatranj Ke Khilari* is its world-building. Watching the film, it is impossible to believe that it had been directed by someone who, by his own admission, had very limited working knowledge of Hindi and almost no knowledge of Urdu or Awadhi. And that's just the dialogues. *Shatranj Ke Khilari* transports us into a magical world of nawabs and nautch girls, of palaces and forts, of hookahs and Peshawari shawls, of cockfights and kite-flying contests, of kathaks and thumris—all with its beautiful cinematography, perfect art direction, immaculate lighting and hundreds of knick-knacks and props, most of which Ray carefully hand-picked. In his book, *My Adventures with Satyajit Ray: The Making of Shatranj Ke Khilari*, the film's producer, Suresh Jindal, says that the amount of research that had gone into the making of the film was exemplary. For a marching scene that hardly lasts for a few seconds on screen, Ray consulted several experts in both India and abroad, only to get the order of the various ranks of troops correctly depicted. From procuring carpets to seeking the loan of an ancient hookah from an acquaintance for use in the film, Ray went all out, as was his usual practice, to ensure that a historical film such as *Shatranj Ke Khilari* was made with genuineness and authenticity.

The film itself is extremely riveting, denying viewers even the slightest opportunity to take their eyes off the screen. Every single frame is like a painting, the colours deliberately muted, to make the picture reminiscent of a bygone era. There is a certain mellow feeling throughout the film, primarily brought on by the hues used. One gets a sense of tragedy looming large, even when the characters aren't speaking or emoting. To add to these, of course, are some of the best performances assayed on screen in a Hindi film. Sanjeev Kumar and Syed Jaffrey play the two noblemen whose love for chess knows no bounds—not even the ones imposed by family. While Jaffrey is the warm, jolly and courteous simpleton oblivious of the fact that his wife is having an affair behind his back, Kumar is the more aggressive of the two friends, both on and off the chessboard.

Amjad Khan plays Wajid Ali Shah with great sensitivity, showing once again his stature as an actor. The Nawab of Awadh, thanks to his softer inclinations, literally gives up his crown without the British army having to shed a single drop of blood. On hearing that the British are coming to overthrow him, when his prime minister breaks down, Wajid Ali Shah remarks, 'Only music and poetry can bring tears to a man's eyes.' His long speech to his ministers upon hearing of Outram's plans is the stuff of cinematic legend, fraught with a mix of angst and defiance, and of tragedy that he would no longer be able to indulge in the things that gave him the greatest pleasure.

One would imagine that in a film about chess, it would be difficult to believably portray the passage of time on screen, but in Ray's able hands, such fears are brushed aside and what transpires on screen is indeed poetry in motion. *Shatranj Ke Khilari* is one of those rare films that make you realise that even without any background information whatsoever, the makers must have made it with a lot of heart. Ray's skilful tackling of the subject resulted in the adaptation of Premchand's short story into a full-fledged politico-historical film—an important commentary on the systematic atrocities of the British in India—one that will be lauded by generations to come.

Joy Baba Felunath

The Elephant God (1979)

SATYAJIT RAY'S IMMORTAL CREATION DETECTIVE PRODOSH Chandra Mitra, more popularly known in literary circles as Feluda, often said that money was never a big enough motivation for him in accepting cases. For Feluda, the lure of a baffling puzzle, one that offered him the opportunity to exercise his brains, was far more interesting. And if, on top of that, he had the chance to duel with an extremely shrewd and intelligent adversary while solving such a puzzle, then nothing like it. Interestingly enough, Feluda did get an opportunity to do both, and in the backdrop of Ray's favourite location in India—the picturesque ancient city of Benares. In his extremely popular novel *Joy Baba Felunath* (The Elephant God), Ray makes Feluda pit wits against a sly and wealthy Marwari businessman named Maganlal Meghraj, who was to appear in two more novels to rightfully earn the position of Feluda's arch-enemy—much like Professor James Moriarty to Sherlock Holmes. It was perhaps this contest between Feluda and his nemesis that made Ray follow up his immensely popular adaptation of *Sonar Kella* with the razor-sharp, crisply edited and beautifully written film *Joy Baba Felunath*.

The year is 1975. Feluda, his cousin Topshe and their friend—the popular Bengali thriller writer Lal Mohan Ganguly (also known as

The trio of Feluda, Topshe and Jatayu still continue to rule the world of Bengali detective fiction.

Jatayu)—have come to Benares on holiday during Durga Puja. There, they are introduced to a gentleman named Umanath Ghoshal, whose family has been living in Kashi for almost six decades. Umanath tells Feluda that a precious Ganesh idol that belongs to the family has recently been stolen from his father's chest, and requests Feluda to catch the thief and find the idol for him. Meanwhile, a sadhu by the name of Machhli Baba has arrived on the ghats of Benares, claiming to have swum the holy river directly from Prayag all the way to Kashi. Needless to say, various eminent people—the 'cream of Kashi'—have started gathering at the ghats to listen to the baba's sermons. Among them is Maganlal Meghraj, whose shady dealings and involvement with a racket of art and antique smugglers are not unknown to the local police. Maganlal was keen on buying the Ganesh idol from Umanath, but Umanath had refused. A few days later, the idol had been stolen. Feluda investigates, but soon realises that the idol is not with Maganlal. Where did the idol vanish? Who had stolen it? And how does Maganlal hope to get his hands on it? When Feluda ignores a chilling warning from Maganlal and continues his search for the stolen idol, he soon finds himself investigating a much more heinous crime—the murder of an innocent old man.

Just like the previous Feluda film was set amid the beautiful, arid deserts of Rajasthan, *Joy Baba Felunath* is set among the age-old ghats of Kashi and its winding lanes and by-lanes, which still capture the very essence of India's heritage in the middle of the twentieth century. Almost every building shown in the film is more than a hundred years old, and there is an old-world charm about the atmosphere that acts as the perfect setting to a mystery thriller. In a brilliant and daring scene, for instance, Feluda follows a man bathing in the river all the way to his home in an old and abandoned palace on the ghats, only to realise that it's the hideout of none other than Machhli Baba himself. In another scene, as the three musketeers are taking an after-dinner walk along the dimly lit and eerily desolate lanes of the city, they see the silhouette of a man staggering out of the mouth of a by-lane ahead of them, only to realise that the poor man has been stabbed. Almost every frame in the film seems like a painting coming alive on screen, straight out of the canvas. The camerawork, the cinematography and the art direction are of extremely high quality, and they all help build a fittingly sinister atmosphere for the crimes.

The performances are all spot on, with the right doses of comic relief coming at the right points in the film. Soumitra Chattopadhyay is once again brilliant as the smart and sharp-witted detective Feluda and Utpal Dutt's performance as Maganlal Meghraj is, of course, one of the salient features of the film. But stealing the show from both the hero and his worthy adversary is the performance by Santosh Dutta, as the much-loved Jatayu, who earns the wrath of Maganlal Meghraj and is made a target for a knife-throwing show by an impossibly old artiste employed with the shrewd tycoon's private circus. That one scene in itself is worth a million bucks, as Jatayu's nervous optimism at being martyred for a good cause leads to a highly comical situation within the dark confines of Maganlal's home. Feluda, of course, does not take the matter lightly and vows to avenge the insult to his friend. And he does that, in true Feluda-style, as he re-stages the private circus show in the thrilling climax of the film.

Joy Baba Felunath is certainly not one of Ray's most important films; nor is it one of his best. But just as the previous Feluda adaptation, it is a beautifully told story with a brilliant twist at the end, and with all the ingredients that make for perfect entertainment. For millions of Feluda fans all over the world, then, *Joy Baba Felunath* is not just a motion picture—it is an emotion. It is a gentle pluck at the strings of our nostalgia, a throwback to the good old days when life was simple, Topshe's unwavering devotion towards his cousin meant something to us, Jatayu's grit and courage towered way over his buffoonery, and the smart, sharp and incorruptible Feluda was our one true hero.

Hirak Rajar Deshe

The Kingdom of Diamonds (1980)

IN 1968, SATYAJIT RAY'S *GOOPY GYNE BAGHA BYNE*, BASED ON A short story written by his grandfather Upendrakishore Ray Chowdhury, went on to become one of the biggest commercial successes of Bengali cinema, and the characters of Goopy and Bagha became so popular that the inevitable happened. Twelve years after the film was made, Ray decided to follow it up with a sequel—*Hirak Rajar Deshe* (The Kingdom of Diamonds).

In *Hirak Rajar Deshe*, Goopy and Bagha, who are now the sons-in-law of the kings of Shundi and Halla, respectively, are invited to the annual festival of the Kingdom of Diamonds to sing and play the dhol, and enthral the king and his guests with their music. When the duo reaches the kingdom, they learn a dark secret—that beneath the surface of apparent warmth and generosity, the King of Hirak is, in fact, an evil man, who exploits his subjects ruthlessly. Most of the poor subjects have no option but to work day in and day out in the farms and the mines, only to hand over all their income to the king in taxes. The ones who protest are mercilessly subdued with the help of a brainwashing device that the royal scientist has invented. When a spirited and fearless teacher rises in rebellion against the king, Goopy and Bagha join forces with

The King of Diamonds with the court jester.

him, aiding him with the help of their magic to pull the evil king down from his throne.

As with his previous film with Goopy and Bagha, in *Hirak Rajar Deshe* too, not once does Ray artificially sweeten the message of the film to make it suitable for children. In fact, he makes the best use of the opportunity to pass on a very important message to them—that the only war worth fighting is the one against oppression, a war that is bloodless and yet one that aims to dethrone the greatest enemy of the common man. The film's biggest asset is that it does not treat its primary audience—children—as any less intelligent than adults. It makes them understand the difference between right and wrong, and urges them to rise in rebellion when the need arises.

Just as the first Goopy–Bagha film, this one, too, relies heavily on music, and keeping his audience in mind, Ray's compositions are simple, melodious and extremely pleasing to the ear. One of the most beautiful songs in the film is titled *E Je Drishyo Dekhi Onnyo* ('These strange sights I see'). It is sung when Goopy and Bagha venture into the forest, admiring the ancient trees towering over their heads with awe and wonder. In another song, titled *Paaye Pori Baagh Mama* ('We bow to thee, o king of beasts'), based purely on Indian classical ragas, Goopy and Bagha try to placate a full-grown, ferocious Bengal tiger guarding the keys to the palace's treasury, giving rise to a hilarious situation of confusion and tension. But perhaps the best song of the film comes right at the end, during the climax, when the evil king and his posse of ministers are rounded up by Goopy and Bagha in the royal laboratory, to be 'taught' the lesson of their lives. Titled *Nohi Jontro* ('I am not a machine'), it is an excellent protest song and denudes the king, laying bare his incapacity to look after the welfare of his people.

Another salient feature of the film is that almost all its characters speak in rhyme, with the exception of the rebellious teacher Udayan Pandit—perhaps symbolising that he is different from the rest. Despite all its charms, though, the film is not without its flaws. The editing is sloppy in not one but several scenes, and some of the performances look too melodramatic for comfort. The humour—which was such a naturally integral part of the previous Goopy–Bagha film—also comes across as slightly forced at times. But even with these minor glitches, it is virtually impossible to take one's eyes off the screen even for a second, so strong is the message of the film. Ray highlights several important issues in the film—the tragic 'creation' of a terrorist, the dangers of state-sponsored scientific advancements, the angst and frustration of talented people in the regime of tyrants and the importance of education and enlightenment.

Tapen Chatterjee and Rabi Ghosh are once again effortlessly brilliant as the lovable duo of Goopy and Bagha, respectively. Veteran actor Utpal Dutt plays the King of Hirak with the right mix of humour, callousness towards the plight of his subjects and seething fury at being unable to quell the mutiny.

But despite being a film about the adventures of Goopy and Bagha, the real 'hero' of the film is Udayan Pandit—the teacher who is forced to turn into a rebel. It is through him that Ray speaks throughout the film. In a brilliant scene right after his school is shut down and his home destroyed, Udayan goes on the run, only to stumble upon Goopy and Bagha and vow to them, 'The school will open again. *I* will open it.' The strength and grit on his face when he utters those few words are perhaps the same emotions with which Ray himself had set out to write and direct such a powerful film against the ever-deteriorating condition of state administration and public welfare in the country. At its core, then, *Hirak Rajar Deshe* is much more than a children's film. It is, by far, one of the best satires against state oppression that the Indian film industry has ever produced. It was relevant then, way back in 1980; it is relevant even today; and will perhaps continue to be so over the years, reminding us, again and again, that every time an evil king attempts to exploit the farmers, the labourers and the rest of the very people who make the kingdom a kingdom of diamonds—the common man—will rise in rebellion and pull him down.

Pikoo (1980)

IN 1980, WHEN HE WAS AT THE PEAK OF HIS FILM CAREER, SATYAJIT Ray was approached by a French gentleman named Henri Fraise, who was an independent film and television producer. Fraise requested Ray to make a film for a French television channel named France 3, assuring him that he would have full creative liberty (apparently, the actual words Fraise used were, 'Even if you place your camera at your window and shoot the house next door, we will accept that')*. For this project, Ray decided to choose one of his own short stories, and adapted it for the screen. In the same year, Ray made *Pikoo*.

Before talking about the story of the film, one must spend some time discussing the original short story on which it is based—Ray's own story '*Pikoor Diary*' (Pikoo's Diary). Ray was essentially a writer of children's literature, though his stories, novels and novellas were read with equal enthusiasm by adults as well. But in his writing career, he did write stories targeted only at adults as well. '*Pikoor Diary*' was one such story, and it was a unique concept that could have taken birth only in the creative imagination of someone as talented as Ray. The uniqueness of the story lay in the fact that it was in the form of a diary, kept by a lonely six-year-old boy. Hence, most of the words were misspelt, there was no punctuation

---

* Andrew Robinson, 'Chapter 23: Two (1964), Pikoo (1980)', *Satyajit Ray: The Inner Eye*, IB Tauris, revised and updated edition, January 1989, p. 253.

Pikoo uses a black sketch-pen to draw a white flower. Ray's legendary understanding of the mind of a child.

at all and the writing was unorganised, unplanned and spontaneous in the true sense of the term. Through the eyes of this little boy, though, what emerges is deeply moving and unsettling—although the boy himself does not realise the significance of most of the incidents he describes. For instance, Pikoo's innocent description of his mother's behaviour with a family friend makes us realise that she is having an affair with the man. His childlike excitement on receiving gifts from this 'uncle' is genuine and honest—and yet, we realise that he has merely been bribed to go out into the garden and play so that the lovers can have some time alone. When Pikoo finds his ailing grandfather (his only friend) lying dead in his room, he doesn't quite realise what has happened and simply describes what he sees matter-of-factly.

While such a magnificent creative exercise can work in the medium of literature, how does one transform it on screen? Ray takes up the challenge and makes a few changes in the story and the way it is told. No longer do we see events unfolding only from the viewpoint of Pikoo. To compensate for this change, Ray brings Pikoo's innocence to the forefront through his reaction to things and happenings around him. For instance, when he is loitering around aimlessly on the terrace, Pikoo hears a neighbour's dog barking incessantly. He listens to it for some time and then suddenly yells—'Hush!'—at the top of his voice, and quite magically, the barking stops! Later, when he hears his mother and her lover arguing over something behind closed doors in the middle of the afternoon, he once again yells—'Hush!'—and lo, the fighting stops yet again! It is the genius of Ray that creates moments such as these throughout the densely packed twenty-six-minute film. As with several of his previous films, Ray shows us once again that tragedy works best when juxtaposed with its radically opposite emotion—wit and comedy.

Aparna Sen plays the role of Pikoo's mother—and it's a difficult part to play. For she is not heartless, she is just tired of a failed marriage and her guilt keeps tearing her away from her lover—as is evident from their frequent quarrels. In perhaps the most beautiful scene of the film, after Pikoo has been cleverly dispatched to the garden with his new gift—a painting set—and given the 'assignment' of painting every single flower he lay his eyes upon, his mother and her lover shut themselves in the bedroom for an amorous afternoon adventure. But confused at not finding a white pen in his set, Pikoo yells from the garden, calling out to his mother and letting her know that he is using the black pen to draw the white flower instead. Pikoo's innocent, childlike remark is deep and layered, for here's a child that doesn't think twice before exchanging the white with the black. It is only in the adult world that we truly understand the significance of such an act—especially in the context of his mother's infidelity.

Victor Banerjee plays the role of Hitesh, Pikoo's mother's lover, and brings a certain cut-throat transactional indifference to the part. It is quite evident that he is merely interested in the carnal aspect of the relationship and nothing more. Shoven Lahiri plays Pikoo's father, and in less than a minute of screen time, makes us realise another kind of indifference—the one that busy and successful executives often show towards their wives. Veteran actor Promode Ganguli plays Pikoo's grandfather, an old man who has survived two heart attacks, which have managed to confine him to bed. When the innocent Pikoo inadvertently blurts out what his parents have been saying about his grandfather, the poor old man realises that he is nothing but a burden on the family.

But the star of the film is undoubtedly its little braveheart, the mischievous and very, very lonely protagonist. In the complex world that surrounds him, his views are simple. We can't help but feel for the little boy as he quietly watches the chowkidar have his meal, finally asking the latter how on earth he can eat so many green chillies. Or when he smiles brightly on receiving gifts from his mother's lover. And certainly not when, upon realising that his grandfather will never talk to him again, he doesn't tell anyone, instead choosing to simply sit in a chair on the verandah and keep painting. *Pikoo* is a magnificent study of a child's mind and a reminder that it is only when we adults see ourselves through the eyes of a child that our actions look so distinctly odd to us.

Sadgati

Deliverance (1981)

What happens when one of the greatest filmmakers our country has ever had decides to make a film from a story written by one of the most loved and respected writers of our literature and asks two of the finest actors to have ever graced our screens to act in it? Read on to find out.

In Hinduism, there's a belief that after the death of the body, the soul tends to remain within the periphery of the place of death, and unless it is freed from its earthly ties and granted peace and passage by a representative of god, it continues to remain in the mortal world, to be tormented for all eternity. This deliverance by an agent of god is considered a holy necessity, and in the early years of the previous century, the great writer Munshi Premchand himself wove a beautiful tale around this practice, to be adapted for the screen by Satyajit Ray several decades later. This film, which Ray made for Doordarshan in 1981, was *Sadgati* (Deliverance).

The film tells the story of a poor low-caste village couple named Dukhi and Jhuria (played brilliantly by Om Puri and Smita Patil). Dukhi and Jhuria are chamars—an untouchable caste shunned by the members of the upper caste for their involvement with the traditional practice of tanning. Dukhi and Jhuria want to give away their daughter—a girl

*The untouchable Dukhi chops
away furiously, only to drop dead
moments later.*

barely into her teens—in marriage. To have the almanacs read and an auspicious date and time announced for the marriage, Dukhi goes to the village priest's house and invites him back to his hut. On seeing an opportunity to get some free labour in return, the Brahmin priest makes Dukhi carry out a series of strenuous tasks under the scorching and unforgiving sun. The poor man, who has just come out of a bout of fever, completes all the tasks without uttering a single word of protest. Weak and shivering, with an empty stomach and the midday sun over his head, Dukhi is then asked to chop a massive chunk of wood into fine splints. Drained, Dukhi attacks the monstrous log with a blunt axe and the last remaining strength in his body, but can hardly make a dent. When the Brahmin priest reprimands him for not being able to do his job properly and threatens to announce an inauspicious date and time for the young girl's marriage, Dukhi is scared and chops away at the log—blow after blow after blow—until he collapses and dies right at the spot.

The priest now finds himself in a fix, because there's a corpse lying near his house that no one will touch. The chamars refuse to take the body away and accuse him of working Dukhi to death. The other Brahmins accuse him of causing them much inconvenience because the corpse is lying on the way to the village well and none of them want to see a dead chamar on their way to the source of their drinking water. As the skies burst open, the rains make matters worse, because the corpse starts to decompose sooner than expected. Left with no option, the priest then 'delivers' the corpse to its rightful place, tugging it along the roads of the village with the help of a rope in the early hours of the morning and dropping it heartlessly amid the decaying carcasses of cattle in the outskirts of the village.

While Premchand's story is a scathing account of the tragic lives of the untouchables in this country and the horrors of superstition and blind submission to the self-proclaimed voices of god, Ray's handling of the subject lends a sense of failure and dejection to the entire affair, even when Dukhi is alive—as if it's all over, and as if nothing can be done to help the poor man. Even as Dukhi seethes in rage and directs his fury at the log instead of at his oppressor, muttering expletives at the lifeless piece of wood, we cannot help but accept that we have failed him in every possible way. We feel as if his mere existence, his entire life, all up to this point, has been a lie—that he was born a slave and that he would die a slave, never to question his master, never to stand up to him, or face him, or look him in the eye to show that he resents him and everything that he stands for. It is with this sense of hopelessness that Dukhi collapses to his death. The failure is so impactful that we hardly even get a chance to pay any attention to the other injustice happening right in front of our eyes—the marriage of a young girl child.

Smita Patil plays Jhuria with the feminine grace and anxious uncertainty that is so apt for a poor, rustic, helpless, untouchable woman. Her crude and tragic lament at her husband's death rings in our ears, even as the rain continues to wash her tears away. Mohan Agashe's performance as the cruel Brahmin priest is haunting, and he fills the role with just the right amount of vileness, careful not to turn his character into a caricature at any time. Om Puri looks as if he was born to play Dukhi—his silent submission to his fate is so vivid, so tragic that it makes our hearts ache. When, long after the film is over, you are finally able to separate yourself from the story and look at *Sadgati* as a film, you realise why these actors are considered to be some of the greatest in Indian cinema.

And in the end, there is something that needs to be said, because one can't help but wonder. The story of *Sadgati* was written almost one hundred years ago. The film itself was made forty years ago. But even today, the evil shadow of untouchability and caste crimes hover over us. Even today, in a free state such as ours, poor, ignorant, helpless people from the lower castes are beaten to death, maimed and lynched in public, humiliated and raped and stripped of their basic right—the right to live. All because they belong to a so-called lower caste. There is no dignity for them, no justice whatsoever, and certainly no deliverance.

Ghare Baire

The Home and the World (1984)

IN HIS THIRTY-SEVEN-YEAR-LONG FILM CAREER, SATYAJIT RAY adapted the works of Rabindranath Tagore five times. In order of chronology, these films were *Postmaster, Monihara* (The Lost Jewels) *and Samapti* (The Conclusion)—all three part of *Teen Kanya, Charulata* (The Lonely Wife) and *Ghare Baire* (The Home and the World). While the first four of these films received high critical acclaim, *Ghare Baire* received a lot of flak from critics and the common man alike. Some have even gone on to say that it was one of the three weakest films of Ray's career, let down by poor writing, terrible casting choices, and a frightful lack of economy and disjointed set pieces that just didn't hold together.

Ghare Baire is an adaptation of Rabindranath Tagore's 1916 novel of the same name. The film revolves around three central characters. There's Bimala, the wife of an early-twentieth-century aristocrat in Bengal. There's her loving husband, Nikhilesh Chowdhury—an educated, soft-spoken and revered nobleman of refined tastes. And finally, there's Nikhilesh's friend Sandip Mukherjee—a charismatic revolutionary waging war against British rule in India through the Swadeshi movement. Bimala and Nikhilesh live a happy and prosperous life together. Having received his education in the Occident, Nikhilesh does not believe in keeping his wife confined to the interiors of the household. He appoints

Nikhilesh and Bimala in a tender moment from the film.

a British music teacher for her, converses with her on a vast range of subjects and generally encourages her to come out of the house and step into the world outside. Bimala is happy receiving the tutelage of Mrs Higgins, singing highland ballads, playing the piano and leaving the supervision of household chores in the hands of her not-so-fortunate and widowed sister-in-law. But things change when Nikhilesh's friend Sandip comes to live with them for a few days. Sandip leads the revolt against the British empire, and his fiery speeches, magnetic charm and unshakeable conviction to the cause stir up several emotions in Bimala's heart—those that she had never experienced before, ever since she had been married into the Chowdhury household as an underage girl.

Sandip takes advantage of this and embarks upon a dangerous game of seduction, drawing Bimala closer to himself bit by bit, knowing fully well that the coveted path to Nikhilesh's coffers runs through the heart of his beloved wife. Bimala finds a sense of purpose in Sandip's movement, and without understanding the true nature of it or its far-reaching implications, she submits to it with full devotion. What the unsuspecting woman does not realise is that Sandip is not who he says he is, and that in the garb of a revolutionary, he is just a scheming profiteer, rolling in the same pleasures that he encourages others to give up. Nikhilesh himself is opposed to the British rule in India, but he does not believe in the radical approach of the Swadeshi movement, because he knows that such a movement will cause irreparable financial harm to the livelihood of the poor. He prefers the other, the seemingly more civilised approach of debate and discourse to get the British to leave. Despite this, and despite realising that his wife is slowly being enamoured by his friend's charms, Nikhilesh allows Sandip to stay in his house. And by the time Bimala sees Sandip's true colours, it is too late, in more ways than one.

The greatest strength of *Ghare Baire* is its story. The biggest weakness of the film is the execution of that same story. While Tagore weaves a beautiful tale of love, companionship, deceit and freedom (in the most wholesome sense of the term) against the backdrop of the nationalist movement after Lord Curzon's partition of Bengal, Ray stretches the story too thin with unconvincing portrayals of its trio of characters. The film is held together by nothing other than over two hours of dialogue; the camera seems too lazy to do anything other than stay on the face of the characters delivering their lines. There's hardly any emoting, and wherever there is any, it tries to overcompensate, leading to disastrous results. More than anything else, *Ghare Baire* is perhaps the first film in which Ray seems to have lost his 'grip' on his audience. It is not like he hadn't made sub-par films in the past, by his own standards. But never before had he completely misread the pulse of those who would watch his film. Whatever precious little works for the film is only because of the story, and the story alone.

It is painful to see frequent Ray collaborator and veteran actor Soumitra Chattopadhyay struggling to grasp the character of Sandip throughout the film, resulting in nothing short of a debacle. He simply isn't convincing enough, and not for want of trying. Chattopadhyay has played flawed characters in Ray's films before, but this time, his charms simply don't work. Swatilekha Sengupta is a misfit in the role of Bimala—a casting error of epic proportions. To put it mildly, her acting is wooden, her face devoid of any emotion whatsoever and both in physical features (which is understandable) and in her performance (which is not), she is a far cry from Tagore's Bimala. Perhaps the only saving grace of the film, when it comes to the subject of performances, is Victor Banerjee in the role of the reticent and mild-mannered aristocrat Nikhilesh Chowdhury. In most of his scenes, Banerjee manages to get under the skin of his character and plays it with the right mix of cautious optimism and silent despair. You can't help but feel for him in that one scene in which Bimala realises her mistake, breaks down and apologises to him, and he simply embraces his wife, saying, 'It's not your fault—for the last ten years, I am the only man whose face you've seen.'

Ghare Baire remains that rare Ray film that is not just weak but also a tragic loss of opportunity. What could have been a wonderful adaptation turns out to be an underwhelming coming together of the greatest mind in Indian literature and the brightest gem of Indian cinema.

Sukumar Ray (1987)

It is well known that Satyajit Ray came from an illustrious family of artists, writers, mathematicians, sportsmen, publishers and musicians—all of whom played important roles in what is now known as the Renaissance of Bengal. His own father, Sukumar Ray, was a literary mind with a fertile imagination, a fantastic sense of humour and an undying passion for enriching young minds through children's literature. When young Satyajit was just two and a half years old, his father passed away at the age of thirty-six, after battling an incurable disease for several long years. In that sense, Satyajit Ray never met his father, but if one were to go through the literary and visual works of Sukumar Ray carefully, one can clearly see where his son—inarguably one of the greatest creative minds of the twentieth century—got his artistic genes from. In 1987, on the occasion of the birth centenary of Sukumar Ray, his son Satyajit Ray created a documentary film on his life and works as a tribute to a father he only knew through his writings, sketches and letters.

The documentary begins with a detailed look at Sukumar Ray's family background, especially at his father—the renowned publisher, writer and entrepreneur Upendrakishore Ray Chowdhury (whose short story 'Goopy Gyne Bagha Byne' Satyajit Ray adapted for the screen years later). From the documentary, we know that Sukumar Ray's literary ambitions began quite early in life and that when he was in college, he founded a club named 'The Nonsense Club', whose primary objective was the pursuit

Sukumar Ray with his wife Suprabha Ray.

and perusal of the genre of nonsense literature. It was for the handwritten magazine of this club that Sukumar wrote two famous plays, *Jhalapala* and *Lakshmaner Shaktishel*. The documentary shows two scenes from the two plays, enacted by stalwarts of cinema and stage such as Utpal Dutt, Soumitra Chattopadhyay and Manoj Mitra. Laced with subtle humour, wordplay, wit and sarcasm, the two scenes immediately make it evident why Sukumar Ray is considered one of the most renowned humourists in Indian literature.

Later, as we are told, Upendrakishore sent his son to London and Manchester, where Sukumar Ray learnt the crafts of photoengraving, chromolithography and litho-drawing over a period of two years. Upon his return to India, Sukumar married Suprabha and began helping his father publish a children's magazine named *Sandesh*. This remarkable magazine was a treasure trove of stories, plays, poems and articles on subjects as varied as science, sports, mythology, history, geography and the arts, with riddles and puzzles and beautiful illustrations to enrich the impressionable minds of young readers. Two years later, after Upendrakishore's sudden death, the responsibility of running *Sandesh* fell upon Sukumar Ray. Under his care, *Sandesh* became an important milestone for children's reading in Bengal, with literary contributions from such eminent people as his father's friend and contemporary, none other than Rabindranath Tagore himself.

Sukumar Ray was also an active member of the Brahmo Samaj in Calcutta, and from the documentary, we learn that he played an important role in electing Tagore as an honorary member of the Brahmo Samaj. Among Sukumar Ray's other achievements was the founding of the Monday Club in Calcutta, whose members were invited and encouraged to hold healthy and erudite discussions on any subject of their choice. It was, without a shred of doubt, a meeting of some of the most brilliant minds of those times, to discuss topics such as politics, philosophy, science, poetry, literature and art, but never sacrificing the underlying allegiance to humour, as was evident from the many pamphlets, posters and flyers designed by Sukumar Ray himself, making important announcements and invitations in the wittiest of ways.

In 1921, the same year his son Satyajit was born, Sukumar Ray fell ill and was diagnosed with a severe form of infectious fever, the notorious 'kala-azar', for which no cure existed in those days. What is most astonishing to note is that it was while he was battling this fatal disease that he wrote two of his best books, *Ha Ja Ba Ra La* (inspired by Lewis Carroll's *Alice in Wonderland*) and *Abol Tabol*, a collection of nonsense rhymes for children. How an ailing man battling for his life could write something so beautiful, so rich, so dense with remarkable ideas and unbridled imagination, and so full of life and laughter, one can only wonder. His undying passion to tell children the most wondrous stories from all around the world, to understand their little minds and let their imagination run free, to excel in the serious business of nonsense art and to urge his spirit to fight and write till his last breath—all of these will endear Sukumar Ray to readers for generations to come. For here was a man, who, in thirty-six precious years, single-handedly did what no other savant in our country could do—ever before or ever since. He taught children how to dream.

Satyajit Ray's documentary on his father is a film that everyone must watch. Because through his rich and flowing music, his fondly scripted narrative and the use of numerous photographs, sketches, doodles, illustrations, paintings and poetry by his father, Ray offers a glimpse into the mind of a genius. Five years after he had paid this beautiful tribute, the illustrious son of the illustrious father himself passed away, and that was, perhaps, the end of the renaissance of Bengal.

Ganashatru

An Enemy of the People (1990)

IN 1881, NORWEGIAN PLAYWRIGHT HENRIK IBSEN WROTE A PLAY titled *Gengangere* (Ghosts), which led to widespread public protests because of the subjects it dared to deal with. The play was a scathing commentary on nineteenth-century Victorian morality and tackled topics such as incest, euthanasia and the dangers of blind religious faith. When the play was staged, Ibsen was strongly criticised and treated as an outcast. In response to such reactions from all quarters of the society, he wrote another play the following year titled *En folkefiende* (An Enemy of the People). Strangely enough, as many as eighty years later, in another part of the globe, history repeated itself, and the same story played out—in 1960, Satyajit Ray made a film titled *Devi* (The Goddess), which was a scathing commentary on the dangers of blind superstition and religious orthodoxy. Ray had to face unprecedented public criticism for the film, with allegations against him ranging from trying to malign a religion he was not part of to hurting the sentiments of Hindus all over the world. In response to such an ugly and baseless public outcry, Ray decided to make a film towards the end of his career. And what better way to register his protest than to adapt Ibsen's play *En folkefiende*? In 1990, then, Ray made *Ganashatru* (An Enemy of the People).

Dr Ashok Gupta is constantly interrupted by his brother
Nishith, as the former tries to warn the townsfolk of
impending danger.

For the adaptation, Ray remained extremely loyal to his source, changing only the setting to a modern-day Indian town. Dr Ashoke Kumar Gupta is a highly revered, honest, hard-working and principled physician working in the township of Chandipur in Bengal. The town is known for its charming weather, and for a temple that attracts devotees and tourists in large numbers throughout the year. The members of the town's municipal board are working towards positioning Chandipur as a tourist destination, which, in turn, will help the town's economy. But when Dr Gupta finds out that the *charanamrita* (holy water) from the temple has recently been contaminated with germs of infective hepatitis, thanks to poor-quality underground sewage pipelines, he tries to warn the people of the town, advising them to refrain from visiting the temple until the sewage pipelines have been repaired. This leads to a huge public outcry and Dr Gupta soon finds out that in return for speaking the truth, he has been branded an enemy of the people.

There is a common belief among film enthusiasts, particularly among those who have watched Ray's films keenly, that *Ganashatru* is, by far, his worst film. While that belief is a subjective point of view, and while it is undeniably true that the film suffers from some extremely poor technical treatment, a few things need to be said about some of the other criticisms against it.

Certain characteristics mark any film that has been adapted from a play. One finds these characteristics almost inevitably in all such films, to the extent that if one were to watch them closely, even without any knowledge of the source, one would be able to surmise that the film has been adapted from a play. Chief among these characteristics is the overdependence on dialogue. Set in a limited and often confined space, such films take the story forward only when the characters verbally communicate with each other. The filmmaker does not have the luxury of subtleties. Speech is the primary vehicle here. *Ganashatru*, too, is marked by this feature, which, mind you, is a huge departure from Ray's usual style of filmmaking. This leads one to conclude that the film is unlike any other Ray film.

But then, one might argue that even some of his later films—*Agantuk* (The Stranger), for instance—are heavily dependent on dialogue and discourse. Why is it, then, that these films are so popular? One of the possible responses to this question can be that *Ganashatru* suffers from two primary faults. First, the story becomes quite mundane over the period of hundred minutes and that it is quite predictable (another un-Ray-like feature). Second, the editing of the film is unbelievably shoddy, with a lack of continuity, background characters staring into the camera or standing still like a statue or not knowing what to do when they are not speaking—everything that would normally make a director demand another take. It almost feels as if the film was hurriedly put together (which it was). But then, perhaps we should not forget that the man who used to make one film every year was returning to make a feature film after six long and physically devastating years of battling a prolonged and life-threatening illness. The result was for everyone to see. The actors in the film try their best but the editing doesn't do its job of 'hiding' their faults. Soumitra Chattopadhyay is brilliant as the upright and fearless doctor, and so is Dhritiman Chaterji as his jealous brother, who also happens to be the chairman of the municipality. Mamata Shankar is effortlessly natural as the good doctor's daughter, but the rest of the cast, which includes some terrific actors, seem simply there to fill the screen.

Is *Ganashatru* essentially a bad film? The question merits debate. In isolation, as purely a work of art, perhaps it is. But it is also undeniably true that no art is independent of its creator and his or her state of mind. Ray's biggest crime, if one might take the liberty of saying so, in making *Ganashatru* is that he was perhaps more loyal to the source than he should have been. What had worked on the stage—that, too, in 1882—does not work on screen more than a century later, unless treated in a certain way. A master of adaptations, Ray for once seems to have overlooked this simple fact in his otherwise illustrious and impeccable film career.

Shakha Proshakha

Branches of a Tree (1990)

Towards the fag end of his career, the films that Satyajit Ray made were a clear reflection of two things—first, his failing health and exhaustion, and second, the fact that he was finding it increasingly difficult to cope with the rampant unscrupulousness of the society around him. Almost devoid of his smart humour, perhaps because he was too tired to use it by now, even the most casual watcher could tell the master's growing irritation and helplessness shadowed in these films, as he found himself surrounded by the death of ethics. One such film is his penultimate one, titled *Shakha Proshakha* (Branches of a Tree).

The story of the film is simple. Ananda Majumdar is a retired industrialist, who has risen from the position of a trainee in a mica-manufacturing firm in a small town in the Chota Nagpur plateau all the way up to the position of partner in the same company, by dint of sheer industry and exemplary honesty. Thanks to his upright character and philanthropy, the people of the town worship him, so much so that they have named the entire town after him. He has four sons, and after three of them move to the city and go their own ways, Majumdar lives with his second son, who was once a bright and promising young man but who has now been reduced to a mentally ill individual after surviving a nasty accident in London. On the occasion of his seventieth birthday,

As the Majumdar family dines, the cracks begin to show.

the patriarch of the family suffers a massive heart attack and his three sons and their respective families hurriedly gather around him. In the week that follows, tensions mount and, unknown to the old man, it is revealed that none of the three brothers, who are considered to have successful careers, have inherited the honesty and strength of character that their father is known for.

The two female characters in the film exhibit their mute strength in their own ways. Not entirely unfamiliar with their husbands' dishonourable ways and means of bringing money home, they suffer silently, knowing well that there's no way out any more. The wife of the third son, Tapati—played beautifully by Mamata Shankar—finds herself in a failed marriage and is increasingly drawn to her brother-in-law, the youngest son of the family, whose Marxist ideologies make him give up a cushy and lucrative job in an advertising agency to take up a career in professional theatre. When the same man confesses to her that he has fallen in love with another woman, Tapati is hurt and bruised. Her only solace is her eight-year-old son, and although she is unhappy, she stays back and makes a genuine attempt to protect her marriage, all for the sake of her child.

Set against this gloomy backdrop is the second son Prashanta's seemingly useless existence. He sits in his own room with a candle burning in one corner and listens to Bach and the Gregorian chants. The scenes depicting him in his dimly lit solitude seem to come straight out of an oil painting from the days of yore. Every now and then, he exhibits glimpses of his erstwhile spark—a deep knowledge of music, literature and philosophy—and also, rather surprisingly, a brilliant sense of humour. Played beautifully by legendary actor Soumitra Chattoapadhyay, it is endearing to see him suffering from the agony of a memory loss and yet casually walking up to his father and touching his feet to take his blessings when he learns that it is the old man's birthday. In perhaps the most hard-hitting and masterfully written scene of the film, the same Prashanta, ignored and relegated to the background, protests in his unique way when the family gathers over lunch but ends up throwing allegations of corruption and vices against each other. He is a madman, but a madman who hasn't forgotten his principles. Once again, if there's one thing that gets portrayed in this scene, it is the ageing filmmaker's tragic helplessness and angst at finding himself more of an exception than a rule in the midst of a lost cause.

If one were to do an honest assessment of the film, one would have to say that despite the relevance of the message, the usual brilliance of Ray's style and filmmaking, and several admirable performances by the actors, the film is not without its flaws. One of the principal criticisms of the film could possibly be around its use of dialogue. In an essay written in 1963, Ray himself says, 'Perhaps the most important thing to be said about dialogue in film is that the screenwriter ought to be able to completely obliterate his own existence, enter the minds of his characters and then express the nature of these characters through the words that *they* would speak. One must also remember, that in film, time is a very valuable commodity. The more you can express in as few words, the better. And if you can do it through gestures instead of using words, well, nothing like it. [translation mine]' Sadly, it is this economy of dialogue—which Ray once professed so strongly and practised with zeal in every single one of his early films—that is lacking in *Shakha Proshakha*. The dialogue looks rather forced at places, and this affects the screenplay in many ways. The film could have done with better editing as well, and Ray's handling of the child actor in the film also leaves us less than satisfied.

And that brings us to a point that is worth considering before judging the film too harshly. The subject of the film, the message within and the way this message is delivered—by juxtaposing the so-called 'success' of the three accomplished sons against the seemingly worthless but selfless love of the ignored one for his dying father—are all so relevant in today's world that one is forced to ignore these minor blemishes and take a moment to reflect and make an effort to tell the gainfully wrong from the morally right. And it is in that sense that *Shakha Proshakha* succeeds as a film—for what is a good film but a moving image of life that makes you think?

Agantuk
The Stranger (1992)

WE HAVE REVISITED, DISSECTED AND ANALYSED SOME REMARKABLE films by Satyajit Ray. These include feature films, short films and documentaries. As many as thirty-nine films together constitute the entire body of work that one of the greatest filmmakers in the history of world cinema has left behind as his legacy. Of all the films that Ray made, perhaps the most intellectual, the most thought-provoking and the one that compels us to question ourselves over and over again is his final film. And yet, very few people know that this film is based on what can best be described as a children's story, written by Ray himself. In 1992, merely a few months before he passed away, the legendary director gave us *Agantuk* (The Stranger).

As with all great films, the story of *Agantuk* is a very simple one. Anila Bose, a young, educated lady in south Calcutta, receives a letter one day, written by a man who claims to be her long-lost uncle. The stranger, who claims to have roamed the globe for the past thirty-five years, has invited himself over to her home as he is passing through India. While Anila's son Babloo is excited about the arrival of 'a man who may or may not be Dadu', her husband, Sudhindra Bose, is cautiously sceptical of the stranger's motives. During his stay at the Bose residence, the stranger, who introduces himself as Manomohan Mitra, comes across as a man of

Manomohan Mitra's only surviving blood relatives arrive to
take him home.

simple tastes, good humour and gentle manners. And yet, the seeds of doubt are not entirely dispelled from the minds of Anila and her husband. Is the man really who he says he is? And if he is indeed Anila's uncle, why did he return to Calcutta after thirty-five years? Is it because of the money that his father left behind for him? Or does he have an ulterior motive? As all these questions continue to bother Anila and Sudhindra, the stranger continues to impress them with his deep knowledge, rich experiences and profound views of life, until a shocking discovery at the end leaves them astounded.

At its very core, *Agantuk* is a philosophical film. It raises more questions than it answers, and each of those questions makes us wonder about ourselves. In trying to reveal the stranger's true identity, when Sudhindra's barrister friend grills him about his whereabouts over the past three and a half decades, what is revealed is truly astonishing. The stranger claims to have lived almost all his life amid tribesmen in various remote jungles of the globe. He argues that the very notion of civilisation needs to be re-examined. It is his belief, he says, that the so-called uncivilised people—the tribal folk and forest-dwellers—have achieved much more by way of science, technology, architecture, medicine and art than their more civilised cousins living and working in cities. Religion, he argues, is a by-product of civilisation—and it has done very little other than dividing people—creating groups, classes and sects within the very people who practise it. Of what use is such a religion, then, he asks? When questioned about the unthinkable progress that space technology has made, the stranger argues that the success of NASA is no more important than the success of a tribesman who can build a hut that protects him from the elements, or that of an Eskimo who uses opaque slabs of ice to build the walls of his igloo and transparent ones to build the windows.

The stranger's views on life are quite simple, and yet he looks at the world like no one usually does. In explaining the phenomenon of eclipses to Babloo and his friends, for instance, he wonders how the moon and the sun were both placed at such precise distances from the Earth that in the sky, the two of them appear exactly the same size, despite the latter being much bigger. It is, in his words, an inexplicable phenomenon, the greatest magic trick in the entire universe!

Utpal Dutt gives one of the best performances of his career in the film, as the stranger who calls himself Nemo—or 'Mr No One!' An extremely learned and scholarly gentleman himself, Dutt gets right into the skin of his character with such ease that it becomes impossible to imagine anyone else in the role thereafter. Dipankar De also gives a fantastic performance as Sudhindra, and in a short but significant role, Dhritiman Chaterji is brilliant as the tough-talking lawyer who, out of sheer frustration at not being able to win a debate against the learned Mitra, chooses to hurl insults at him instead. Mamata Shankar is perfect as Anila, in what almost seems like a role written for her. Towards the end of the film, when the family is gathered to witness a tribal dance next to a meandering river, the joy and excitement on her face is vivid, so much so that on the first insistence of her husband that she should go and join the dancers, she promptly does so, leading Mitra to comment, 'I had a doubt if she really was my niece. Now I don't!'

Avid film lovers—at least those who have followed Ray's films, his literary works, his essays and his life in general—will tell you that when they see Mitra on screen, they know that it is, in fact, Ray himself speaking. Never one to conform to any one religion and yet keeping an open mind about all forces and phenomena that science fails to explain, Ray never believed in organised religion and offered several critiques of it through his films. He was, however, quite aware of the presence of a supreme force that drives us all, and he refused to label it or try to explain it in any way. To him, this mere awareness was enough, and it was a deeply personal experience and belief.

Similarly, he had managed to raise himself above all political discussions, and like a true artist, believed that one lifetime is too short to soak in everything beautiful that nature has to offer. Refusing to waste his time on futile debates of divisive politics, he turned his attention to the human condition instead. To him, it was a far more fruitful and interesting exercise—one that quenched his thirst and gave him great contentment. Like Mitra, Ray tried to live his life amid simple people, and his experiences taught him that civilisation was nothing but an illusion. It was these precise thoughts that he wanted to portray in his swan song. It is said that on the last day of shooting, after the final shot was over, Ray threw up his hands in the air and announced to his wife, 'That's it. That's all there is. I don't have anything more to say.' A few months later, he passed away in a nursing home in Calcutta, leaving behind a rich collection of films that continues to enthral us today. As film lovers, we are deeply in his debt—and will continue to remain so for as long as there is the magic of cinema.

PART II

MEDITATIONS
ON RAY,
HIS FILMS,
HIS FILM-MAKING

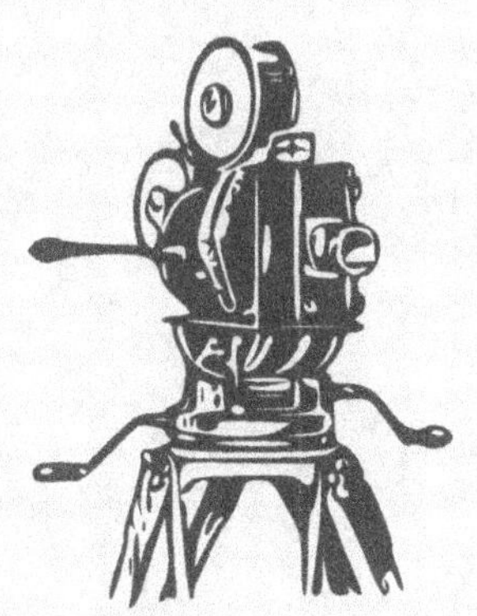

Aparna Sen

'Ray's greatest strength was his power of suggestion'

Aparna Sen acted in four Satyajit Ray films—*Samapti, Aranyer Din Ratri, Jana Aranya* and *Pikoo*. In her own words, none of these were very elaborate or complex roles. And yet, anyone who has watched these films will vouch for how she left an indelible impression on her viewers with her beautiful and dedicated performances. Daughter to a renowned film critic, and an internationally celebrated and widely laurelled filmmaker herself, hers is one of the most important voices we must listen to if we truly want to understand the man behind the legend. In this interview, Sen speaks of the great admiration she has for her Manik Kaka and why this admiration also gives her the right to understand and accept his mistakes.

What are your earliest memories of Calcutta Film Society, of which your father Chidananda Dasgupta and Satyajit Ray were founding members?

The film society was already in existence by the time I was old enough to realise anything. I don't remember a great deal about the society, except that both my parents were members of it. I think it was in 1952 that the society had its first film festival, although I have no recollection of it at all. When I grew older, probably at the age of ten or eleven, I remember these meetings that used to happen at our home in Palm Avenue. There used to be an 8-mm projector set up in our large balcony and the films were projected onto a screen. A lot of film-society members used to come for these meetings and screenings. We children were encouraged to watch the films too, as my parents never distinguished between adult films and children's films, as long as they were just good films. I remember having watched such films as *Alexander Nevsky*, *Ivan the Terrible*, *Battleship Potemkin* and even *The Passion of Joan of Arc* at these screenings. In addition, we used to attend other film-society shows. My parents took us for *Hiroshima Mon Amour*, which I didn't understand at all then but it left a deep impression on me. It was like growing up in a house full of musicians where the ragas have not been explained to you, but you pick them up anyway.

Did the society have a significant number of female members as well?

My mother was a founding member of the film society. Siddartha Shankar Ray's brother's wife—Rita Ray, a film critic, who wrote under the pen name Kobita Sarkar—was also a member. An avowed film buff named Vijaya Mulay, who was addressed as 'Akka', was also a member, though she did not live in Calcutta. I think Akka was very active when the Federation of Film Societies of India was formed. Satyajit Ray's wife, Bijoya Ray, was also a member. Perhaps male members outnumbered their female counterparts. But I do remember seeing a lot of women at the film festivals or at the film shows, where I saw [Akira] Kurosawa's *Rashomon* and *Red Beard*, among many other films.

Your father and Ray were lifelong friends. Were you ever encouraged by your father to look at Ray's films through a critic's lens and not just as a film fan?

I never used to see any film as a film fan. There were films that I didn't understand. I sometimes asked my parents to talk about them, and we exchanged ideas. I still remember, sometimes I used to complain bitterly as I wasn't allowed to see the popular mainstream Bengali films at all. We were taken to the theatres to watch Chaplin and Marx Brothers, and so on. I must have been eight or nine when my father said, 'I will take you to see Manik's film when it comes out. It will be out next year.' *Pather Panchali* was released in 1955. When I was older, my father and I often discussed Ray's films. I remember our discussion on *Devi*, for instance. We talked a great deal about the father-in-law's interest in the daughter-in-law's love life. The father-in-law kept asking the daughter-in-law about the letters his son wrote to her. That's something that a father-in-law normally won't do. It was a very psychologically interesting aspect, because just after that, he has a dream where he sees the daughter-in-law as a goddess, thus making her sexually inaccessible to his son.

Is it true that you also held the belief that Ray was not very good at depicting scenes that involved sexual activity between two people?

Ray's greatest strength was his power of suggestion. He was more comfortable depicting legitimate marital relationships. There is a kissing scene in *Devi*, even though it is in silhouette. There is also a lovely shot in *Apur Sansar*, in which Apu finds Aparna's hairpin under the pillow. It suggests a happy sexual relationship. Explicit lovemaking scenes— for instance, a kissing scene—came only in *Ghare Baire*. In *Charulata*, Charu's interest in Amal both emotionally and physically was evident throughout the film, and it was beautifully depicted.

Then again, in *Seemabaddha*, there was clear sexual tension between Tutul and her brother-in-law Shyamalendu.

You could say that, I suppose. Actually, Tutul had a teenage crush on her brother-in-law and still has a lot of respect for him when she comes to visit them in Calcutta. But there was sexual interest only on the part of Shyamalendu. Tutul was in love with somebody else—a Naxalite boy, whose future was uncertain. I don't think Tutul was sexually interested in her brother-in-law. It was more like she idolised him. She was, in all likelihood, aware of her brother-in-law's interest in her. Yet, by the end of the film, she was disappointed in him. He had fallen in her estimation because of the unscrupulous way in which he handled the crisis in his office.

As a filmmaker yourself, what do you feel about *Ganashatru*?

Ganashatru was not one of Ray's best. It is not up there with his earlier gems. There is no doubt about that. *Ghare Baire* onwards, I think the standard of Ray's performance as a filmmaker fell to some extent. I think that was because of his illness, more than anything else. But then again, in *Shakha Proshakha*, he was very good. He was equally good in *Shatranj Ke Khilari*, where he used a lot of acerbic humour. The relationship between Saeed Jaffrey and his wife—played by Farida Jalal—even as she was having an affair with someone else, was depicted with a delightful playfulness. And Shabana Azmi's pain of constantly being ignored by her husband, who was busy playing chess all the time, has also been treated with humour. The scene where she has removed all the chess pieces and the two players have to make do with vegetables instead is utterly delightful. And yet, despite all this bizarre humour, one can detect a resigned sigh on the director's part at the degeneration and lack of political will of the nobles of the time. By the time Ray came to *Ghare Baire*, he was not nearly as physically fit as he had been before his heart attack. It could be that when all your senses are not functioning at peak level, you cannot make the kind of films that you have made earlier. Creativity is affected by illness too.

Is it true that you were the first choice for Bimala in *Ghare Baire*?

A long time ago, in 1976, when we were on the jury of IFFI [International Film Festival of India], he had told me that he was thinking of me for

Bimala. He couldn't make the film at that time because communal tensions were running high. A few years later, when I cut my hair short, he was very upset. 'Oh, your hair looks like that of a widowed aunt,' he said. 'I can't cast you as Bimala, with your hair like this!' Later, I went to his house one day, and he told me that he had found someone for Bimala. It didn't seem right on my part to question him about it, as it was his vision and his decision. To be honest, he had never really cast me very much in his films. In fact, my role as Mrinmoyi in *Samapti* was also a replacement for somebody else. A girl named Sukriti Tagore was first chosen but her family was not happy about it, so the role came to me. I used to joke with him about this and say, 'You always use me as a stepney, don't you?' But in films such as *Aranyer Din Ratri* or *Jana Aranya*, he really wanted me—even in those cameo roles. He would be shooting in the studios, and I was also then working in mainstream films, so I would often go to his sets to chat with him between shots. He used to tell me that I was a strong actor. Swatilekha could sing as well as play the piano. Perhaps that was the reason for casting her as Bimala. And I think he had seen Swati in *Khorir Gondi*, the Bengali adaptation of *The Caucasian Chalk Circle*, and had liked her very much.

In *Pikoo*, we see a glimpse of a mother's bruised mind as she struggles to deal with her own guilt against her son's pure innocence. Ray had said that it was an extremely complex film. Was it a complex role to play too?

No, I didn't really find it that complex. Perhaps I missed something. I found it very interesting, though. There was a scene in which I was supposed to be looking at my young son in the garden below and crying. Ray and I had a conversation about this before he filmed the scene. He said, 'You are crying because you see your innocent son in the garden and feel you have cheated him.' I said, 'But I haven't cheated *him*. I have cheated on *his father*.' And he said, 'It's the same thing.' I didn't agree with this interpretation at all. But I was a professional, so I went ahead and did the scene. He seemed quite happy with the result.

You were fifteen years old when you played the role of Mrinmoyi in *Samapti*. How did Ray explain the complexities of the character to you?

I was fourteen, in fact, when I started *Samapti*, because we started shooting in 1960 and I turned fifteen later that year, on 25 October. Ray didn't explain anything to me, nor did he ever delve into the psychology of the character. It wasn't a very complex character anyway. Mrinmoyi didn't have to do anything that I couldn't understand. The most complex part was where she changed from a girl into a woman. He filmed that scene beautifully in three close-ups of Mrinmoyi, where he kept changing the lights. In the last segment, where Mrinmoyi had come to terms with herself and realised that she did love her husband, Ray did not explain anything. He just asked me to put my thumb in my mouth and think of 'lovely, wonderful things'. I was old enough to understand what he meant, of course! Most of the time, I was just following instructions and I used to wish rather wistfully that I would get a chance to show him that I could act. One day, I did get the chance and that day has remained very memorable to me.

In the scene being filmed, I was supposed to have my squirrel, Chorki, in my hand and show it to my friend Rakhal, who was sitting in the living room where his sister was being presented to Soumitra as a prospective bride. I was at the window, calling Rakhal and asking him to come out and play with me. But he didn't want to come and wanted to keep sitting in the room. As I tried to tempt Rakhal by showing him my new pet, Chorki was supposed to slip out of my hand and into the room. I would then have to run into the room to locate Chorki and turn the place upside down in the process. Normally, Chorki would invariably try to slip out of my hand, but on that particular day, he decided to stay put. I didn't want the shot to be rejected on my account. So I pretended to put it down on the windowsill so that Rakhal could see it better. Then I acted as if I had suddenly realised that Chorki was gone, and rushed out after it. I remember Bansi Kaka—Bansi Chandragupta, the art director—shaking his head and saying, '*Holona, holona* (No, no! That didn't work)*!*' But Manik Kaka was laughing a lot. He stuck his head out from behind the camera and said, 'I rather liked it!' So that was that. The shot was retained in the film. That was my one little moment of triumph.

There was this other time when I was supposed to cry. I was terrified and told everyone that I would never be able to cry convincingly. But after I did the shot, both Manik Kaka and Monku Mashi [Bijoya Ray] said, 'Who said you can't cry? Look how beautifully you did it!' There wasn't too much to do by way of acting, really. I did what he asked me to and I understood his instructions. Of course, there were some things that did come from me. For instance, I was supposed to write a letter to my husband, '*Tumi phire esho* (Please come back).' Nobody had asked me to write as an uneducated girl would. But I wrote those words in an uneducated hand anyway. Ray probably liked that, as he didn't cut the shot. Anyway, most of the time, when I did as I was told, it came through quite well. Actually, when Ray read out the dialogue before a scene, if you simply imitated him, 50 per cent of the job was done!

It is said that his script narrations were events in themselves. And that he never used to theorise his characters too much.

He may have narrated scripts to Soumitra and Sharmila and some other actors, but he didn't read the script of *Samapti* to me. My role was comparatively small. I think he just narrated the script of *Pikoo* to me. As for explaining the characters in great detail, I think he may have done that with Soumitra because Soumitra used to keep a diary or a journal for his character of Apu, and they used to talk about that a lot. I know that Ray had this sort of a relationship with Soumitra, because Soumitra himself had told me so. I acted in two of his short films—*Samapti* and *Pikoo*—and had a couple of cameos in two other films—that's it! And I felt quite peeved about it then, to be honest. I would have loved to play Bimala. But that's in the past and doesn't really bother me anymore.

There's been considerable lament among the female readership of Ray's literature around the inexplicable dearth of female characters in his stories. But in his cinema, Ray had written and imagined strong female characters—Charu, Aparna, Mrinmoyi, Karuna, Anila—one could go on. Not just as a filmmaker but as a woman, do you think Ray understood the mind of a woman well?

My elder daughter, who is a die-hard Feluda fan even as a mother of two grown children today, used to bitterly complain to me as a child about the lack of female characters in the Feluda stories. Manik Kaka was aware of this himself. He told me that he received many letters from young female readers who complained about it. When I asked him in an interview about the reason for this lack of female characters in his stories, he said, 'If I have a little girl of Topshe's age in the stories, what would her relationship with Topshe be like?' This seemed to be a problem that he simply didn't know how to solve. But I never quite understood where the problem lay, as there can be different kinds of relationships between two teenagers, not necessarily a romantic one. But there was this one female character in one of the Feluda stories whom Manik Kaka described as 'masculine' because she could ride a horse and fire a rifle. He seemed to have very clear-cut notions of what was feminine and what could be masculine. In that same interview, I asked him, 'What do you think of women?' He replied, 'Since women are not physically as strong as men, I think that makes them morally stronger.' That was rather difficult for me to understand. I never quite agreed with him on that point, as I think women can be just as immoral. But Ray has created truly unforgettable female characters in his films. Arati in *Mahanagar* was a wonderfully strong character created by him. Even Sarbajaya, who brought up Apu on her own, showed great strength of character. In *Jana Aranya*, the girl who decides to be an escort was an equally strong character. Despite the difference in our ages, Ray and I became good friends after being on the jury of IFFI in 1976, and we used to discuss a lot of things. He would often call me up and discuss problems he was facing when writing certain scenes in his script. One day, he called up and said, 'How can the protagonist ask his friend's sister to become an escort? It doesn't seem right!' I remained quiet. It was not my place to offer solutions. A couple of days later, he called me again and said, 'I think I have found a solution. What if she herself insists? What if she asks the protagonist to stop interfering and ruining her business?' That seemed to make perfect sense. I was gratified that he chose to discuss these things with me. I must confess that I still miss those discussions.

In Sandip Ray's *Phatik Chand*, the character played by Kamu Mukherjee does not accept the reward money at the end. I had asked Ray, 'Don't you think it would have been more interesting if he had faced an internal dilemma? After all, he is poor, and all that money must have been very tempting for him! Don't you think it could have given the character another layer?' He said, 'No, I never thought of it that way. The thought never struck me. It was a children's film, after all.'

How about your own character in *Pikoo*?

In *Pikoo*, there were layers to my character. I was obviously not quite happy in the relationship with my husband, certainly not sexually. But I was torn between the guilt of deception and the need for sexual gratification. I think Indir Thakrun, too, showed interesting contradictions. Recall how she walked out of the house in a huff when Sarbajaya rebuked her, but when Sarbajaya choked on her food, Indir immediately tried to comfort her. I think there was a dichotomy in Sarbajaya as well. She was angry with Indir Thakrun, but that is only because there were too many mouths to feed and too little money. I think the characters in Ray's earlier films had more layers—they were more Chekhovian than his later ones. One of the most interesting characters I have come across in a Ray film is that of Siddhartha in *Pratidwandi*. Throughout the film, he was not really sure about what he felt. And as a filmmaker myself, I have always found contradictions in people very interesting.

Was Ray open to criticism?

No, he wasn't. I didn't ever criticise him, though. When I discussed things with him, it wouldn't be by way of criticism—it would be more of a discussion, just like the discussion I had with him on Kamu Mukherjee's character in *Phatik Chand*. And he listened to me patiently. When I interviewed him, I did pose some uncomfortable questions, but in a very respectful way. That was not difficult, because I did respect him hugely. But even though my father was an old friend of his, if he wrote anything critical about his films, Ray would always hit back.

I have thought at length about this. Ray lost his father at a very young age and he was brought up by his mother. Perhaps the insecurities of his childhood, having to stay as long-term guests in his uncle's home ... these things left a deep impression on him. Perhaps it was due to these insecurities that he was not very good at taking criticism. Perhaps it was an act of overcompensation, an instinctive protectiveness for himself. Mind you, he was very aware of his mistakes himself, but he never discussed them, except with the people he trusted most—his wife and his son. Why else would he talk of *Charulata* as the film where he had made the least mistakes? Strangely, he was quite protective of me as well when I faced criticism for the first film I directed. I came to know of this at a film party. Someone said to me about *36 Chowringhee Lane*, 'It was good, but it was far too long.' Later, Manik Kaka said to me, 'How awful of him to say that! I didn't like it at all!' I said, 'But it *was* a little too long, wasn't it? He was just giving me his feedback.' He said, 'Still, it feels very bad to hear things like that!' Do you see what I mean? Nothing was said about any of *his* films, but he was upset when *I* was criticised. That was just how he was.

Do you consider yourself a protégé of Ray?

Do you mean have I learnt a lot from him and his cinema? Oh yes, I most definitely have. I have written and spoken a lot about Manik Kaka and his cinema on various forums. When I wrote about the ten favourite films that I would take to a desert island with me, one of them was *Apur Sansar*, despite the fact that *Aparajito* is my favourite of the trilogy. In *Apur Sansar*, one identifies so completely with Apu and Aparna that when Aparna dies, one doesn't even think about the child she has left behind. We are so engrossed in Apu's grief, it has affected us so much, that it is only much later that we think of the child.

When I think about it, I feel Ray had mastered the art of making highly sensitive, artistic films that would also appeal to ordinary people. His great strength was in being able to make audiences care about the characters he had created. The observations I have made about Ray here in no way diminish him in my eyes. I do not believe in blind devotion, but there is no doubt in my mind that he is the greatest filmmaker we have had so far. Satyajit Ray worked with outdated machines and limited resources, and yet managed to make films that shook the world. I have the greatest admiration for him. But it is *because* I have so much admiration for him that I also feel that one must not turn him into a god who is above all criticism. Just like Rabindranath Tagore. There is a predilection among Bengalis to turn Tagore into a god. But that, in fact, is a way of diminishing him, really. To my mind, accepting the fact that he was human and fallible but at the same time a genius is the mark of true respect.

Barun Chanda

'*Seemabaddha* is an accurate depiction of the rat race in the corporate world'

In Satyajit Ray's *Seemabaddha* (1971), Barun Chanda played the smart, suave and ambitious corporate bigwig Shyamalendu Chatterjee, who is on an accelerated growth path but has to take a difficult moral decision to reach his goal. Chanda did only one film with Ray but left a mark with his distinct style, good looks and impeccable diction. A fun-loving man who is always up to some prank or the other in real life, he speaks both fondly and passionately of his days with Ray.

Did you begin your acting career with Satyajit Ray's *Seemabaddha*?

Not exactly, and I'll tell you why. To begin with, if you think about it, haven't we all been acting in one way or the other all our lives? Take a job interview, for instance. You memorise your lines, you put on a serious face, you throw your voice in a particular manner, you try to be presentable and likeable, and you do your best to think on your feet and improvise as you go along. What would you call that?

Then again, when I was in school, in Ramakrishna Mission Vidyapith in Deoghar—a rather austere and sombre academic environment, I must say—I played the role of Shakuni in the dramatisation of a portion of the Mahabharata. I think I got that role because I could raise one of my eyebrows quite alarmingly higher than the other one—not unlike the Hollywood actor Gregory Peck! Anyway, I happened to win a standing ovation and an award from Bhabatosh Maharaj for my acting once the show was over.

The second time I appeared on stage was during my final year of English studies at Jadavpur University. The venerable head of the department, Mr Guha, had retired from Dhaka University to join the College of Arts at our university. Those were the early days of the college, and I had played Hamlet. Dr Triguna Sen, who had become the central minister for education under the Congress regime and who was a very learned man, was patient enough to watch the play till the end, and he announced a special award for me.

How and when did the role of Shyamalendu in *Seemabaddha* come to you? Did you audition for it?

No, I didn't. My young pride prevented me from doing so. There was an audition, but I never went after Satyajit Ray seeking a role. There was a friend and colleague of mine who used to moonlight for a magazine called *JS* (*Junior Statesman*). *JS* was the first youth magazine in India. I went up to the editor, Desmond Doig (who was also a fantastic illustrator), and told him that I wished to interview Mr Ray on behalf of his magazine. He said, 'Why not? Go right ahead.' So I borrowed a Gerard recorder with six-inch spools (the cassette recorders hadn't arrived yet) and went to interview Satyajit Ray. The interview couldn't have begun on a worse note, because the recorder simply refused to work. After fidgeting with it for a while, Ray said in that booming voice of his, 'All right, let's interview without the recorder.' Now, I hated the idea of reading out questions from a sheet of paper, so I hadn't even bothered to carry a questionnaire. My face turned white and I could sense that he was watching me all the while and rather enjoying my discomfort. Somehow, I recovered my senses and recalled the questions I wanted to ask him, and the interview began.

I remember I threw him one question that he mustn't have expected. He had just made *Aranyer Din Ratri,* and I had read the book by Sunil Gangopadhyay. So I asked him, 'This film that you've made, do you realise that this is the first youth-oriented film that you have made so far?' That seemed to throw him off a little, perhaps because it had not occurred to him. When the interview was over, he asked me if I would show the transcript to him before it went to press, just so he could check if I had written everything in a manner and meaning that he had intended. And I assured him that I would. But when I walked out of there, again in my youthful, arrogant pride, I thought, 'Over my dead body. Why should I show the interview to him?' I had asked for an interview; he had agreed. He had said what he wanted to say and I had listened to him. I had the faculty to understand what he had to say. So, as usual, the interview came out and I sent him an advance copy. And he was rather impressed with the fact that I had remembered every word of what he had said and was able to reproduce it back in my office. In hindsight, I now think that was when he had become interested in me.

But having said that, when he made *Pratidwandi,* I was quite sad that he hadn't cast me or called me. I wanted to do that role, because, oh, what a role that was! But later, when I saw Dhriti (Dhritiman Chaterji) do it, I stopped complaining. He was the living embodiment of Siddhartha. However, it's not that I was completely absent from *Pratidwandi.* I had played a small role in it, although only my back and my hands were seen in the film. I was one of the political acquaintances of the hero, whom he met at a café and offered him a job outside the city.

But the voice of the character was not yours, was it?

No, it wasn't. When the day for dubbing came, Ray must have looked for me, but I was in Bombay, shooting. I used to make ad films and documentaries. He couldn't wait for me, so he had to dub his own voice onto my character. When I returned to Calcutta, he was furious with me. He said, 'You made it quite difficult for me, because although your back was to the camera, your gestures, etc., were so on point, so natural, that it was tough for me to do the dubbing in my voice.'

So that is why you said at the beginning of this interview that *Seemabaddha* was not exactly your first Ray film?

That is correct. Even when he was making *Seemabaddha*, he didn't quite approach me with the role of Shyamalendu—certainly not in the conventional sense of the term. It was the year 1969, as far as I can remember. I was visiting him on and off by then. One day, he asked me, 'Do you read Bengali stories?' I don't know what gave him the impression that I was anglicised—I certainly wasn't. But anyway, I didn't take umbrage to the question and I said I did read Bengali literature. And he gave me a couple of magazines and books, and asked me to read two stories. One of them was a novel by Mani Shankar Mukherjee, *Seemabaddha*. The other—and very few people know this—was a long short story by Sunil Gangopadhyay called 'Shaada Bari Kaalo Raasta'. No one has ever mentioned this—that he may have contemplated making a film on this story.

Anyway, I went to Rajasthan on a holiday, and I read *Seemabaddha* on this trip, and when I came back to Calcutta, he made it known to me and others that he was writing a script on the story. He would call me often and say, 'Listen Barun, it's been a long time since I have had any sort of connection with the world of advertising. Why don't you come over one of these days and tell me how you make these commercial radio jingles and play them for your clients?' Based on my inputs, he made those ad pitches that you see in the film. Another day, he asked me to come over to his place and said, 'Don't you write copies for ads?' I said I did. Then he asked me to write a copy for an export ad on ceiling fans. The one that I ended up making for him was, 'The breeziest export story of the year', and you can see it in the film. He asked me, 'Where do you make these jingles?' I said we did them at Arup [Guhathakurta]-da's place—Ad Makers. He said he knew them, Arup-da being Ruma [Guhathakurta]-di's husband. That's where we got the two jingles made—one in Bengali and the other in Hindi.

Finally, he called me one day; he didn't mention why. I went to his home and he pulled out his famous thick red book, which I knew he used to write his screenplays. Then he looked at me and said, 'You've never considered acting, have you?' Once again, my young pride was acting up. He had asked me an indirect question, and I decided to give him a suitable answer. I said, 'I've never said no, have I?' And he laughed and laughed. Then he became his normal self again, and said, 'I'm going to read out the script of *Seemabaddha* to you.' After two hours, during which there were no breaks or interruptions of any kind, he finished reading, turned towards me and said, 'What do you think of it?' I had lost my voice by then. I somehow managed to croak, 'It's good!' He must have been furious with such an impassive response, but he didn't show it. Instead, he told me that I was playing Shyamalendu. But he made it very clear that I had to go through a process of audition for that role.

Ray has made several films on the old-versus-new commentary. In some of them—for instance, in *Devi* and *Jalsaghar*—he has shown the demerits of holding onto the archaic at the cost of logic and practicality. In others—*Seemabaddha* and *Shakha Proshakha*, for example—he has spoken about the dangers of moving too fast and too far away from tradition and ethics. In *Seemabaddha* in particular, a wise old man cautions your character against raging ambition. One wonders, then, what kind of a man Ray himself was. Where, in the spectrum of tradition versus modernity, would you see him?

I won't give you a straight answer to this. I think it was after *Mahanagar* that he began to work on the complications of the urban society, and I suppose it came as a response or a reaction to the general thinking of people—even those outside the country—that Ray was a comfortable filmmaker, making only period films, dwelling only in the past. All of the films that he made during this phase of his career had one central theme—that of unemployment and the resulting unrest, the entire Naxalite movement.

Ray has often been criticised for not being openly critical of the political scenario of the country and Bengal in his films, in his art. Do you think his films were, for lack of a better word, 'safe' films? Not scathing enough? Not unafraid?

He has given a pointed answer to that in an interview. He was very well aware of this criticism and had commented that in hindsight, probably he would not have made his urban films any more committed than he already had. He had dealt with all the urban problems of the present system in his own way and had felt that if he would have made *Pratidwandi*, *Seemabaddha* or *Jana Aranya* any differently, perhaps with a more scathing commentary, it would have made no difference to society at all. Mind you, he had never said that film is merely a work of art and not an act of propaganda. But if one listens to him carefully, one will understand that he was being rather guarded in his response to the criticism against him. He even mentioned that Mrinal [Sen] would have probably made more committed films. He went on to say that some people had made more committed films than he had and made quite a bit of news, but society, in general, didn't change as a result of that, because the film meant nothing to those in power. It was a very angular kind of an answer. He added, 'I am first and foremost a storyteller, and if I find a story interesting and relevant, I will go for it.'

You were part of the corporate world for almost all your life. Do you think the story of *Seemabadhha* is an accurate description of the corporate world in general or is it just another story, a work of fiction?

After watching *Seemabaddha*, many people from the corporate world found the film a much superior one than *Pratidwandi*. They felt it was a profound reflection of the harsh realities of the corporate world. But I didn't think so. I believe *Pratidwandi* is a brilliant film that truly has the power to shake you up. When you are talking about *Seemabaddha*, you are talking about the tip of the pyramid, whereas films such as *Pratidwandi* and *Jana Aranya* are talking about the masses and were successful in shaking up the foundations of society. But to answer your question, yes, *Seemabaddha* is an accurate depiction of the rat race in the corporate world.

In the film, the sexual tension between Shyamalendu and Sudarshana is crackling, to say the least. Ray heightens this with music, silences, gestures, mellow lighting, a gentle breeze, the fascinating use of space and distances, and sheer body language—both yours and Sharmila Tagore's. What was his explanation to you for this aspect of the character of Shyamalendu?

I had a full-scale discussion on this with Mr Ray. He had never given me a script, fearing that I might memorise it. By that time, I had also got accustomed to the norm of addressing him as Manik-da. And I told him that I wanted to discuss something with him. I asked him a simple logical question. In the film, Tutul, or Sudarshana, eventually rejects me—and that makes *Seemabaddha* a tragedy. But how can there be rejection if there has never been an acceptance in the past somewhere? Or somehow? If you remember, the scene of the morning after the party is almost like a game of chess. I walk up to her, she moves away; I follow, she returns, until finally she goes to a bookshelf, where I corner her. She has nowhere else left to go. If these are not sexual advances, what are they? It was then that Manik-da mentioned Tagore's *Dui Bon** to me. He explained to me that we couldn't go beyond a certain level of implying specific things. He said that there were already sequences in

---

* In *Dui Bon*, Rabindranath Tagore tells the story of a man who must choose between his love for his wife and her sister—two women of entirely different personalities.

the film that implicitly expressed the warmth of the intimacy between the two characters. The sequence at the racecourse, for instance, where she [Sharmila Tagore] grabs my jacket in excitement and I look at her. She hasn't touched me unknowingly but because she feels she can, that too in a public place. In another scene, she says that when I used to come to her home in Patna to meet her sister, she used to envy her.

How did Ray treat newcomers and non-actors?

He always used to make an effort to find out the comfort level of a newcomer so that the new actor didn't have to face any difficulties. When he wanted a retake, he would simply say, 'This is good. Let's have one more please.' Sometimes he would walk up to the actor and whisper advice and suggestions for improvement of their performance. Never would he make anyone feel embarrassed or humiliated in any way.

There are some films in the history of cinema that make fascinating fashion statements. This aspect of *Seemabaddha* is hardly spoken about. Those beautifully cut suits, those fashionable neckties and cufflinks, those gorgeous saris and sunglasses. Please tell us about the fashion of *Seemabaddha*.

A lot of people still tell me that for several years after the film was released, I was their idol. They wanted to emulate the way I talked, the way I walked—everything. The outfit I wear for a brief sequence when the young man comes to thank me for recommending him for a job at the factory. Or my golfing tees. These are some of Manik-da's well-thought-out fashion ideas. He took me to a big shop in Park Street and chose the material for my suit. And he asked me, 'Who is your tailor?' I replied, 'He lives in Rashbehari Avenue, near Gariahat. Will you go there?' The name of the tailor was Jahar Banerjee, who was sent abroad by his father to be a barrister but returned as a tailor. When I told Manik-da his story, he became so interested in the man that he readily came along. As Jahar-da took my measurements, Manik-da simply sat there and watched him, occasionally asking him questions about his life.

The only thing Manik-da didn't personally choose for me was my pair of shoes. He selected a special kind of shirt, though, with double-folded cuffs. We used to wear those kinds of shirts underneath suits. But look at the genius of the man, he left Pradip [Mukherjee, the protagonist of Ray's *Jana Aranya*] completely spontaneous about his costumes, even going to the extent of giving him the liberty to be comfortable in his sandals when he said he wasn't comfortable wearing shoes. Whereas he took a lot of care with my wardrobe, about the cufflinks, about every single detail. Then I understood that this was deliberate as he wanted to project a well-groomed, cautiously attired corporate bigwig.

Chandak Sengoopta

'Ray is profoundly out of fashion in academic circles'

Chandak Sengoopta is a professor in the Department of History, Classics and Archaeology at Birkbeck College, University of London. In research, his three major areas of interest are the history of European medicine, the history of modern science in India and the cultural history of modern India. Among his many published books are *Imprint of the Raj: How Fingerprinting Was Born in Colonial India* (Macmillan, 2003) and *The Rays before Satyajit: Creativity and Modernity in Colonial India* (Oxford University Press, 2016). Professor Sengoopta is currently working on a new biography of Satyajit Ray, emphasising the historical, cultural and ideological contexts that shaped his work and impact. A major aim of the study is to analyse how Ray's films, in spite of their profoundly Bengali/Indian setting and tone, came to be seen, especially by Western critics, as timeless and universal.

How and when were you introduced to the cinema of Satyajit Ray?

I have often thought about this myself. As far as I recall, I was taken to see a rerun of *Pather Panchali* when in school in the mid-1960s, but I don't remember anything about the experience. There was no significant impact. The second time was *Pratidwandi*—I was still in school—but again, I don't remember much about the experience, which is mortifying, since it is now among my most beloved films and the one I identify with myself. *Ashani Sanket* and *Sonar Kella* I saw when they were first released and although I loved both, there was nothing like the impact of *Jana Aranya*, which just overwhelmed me—and I never looked back after that. Upon hearing that Ray personally replied to all his letters, I wrote him a long screed about how much I loved *Jana Aranya* and whined about not having seen many of his films because they were rarely re-released. (This, of course, was an age without any home-viewing options.) Anyhow, he replied briefly in his well-known handwriting, and I was a hero at home for a while!

I finally caught up with all his films in 1981 at the retrospective to mark the twenty-fifth anniversary of *Pather Panchali* and realised that my experience of *Jana Aranya* was not a one-off. True, there were some films I liked less but most of them I just adored, including the ones that had previously left me cold. My love for *Pratidwandi*, for instance, began at that retrospective. I was in college by then and my sensibilities had developed a little! Ray, of course, was still very active and probably at the height of his fame—and I was soon identified as a fire-breathing Ray acolyte by my friends, not all of whom liked him or his work very much.

I suppose it was only from *Ghare Baire* in the mid-1980s that I realised that even if my god didn't have feet of clay—one bad film didn't negate the rest—he was only human. But from *Pather Panchali* to *Sadgati*, I think Ray pulled off miracle after miracle. There were a few that did not impress me much, but the overall quality of Ray's corpus is remarkably high. I still like the same films and my order of preference has changed only very slightly over four decades. I have become fonder of some films I had initially disliked. *Abhijan*, for example, has come up in my estimation— it's not a masterpiece but a creditable piece of work nonetheless. But the firm favourites are unchanged—*Aparajito*, *Pratidwandi* and *Jana Aranya* being the ones I would take to a desert island.

In the history of the Ray family, has there been any known instance of any member before Ray, or his contemporary, who has been involved with cinema or theatre in any way?

Theatre, never. Even a man as liberal as Sukumar Ray, who wrote plays and is supposed to have been a phenomenal actor, embraced the Brahmo opposition to the public stage (because female roles were performed by prostitutes) and the young Satyajit was never taken to the theatre. Cinema, too, does not seem to have interested his direct ancestors. Nitin Bose's mother was Mrinalini, Ray's grandfather Upendrakishore's sister. So, as a youngster, Ray saw the earliest films made by Nitin Bose on a home projector at the Bose house. Nitin Bose's brother Mukul, too, was in the film industry, working as a sound engineer. Even then, Suprabha Ray was perturbed when her son wanted to become a full-time filmmaker—not because of moral reasons, at least not primarily because of them, but more for the financial insecurity he might experience. It was not an irrational worry, for Ray was then the art director at DJ Keymer and earning a pretty large salary (Rs 2,000 in the early 1950s). I don't know exactly how much he earned as a filmmaker, but it's clear that his financial status remained rather unstable until he started writing regularly. Even then, he did not become rich and would probably have earned more had he remained in advertising.

Please tell us a bit about the film society that Ray and his friends founded in Calcutta.

Ray was not quite the prime mover, as commonly assumed. Nor was Calcutta Film Society the first of its kind in India. There had been a couple of film societies in Bombay earlier, and in Bengal a forum for the discussion of cinema had been founded as long ago as 1931 by the poet Narendra Deb (1888–1971) and his friends. But Calcutta Film Society, although not the first, was certainly the most influential. The idea of starting it came from two young Bengalis, Purnendu Narayan (a prince of the Cooch Behar royal family) and Manojendu Majumdar, after they had read Roger Manvell's *Film* (1944), a pioneering survey of the art, craft and connoisseurship of the cinema that was rooted in British ideas of raising the quality of films and deepening the public's appreciation of 'quality' (as opposed to standard commercial) films. It was the book's final chapter ('Why Not Start a Film Society?') that galvanised them into contacting Chidananda Dasgupta, who was Purnendu Narayan's brother-in-law. Dasgupta was thrilled at the idea and took them to meet Ray, who signed up immediately. The society was registered in October 1947, with Ray and Dasgupta as joint secretaries, Narayan as librarian and Majumdar as treasurer.

The four founders quickly inducted their friends and acquaintances into the society. Dasgupta, who was also Ray's neighbour, offered the use of a room in his house and Ray contributed his collection of film books and magazines such as *Sight and Sound* and *Sequence*. Ray's friend and future art director Bansi Chandragupta came in early, as did the cameraman Ramananda Sengupta. Asit Sen not only joined the society himself but brought in the colourful Harisadhan Dasgupta, who had been Sen's school friend and had just returned from the US, where he had gone to study nuclear physics but had spent most of his time in Hollywood instead.

The better-known founders of the film society were intellectually sophisticated young men. As with most Bengali associations from the nineteenth century until fairly recently, it was established entirely by men, although several female members were to join subsequently, who were concerned only with 'good cinema'. There were some British members—mainly executives of British firms—although they do not seem to have been particularly active. Dasgupta and Ray were reportedly quite wary about admitting anybody who was not a serious student of cinema. Although the film cognoscenti of Calcutta would become highly politicised from the mid-1960s and champion the cause of radical cinema, the founding generation was concerned largely with questions of aesthetics and social realism. Interested almost exclusively in 'realist, neo-realist, modernist' films, they had no patience for arcane experimentation or overtly political cinema.

Despite differences in detail and approach, most British film societies of the mid-twentieth century—there were more than two hundred by 1949—shared the same preference. Once again, Manvell's *Film* was a crucial influence. For Manvell, the ideal film society was a forum for the 'generally educated', not the avant-garde. It was expected to follow a 'middle path between the egocentrism of artistic experimentation and the seductive individualism of mass cinema's narratives', never forgetting that 'a minority art is a closed art'.

The very first screening of Calcutta Film Society, Ray recalled, was of Sergei Eisenstein's *Battleship Potemkin*. (Other founding members had different memories, however, and claimed that the society's first screening was of *The Great Waltz*, a 1938 American film on Johann Strauss II, directed by Andrew L. Stone, which was screened on a rented 16-mm projector at Ray's maternal uncle's home, where he and his mother still lived.) But *Battleship Potemkin* was undoubtedly the first major film screened for the members. They had all read about the film and its extraordinary Odessa Steps sequence in Manvell's book, and the British Film Institute's (BFI) library in London had then been approached for a print. After a lot of correspondence, they were sent a 16mm print on the understanding that, as Ray recalled, 'we would pay for it as soon as we had the funds—that time never came and the BFI was generous enough never to take action against us.' Subsequently, the society rented out the print at Rs 50 a go, which helped raise funds for the society but the BFI, as far as one knows, was never paid. But the institute's generosity was not wasted on Calcutta Film Society. Seeing the film, Ray said, 'transformed our very understanding of the film medium' and at least once, *Battleship Potemkin*'s impact was reinforced by music. Ray, who had grown up with silent films accompanied by live music, played excerpts from gramophone recordings of Sibelius to accompany Eisenstein's images.

Soon enough, Calcutta Film Society discovered that they were not exempt from the countless regulations for film exhibitors in India. In the UK and the US, film societies were exempted from censorship, but not in India, not even after Independence. The authorities treated film societies no differently than commercial exhibitors. A fee of Rs 40 per reel had to be paid for films longer than 2,000 ft and eight copies of a complete script had to be submitted before a film could be cleared for screening. Film societies also had to pay entertainment tax at the same rate as commercial cinema. Finding a place to screen the films was also a challenge. The Bengali middle class might have patronised cinema with enthusiasm but considered the trade itself and its practitioners disreputable. When Calcutta Film Society showed films at people's residences, landlords often objected vehemently.

Obtaining films was not easy either but they managed to keep going with films from the Ministry of Education's Central Film Library, already censored but not extensively distributed films from commercial sources, and films from foreign embassies and consulates. The Soviet Bloc countries, with their nationalised film industries, were usually generous and the Friends of the Soviet Union office in Calcutta supplied some Soviet classics for the society. Sometimes, films worth showing were found by chance among the offerings of commercial distributors. Once Ray and Dasgupta stumbled upon a complete print of *Un carnet de bal* lying mislabelled with a Calcutta distributor and Ray took it home, 'hugging the reels and refusing to let anyone else carry them'.

The membership of Calcutta Film Society was small, rising only to seventy-five in three years. It's clear that the society was quite elitist: Dasgupta himself (and, to a certain extent, Ray as well) were reluctant to open it to anybody other than those already sharing their own ideas on 'good cinema'. Small wonder, then, that the local film industry dismissed the society as a club of young hotheads 'running down Bengali films at meetings and seminars' and interested only in imported products. Despite its diminutive stature, however, the society was pretty active. Among film personalities who visited the society in its early, crucial years were Jean Renoir, Vsevolod Pudovkin (who screened his *Storm over Asia* for the members) and Nikolay Cherkasov.

The idea that Ray and the members of Calcutta Film Society had no interest in indigenous films is not entirely correct. Most of the films shown by the society were indeed from the US or Europe but that wasn't necessarily because of any contempt for Indian cinema. For instance, Ray and his friends did get a chance to see a few Marathi films made by Prabhat Studio, which had been founded in 1929 by the celebrated V. Shantaram, and Ray remembered being 'impressed by them'. One of them, *Ramshastri*, was particularly memorable. 'That,' said Ray, 'seemed like a very serious effort, and impressive.' Dasgupta was even more complimentary. 'It had a period feeling, exciting but natural action, and a sobriety of sentiment which distinguished it from the rest of Indian cinema of that period,' he wrote. 'The film was directed with a quiet sureness of touch without any self-conscious artiness, and although its technique had nothing strikingly novel about it, it avoided the common pitfalls of exaggeration and was singularly apt.' Indeed, Ray was to declare many years later that Marathi cinema 'had caught up with and surpassed Bengal fairly early in the period of sound'. Ray particularly disliked some iconic Bengali films and film actors of the time—Pramathesh Barua was a pet hate—but one should not forget that he did praise an occasional Bengali film such as Charu Roy's *Bangalee*.

Watching *Ramshastri* was an unusual privilege for the members, for few indigenous films were readily available in an Indian city in the 1940s, except local productions or Hindi films from Bombay. We often forget how difficult it was for Indians to watch films from other parts of India well into the 1980s. The 1981 Filmotsav in Calcutta was the only time my generation got to see examples of the 'new Indian cinema', then so much in the news. Only a handful of these films were ever released commercially in Calcutta and there was, of course, no other way of seeing them at that time.

A few years ago, as part of my research, I had reached out to a number of people in the cinema studies department of various universities—both within and outside India. And while I was pleased to see that people were being taught Hitchcock, Chaplin, Buñuel and Eisenstein, I never chanced upon a systematic teaching of the cinema of Ray. Being an academician yourself, do you think that my sample size could have been too small? Or do you think there is indeed a lack of focus on Ray and his films in academia? If so, why?

I have the same impression. Ray is profoundly out of fashion in academic circles and, of course, no longer the hero that he had once been among middlebrow cinephiles in the 1960s and 1970s. The reasons are many and complex. A basic truth is that academics tend to go for subjects that have not been done to death, and quantitatively, the literature on Ray seems to them to be extensive and, therefore, not worth adding to. Moreover, academics and highbrow intellectuals prefer films that are less 'classical' than Ray's and although I do not agree with the notion that all of Ray's films are as rounded and finished, most academics have little knowledge of anything other than the Apu trilogy, and precious few have seen even that. Even though the availability of Ray's films has improved quite a bit in recent years (largely owing to the Criterion restorations), it's surprising to see how many are still unavailable, or available only in very poor prints. So it's a combination of ignorance and prejudice—and the prejudice, I'm afraid, has been reinforced by the consensus that Ray was a classical humanist, not much more than a good storyteller. Bollywood, on the other hand, seems far more exciting, far less 'finished' and, therefore, rich in material for academics to analyse and expatiate on. Ray, I suspect, seems to be 'dull' in comparison, not sufficiently avant-garde to be interesting intellectually or politically, and unlike the commercial cinema of India, too middle-class in his style and appeal. So some film scholars such as Ashish Rajadhyaksha concentrate on the avant-garde while others go for Bollywood—Ray falls between these two types and is neglected.

What is being done to preserve and restore the films of Ray around the world?

Well, I don't know what is happening now with the much-publicised restoration project of the Academy of Motion Picture Arts and Sciences. It began in the 1990s and was, I believe, pushed energetically by the well-connected academic Dilip Basu, who also founded a centre for research on Ray at the University of California, Santa Cruz. But Basu retired several years ago and then died; now it's only the Criterion Collection that seems to be pursuing serious restoration work. Their work on the Apu trilogy is remarkable, but I don't know if they are going to do any more. Obtaining rights from Bengali producers, of course, is often a problem and Ray has never sold very well anywhere except in Calcutta. Good reviews are guaranteed, but they don't keep a business running. In any case, the initiative should come from India, from Bengal—but nothing of importance is happening at that end, except hero-worship.

There has been some criticism around the fact that hardly any member of Ray's technical crew has gone on to become a successful filmmaker. How would you react to that criticism?

I doubt if Ray's early, great collaborators had any interest in becoming filmmakers. Bansi Chandragupta did make a few documentaries, I believe, but I haven't seen them and I feel that he and Subrata Mitra were too absorbed in their own specialist fields to be interested in directing. The same applies to the major collaborators of the later years, such as Soumendu Roy. Other crewmembers came and went but whether they were transient or long-standing, their primary objective was to earn a living and directing could have threatened whatever little security they had. For instance, Ramesh [Punu] Sen, who was an assistant director for many of Ray's films and died only recently, told me that he had turned down several offers for directing a film because he would never get a job as an assistant director once he had directed his film. So, he said, 'what if I flopped as a director? How would I live then?' It was much safer to carry on being an assistant.

More generally, I would want to know how many crewmembers go on to become successful filmmakers in film industries across the world. Did Sven Nykvist become a noted filmmaker? Did he ever want to be one? Great technicians are happy enough doing their job and the not-so-great have no other option, especially in an innovation- and risk-averse place such as the Tollywood of Ray's time.

Do you think there is adequate criticism of Ray's cinema in India—scholarly or otherwise?

By and large, the critical literature on Ray is very uneven, even after one has eliminated the hagiographic effusions. Even some of the best-known studies of Ray's cinema do not question long-held but debatable assumptions. The concept of the Bengal Renaissance, for example, has been debated and, in part, disassembled by historians over the past three decades and more, but those who have written on Ray, including such authorities as Chidananda Dasgupta and Andrew Robinson, seem to be completely unaware of recent historical thinking. A simplistic, monolithic understanding of nineteenth-century Bengali culture pervades their work. Or take the question of Tagore's influence on Ray, on which Dasgupta wrote a well-known essay in the 1960s. Since then, the supposedly Tagorean basis of Ray's thinking has become the absolute truth for every critic. Dasgupta's sweeping generalisation demands re-examination but, instead, it is accepted as an axiom. Ray is not a simple artist to write about and his critics could have done better, had they tried to learn more about his intellectual and social contexts and the history of Bengali thought and culture. An example of what a historically sophisticated critic could achieve with Ray is Reena Dube's book on *Shatranj Ke Khilari*. It is not very elegantly written but is packed with material on nawabi-era Lakhnavi culture, which is of the highest relevance to the film that Bengali critics, as well as sahibs, are unaware of.

Of course, there is an alternative to the historical/biographical/ cultural approach: the theoretical analysis of film texts. Ray's films have not attracted too many theorists, and those I know of (for example, Keya Ganguly) write in a highly esoteric style that I find myself unable to comprehend. Maybe they are great works of critical scholarship, but they are accessible only to a small minority of academics (and from what I know of colleagues belonging to such minorities, they are likely to dismiss Ray as lightweight and middlebrow).

The bottom line, then, is that much more needs to be done, but nothing worthwhile can be done unless critics take the trouble to be genuinely critical. All the old formulas—humanism, Tagore, Renaissance, etc.—need to be reassessed ruthlessly and in deep engagement with relevant fields of scholarship. This, however, can never happen until Ray's films are better-known across the world, and chances of that happening do not appear very high. Here we are, living through his birth centenary and I, at least, do not know that anybody anywhere is undertaking—or even thinking about—significant, large-scale initiatives to raise Ray's profile beyond the tiny world of Bengalis. Much, of course, is being written and published within that tiny world to mark the centenary. I have, as yet, seen few of those and can only hope that they break new ground. But I won't be holding my breath.

Dhritiman Chaterji

'Satyajit Ray did not believe in god'

Dhritiman Chaterji worked with Satyajit Ray in three films—in three extremely important roles. It was about him that Ray once said in one of his essays, 'A star is a person on the screen who continues to be expressive and interesting even after he or she has stopped doing anything', and he went on to cite Chaterji's example as a true star. Since then, Chaterji has played several significant roles in several films, both Bengali and in other languages. But he will perhaps be best remembered as the original angry young man of Bengali cinema, the one who tried to wage a battle against a formidable adversary—the entire city of Calcutta.

You began your acting career with Satyajit Ray's *Pratidwandi*. How and when were you approached for the role of Siddhartha?

There's a backstory to that. When I was doing my post-graduation from the Delhi School of Economics in the mid-1960s, a few of us had set up Delhi University's first film society, which we had called Celluloid. Happily, from what I have been told, the film society still exists. Back then, apart from showing films, we had planned to bring out a magazine. A bunch of us were writing to various people to request them to contribute to it through essays, articles and interviews. From Delhi itself, we got in touch with Satyajit Ray, Mrinal Sen, Shyam Benegal, Shanti Choudhury (who was an eminent documentary filmmaker at that time), and so on and so forth. In connection with that, on one of my visits to Calcutta, I went to meet Ray. Things were much less formal then than they are now, in the sense that there were no mobile phones—you just landed up at someone's doorstep and rang the doorbell. And Ray was very open to that. At that time, he was going to Montreal Film Festival. So he said he wouldn't have the time for an interview just then but that he would be happy to speak to me once he returned. But unfortunately, that interview never happened, because I had to go back to Delhi. Doing an interview on long-distance telephone calls wasn't feasible back then. But that was my first encounter with Ray.

Well, then I finished my studies at Delhi University and came back to Calcutta. We were film society enthusiasts, so we were aware that Ray was casting for *Pratidwandi*. A close friend of mine, who also happened to be part of the extended Ray family (Ray's grandfather's iconic children's magazine *Sandesh* used to be published from my friend's home), told me about the casting and encouraged me to go and meet Ray. I did so, and one thing led to another, and he took a sort of a screen test—and I was cast as Siddhartha.

Was there an audition?

Not really an audition. The thing that Ray used to do was that if he thought that someone was a definite possibility for a particular role, he would have long chats with that individual. Not necessarily about the film, but about this, that or the other. It was only much later that I realised that one of the reasons he used to have these long conversations with his actors—especially if he or she was a newcomer—was to observe the person's body language and how he or she spoke. And he would incorporate some of those traits into his character, including the dialogues, etc. Therefore, I wouldn't really call it an audition or a screen test, but we went to the old Indrapuri Studio, where we shot a short scene. For all intents and purposes, I think he would have already decided to cast me by then.

How much time did it take to wrap up *Pratidwandi*?

I don't remember the exact duration, but after all these years, if I were to hazard a guess, I think it must have been fewer than thirty shooting days. One must remember that in spite of all his fame and everything else, he had to make films in the parallel cinema mode. He had to make them on very limited budgets and resources. He couldn't really afford to have elaborate shooting schedules, which was one of the reasons he was so meticulous with his planning. He used to have everything planned out and was involved with literally everything quite directly. Right from handling the camera himself to paying visits to a newly opened store in New Market to shop for the costumes of the film. Starting from art direction to make-up to editing, he was involved with everything. Since he had so much control over every single aspect of the filmmaking process (and also for reasons of economy), he could afford to have these very tight schedules without compromising on the quality of the output.

What was Ray like on the sets? Was he open to suggestions and improvisations from his actors? Or did he want everyone to stick to the script?

A few things need to be said about this. First, although I never quite had stage fright or things like that, thanks mostly to the fact that I was already doing theatre in Delhi and elsewhere by then, the atmosphere on his sets and locations used to be extremely relaxed and soothing. I never recall there being any sort of tension or yelling or any of that during the shooting of a Ray film. The only disruptions that I can think of were due to the infamous load-shedding and power cuts of Calcutta. But otherwise, it was all very calm.

As for his process of working, from whatever I had observed, I had seen him work with his actors in two distinct ways. For actors he was very confident of, he would simply let them be. He would let them do things their own way, including modifying the dialogues in little ways. I was fortunate enough to fall in this first category of actors. You see, I come from those turbulent times—quite a few of my friends used to be Naxalites—so I had comfortably sunk into the role that Ray had written.

Another set of actors, though, he would direct meticulously. The practice of dubbing had begun by then, so while shooting, he would give a series of directions to some of his actors. Take a step forward, now speak, now take a short pause, turn your head towards the camera—that sort of thing.

There never used to be any major discussion around his scripts. He had another method, which he stuck to until his last film. He would finish writing the script and then ask everyone to gather at his home. Both actors and technicians would be present. And then, in front of everyone, he would read out the script, almost to the point of enacting the scenes. There used to be one or two discussions around that. If someone would have something to say, he would listen. He had the remarkable faculty of putting you at ease, without having to let go of his reticence. This was perhaps why there were never any detailed analyses or discussions around his scripts. He would ensure that you were comfortable doing the scenes in your own way. I still remember, when I was doing *Ganashatru* with him, there were hardly any discussions on the set or during preparations. I sometimes used to feel—am I doing this the right way? Am I making any mistakes? So one day, I walked up to him and asked him. In his usual reticent manner, he said, 'If you make a mistake, I'll let you know.' That was all the discussion I ever had with him! One of the things that I really liked about him was that he was a very practical man. There are several things that people say about his filmmaking, scores of theorisations and all that. But while shooting, he was intensely practical.

Let me ask you a question about Ray that you were once asked in *Pratidwandi*—a question that has since been the subject of significant debate. Do you think Ray was a communist?

The simple and honest answer to that would be—no. That said, one must understand that the milieu, the times that he was born in and grew up in—those were immensely progressive, liberal and socialist times. He was very much part of that intellectual environment, part of the Coffee House crowd (not the College Street one but the Central Avenue one). Among the others from that milieu were such people as Utpal Dutt and Shekhar Chatterjee—people who were sworn communists. And since Ray grew up in such an environment, he was secular and had a clear vision of how society should be to be progressive enough. I would say, in a sense, he was very Nehruvian, rather than being a communist. Because you see, although the RSS [Rashtriya Swayamsevak Sangh] had been born by then, the right wing had never surfaced, not in our consciousness at least. It was never an element that you saw when you went to college and in student union elections and so on. It was an overarching liberal, social, secular, progressive period of Indian history. Even the Presidency College Students' Union in those times wasn't aligned to communist principles. So no, I wouldn't say Ray was a communist at all.

In *Ganashatru*, which was an adaptation of an Ibsen play, you played the role of Peter Stockmann—the corrupt mayor of the town, hell-bent upon stopping his own brother from saving the lives of thousands of townsfolk. What I find fascinating about *Enemy of the People* is that it was as relevant in 1882 as it was more than a century later when Ray adapted it—and is relevant even today, in the present sociopolitical situation in India. And it is this relevance that seems to be a unique feature of Ray's films. What do you have to say about that?

As you know, when he was making *Ganashatru*, Ray had just come out of a long string of illnesses and ailments. His doctors had laid out strict conditions for him to shoot. Shooting would have to happen for not more than certain hours during the day, indoors, under the supervision of his personal doctor and with an ambulance standing by outside the studio. That was one aspect of it. The second was an incident that had taken place—something about snakes drinking up milk, or some such bogus reports that were coming in from everywhere. People were making a big hue and cry about it. Naturally, a rational person such as Ray wanted to address such obscurantism. *Ganashatru* was made under such circumstances.

If you look at Ray's filmography, you'll find that although his films were interesting and entertaining stories in their own right, all of them were pervaded by some social message or the other. There is not a single Ray film, including the musicals, that entertains merely for entertainment's sake.

In fact, there was a time when there was a feeling among cineastes that, as opposed to his contemporaries such as Ritwik Ghatak and Mrinal Sen, Ray was holding back and pulling his punches in his cinema. In many ways, *Pratidwandi* was his answer to that.

Would you say that *Jana Aranya* was also in that league of films? His answer to the criticism that you spoke about?

Jana Aranya was much more direct, much less discreet and darker. The mood in *Jana Aranya* was almost that of despair and gloom.

Some critics have said that purely from a cinematic standpoint, *Ganashatru* was one of the weaker films in Ray's filmography. Would you agree?

Well, there's no denying the fact that cinematically, *Ganashatru* fell short of Ray's own standards. In every aspect. It was all dialogue, dialogue, dialogue. Not the kind of fluid narrative that we had come to expect of Ray's cinema. Some of his core crew members were not working with him at that time and he was not chandling the camera on his own anymore. All that shows in the film.

You have also worked with some of the finest filmmakers in the country. What did Ray's contemporaries think of him?

There used to be a friendly rivalry with Mrinal-da, of course. They had different temperaments, they were different kinds of filmmakers. But, for instance, someone such as Shyam [Benegal] was very respectful of him. While Ritwik Ghatak may have been quite open about his nasty comments on Ray, but with other filmmakers, it was more of a friendly skirmish.

However, it has to be said that since we have put him up on a pedestal, there has been very little critical analysis of his work. It may have happened outside India, but it has certainly not happened here. But even if it were to happen, from whatever I have seen of him, he was not the sort of artist who would be prone to self-doubt. He was confident about what he was doing.

Also, while he could be scathing about the works of some filmmakers, at the same time, he could be very generous about some of them too. For instance, I was once speaking to him, and he was all praise for Ketan Mehta's *Mirch Masala*, a film that was way outside his own style.

Let's talk about *Agantuk*. In an earlier interview with me, you had remarked how Ray was deeply moved by French anthropologist Claude Lévi-Strauss's travelogue-memoir *Tristes Tropiques*, and how that had led to some of the ideas in the film, especially the ones around the mistaken notion of civilisation.

That's because he had become much more sedentary in his ways. He had become much more of a reader, a thinker. When he was reading the script of *Agantuk* to me, he had told me, 'I have told Utpal [Dutt] that you are playing *me* in this film. Whatever I want to say to the world, I will say it through you. As opposed to *Pratidwandi*, *Agantuk* was not just about social and political issues. There were far greater issues at play. Philosophical issues, issues about human civilisation as a whole. That was the stage of life he was in. With age, one starts thinking about such things as mortality. It's only natural.

I agree, and it's quite visible in the film as well. What about the issue of spirituality, though? In *Agantuk*, when your character questions the protagonist about his beliefs around the existence of god, the latter's remarks remain open to interpretation. In his literature, Ray has often been known to say (through his characters) that—and I quote—'my mind is wide open'. This, despite the fact that we know him to possess and profess a great scientific temperament. In all the years that you have worked with him and known him as a human being, did it ever seem to you that he was, in any way whatsoever, a spiritual and/or religious person?

No, absolutely not. He was an agnostic, which, again, was Nehruvian. Ray never disapproved of someone else's belief in god, but he himself did not believe in a higher power. I had done a long interview with him, just after *Agantuk*, which was published in the Bengali film magazine *Anandolok* when he received the Oscar for Lifetime Achievement. I'd interviewed him on several occasions earlier on cinema, his own and that of others. I told him that, this time around, I wanted to talk to him about various things—politics, the environment, anthropology, spirituality. It is probably the most satisfying interview I've ever done. It ran for more than twenty printed pages and was probably his last published interview. He passed on three months after it came out. It was in this interview towards the fag end of his life that he had told me, 'Look, I find it exceedingly difficult to imagine that there's a man with a long grey beard sitting high up in the sky. But these days, my own doctors—men of science themselves, no less—tell me that there's something, somewhere. Some existence of some kind. How else do you explain so many things around you? Now, I have never given much thought to what they said, but perhaps I will.'

I realised that day that it was not an outright dismissal of what other people were telling him. He may not have subscribed to the idea but that didn't mean that he was dismissing it either. But the specific answer to your question is that Ray did not believe in god.

Jai Arjun Singh

'Many of the more mainstream Indian filmmakers felt a bit intimidated by Ray'

Jai Arjun Singh is an independent writer and critic. Among the books that he has written and edited are *The World of Hrishikesh Mukherjee* (Viking, 2015), *Jaane Bhi Do Yaaro: Seriously Funny since 1983* (HarperCollins, 2010) and *Popcorn Essayists: What Movies Do to Writers* (Tranquebar Press, 2011). He has delivered talks—mainly about criticism—at colleges and cultural festivals, and conducted several online courses about cinema and literature. Most of his journalistic work—including columns, features and reviews—can be found on his culture blog Jabberwock (jaiarjun. blogspot.com).

When and how was your first experience of watching a Satyajit Ray film?

Not counting a couple of stray glimpses of *Goopy Gyne Bagha Byne* or *Hirak Rajar Deshe* on TV when I was a child, it would have been *Pather Panchali* and *Aparajito* on videocassette—rented from the library of an embassy or cultural centre sometime in the early 1990s, when, as a teenager, I first developed a strong interest in 'world cinema'. As a Delhiite who had grown up mainly with mainstream Hindi films, Ray's world in some ways was as foreign to me as the worlds of [Akira] Kurosawa or [Yasujiro] Ozu or [Ingmar] Bergman or [Federico] Fellini. These VHS prints weren't great—I watched better prints of both films on a bigger screen at a film festival a decade later. At that festival, I also saw good prints of *Mahanagar*, *Charulata*, *Sonar Kella* and *Seemabaddha*, and it felt like I was truly watching these films for the first time. That was a really enjoyable and fulfilling experience.

What is your opinion on the quality of subtitles in the Ray films? As someone who is not fluent in the Bengali language, do you think you get the full essence of the films?

The subtitling on the videocassettes I first experienced, and on the Ray films I watched during Star Movies marathon '100 Years of Cinema' specials in the mid-1990s, seemed just about serviceable to my inexperienced eyes—I was mainly irritated by grammatical mistakes or typos or half-sentences. But as I realised later, through conversations with Bengali friends, those subtitles may well have been terrible even in terms of conveying the essence of a scene or a conversation, and I must have missed many cultural nuances. But let's be practical: to some degree or the other, this is inevitable when one is experiencing a work written or filmed in another language, even when the subtitling or the translation is very good.

As a film scholar, do you think there are enough discussions, debates and analyses in academic and non-academic circles in India on the cinema of Satyajit Ray?

Oh, I think there have been huge amounts of Ray-related discussions in every field: academic and non-academic books and articles, tributes and comprehensive essays written for DVD releases. I have lost count of the number of Ray-related books—exploring various facets of his craft—that the major Indian publishers have brought out in the past decade or so. Of all Indian filmmakers, I think Ray is absolutely the last one about whom we should worry that he has been neglected or not felicitated enough. Speaking as a viewer/critic who has tried to engage with all sorts of wonderful Indian cinema (popular and arty, across different regions, genres and periods), my peeve would be that so many *other* terrific films and directors have not got their due. For decades, critics outside India seemed to be under the impression that Ray was the only Indian filmmaker worth taking seriously, which I think is an injustice to our many disparate forms of expression.

The question of there being uninterested viewers, including those who favour only mainstream cinema or youngsters who simply aren't interested in films of an earlier vintage, is, of course, a different matter entirely. Those viewers will always exist and it will always be difficult (especially in today's world, when there is so much competing for one's attention) to get them to engage with something they perceive as niche or old-fashioned or whatever. But that isn't something that pertains *specifically* to Ray. Having said that, if one were to try and take Ray and other important filmmakers of the past to the younger generation, it's important to restore as many prints as possible, subtitle them well, make them available on platforms that young cineastes access regularly and promote the films as interestingly as possible, explaining why they are important or relevant or just entertaining.

Which is your favourite Ray film and why? What is it about this film that appeals to you?

Impossible to answer this definitively, since the answer will change from one day to the next, or just depending on what mood I am in at a particular time. But three very different types of films that I have a soft spot for are *Goopy Gyne Bagha Byne*, *Devi* and *Jana Aranya*. *Devi* feels like the best sort of horror story to me in some of its scenes (speaking as someone who has always been deeply suspicious of religion and scared of religious fervour), but I also love the look of the film—the dimly lit indoor compositions, the shots of beds covered with mosquito nets, which creates an other-worldly, shroud-like effect. *Jana Aranya* is such a terrific black comedy—it was one of the last Ray films that I watched for the first time, maybe just a decade ago, and I was happy to see that he could be funny in this particular acerbic way as well. Even though I know a lot of that comes from the source novel.

And *Goopy Gyne Bagha Byne*—too much to say, but apart from the imagination and the constant sense of wonder, for me it is one of those truly self-contained films where one feels like the whole thing is unfolding in a particular dreamscape/environment that has nothing to do with our 'real' world and a camera just happens to be there silently recording it all for us. A few other films, from very different genres, that have had this effect on me include Bergman's *The Seventh Seal*, Herzog's *Aguirre*, Dreyer's *The Passion of Joan of Arc* and Lang's Siegfried films.

Over time, as a film buff, I have become increasingly more interested in specific sequences, vignettes or 'moments' rather than entire films, and in that context there are so many scenes and images from Ray's films that I love. To name just a few, the first appearance of Amal as the stormy wind starts blowing in *Charulata*; the shift from black and white to colour in the quiet opening scene of *Sonar Kella* as the boy draws on his sketchpad; the subtly funny scene in the short film *Samapti* where Soumitra Chattopadhyay's character goes to see a prospective bride and her family. There are lots of others, of course.

Ray has said that in adapting a story for the screen, a filmmaker may borrow the material he likes but must exercise his right to select parts of it, rearrange them and—if he feels the need to do so—modify them. What is your opinion on this?

Yes, of course. As long as the source is acknowledged (something our cinema has very often been careless or irresponsible about!) and it is made clear that the film is 'inspired from' or 'adapted from', as opposed to being a slavishly faithful adaptation.

What also matters is the degree to which something has been borrowed, which can be a tricky call, as you know. With works that are broadly inspired by other, earlier works, where does the point arrive when one has to give official credit, or even ask for permission to use an idea or detail? It has been a very murky question.

While researching for your book *The World of Hrishikesh Mukherjee*, did it ever seem to you that the filmmaker was inspired by Ray and his cinema in any way?

I think by the late 1950s, most filmmakers across India knew Ray was someone special who was doing special things, and therefore in some sense or the other, everyone was influenced by him, either directly or as someone to define yourself in opposition to. He wouldn't have had a formative influence on Hrishikesh Mukherjee—remember that Mukherjee began his career as an editor in the mid-1940s, and after that, if he had a mentor, it was Bimal Roy, with whom he worked closely in the 1950s before becoming a director himself. But yes, looking at interviews of Hrishi-da, one does get the sense that he deferred to Ray's greatness as a filmmaker and an artist. He said in one interview that he would have loved to work as an apprentice with Ray on one of his films.

At the same time, Hrishi-da also defensively said in an interview that Ray was a great artist but that he didn't understand the pulse of the Indian middle class. This was said in the context of the ending of *Jana Aranya*. There is no question that many of the more mainstream Indian filmmakers felt both a bit intimidated by Ray and the need to argue with him once in a while!

M.K. Raghavendra

'Ray himself was a very good critic, though he didn't write much criticism'

The questioning critic is a rare tribe these days, and M.K. Raghavendra one of its last known members. His incisive analyses, fearless critique and cogent arguments are not only well informed but outright honest. He is a man with many distinctions, academic writings and awards to his name, chief among them being the Swarna Kamal—the National Award for Best Film Critic—which was conferred upon him in 1997. In this interview, in his trademark succinct manner, he talks about everything he loves about the cinema of Satyajit Ray, and everything he doesn't. And he does this as all great critics do—by explaining why.

What was your first experience of watching a Satyajit Ray film?

I think it was an unsubtitled print of *Charulata*. I couldn't make much of it but I could see it was different. But you must understand that I was brought up on Hollywood and not Indian cinema, which means that it did not make the kind of impression it might have had if I had watched only Bollywood. I recollect that at that time, the kind of cinema that my parents praised and I adored was stuff such as David Lean's *Lawrence of Arabia* or *Dr Zhivago* on the 70-mm screen. Now I know that that was not great cinema but for someone ten or twelve years of age, that kind of Hollywood would be the best in cinema. It requires maturity to look beyond the immediate sensory experience.

What is your opinion on the quality of subtitles in Ray's films? As someone who is not fluent in the Bengali language, are you satisfied with whatever essence of the films you receive through the subtitles?

There is no way by which I can compare the original language with the subtitles. But I only take subtitles as an aid in the delivery of the story, only very rarely as a literary product in itself. One of the first films in which subtitles seemed literary was in J.P. Rappenau's *Cyrano de Bergerac* (1990), which had subtitles by Anthony Burgess.

You have been a film critic for decades. What has been your overall opinion of the cinema of Ray in all these years?

The first film to really affect me was *Pather Panchali,* which I watched in 1978, I think, followed immediately by *Aparajito* and *Apur Sansar.* The third film was a disappointment. I was a devotee of Ray and went around saying that he was the only artistic genius produced in India. I saw most of his films in a retrospective in 1980, I think. I especially loved *Goopy Gyne Bagha Byne.* Later, I read some of his stories and didn't like them so much. I found them a little timid, as though he could never get beyond the juvenile level in his writing, like ghost stories that are not intriguing or scary. Now I would say that he should be seen in the Indian context, what he did for Indian culture internationally. It is wrong to see cinema out of context and to view every film as 'universal'. European filmmakers come out of a milieu in which artistic expression has progressed much more greatly—because of the notion of the individual—while Ray is from India, in which such individuation is rare among members of the public. An artist must first address his own people, although that could only be the elite and not the masses. Great art is elitist, a fact that would be true everywhere.

There seem to be differing schools of thought in the film appreciation and film criticism circles in India regarding the cinema of Ray. One school of thought is that Ray is—without a shred of doubt—the greatest filmmaker to have ever come out of India and that he was rather infallible, so to speak. The other says that there simply isn't enough critical study of Ray's films in India. One almost gets the impression that it is a subject that is sacrosanct, not to be trifled with. What is your opinion on this?

I would agree that he is the greatest to have come out of India, but more for his craftsmanship as a narrator in cinema than for the profundity of what he was saying. He can be emulated as Ritwik Ghatak cannot be. It is strange that with all the clarity of his approach, he has not been emulated at all. Indian art cinema after him, I believe, is closer to commercial cinema in that its polemical content is more than its observational aspect. But I also think that if Ray had not got international acceptance, he would not have found takers in India and his life might have been unfulfilling. Those who regard him as infallible are generally not able to say where his value lies. He did make some bad films, after all. The basic approach is to see his films as a humanist, but there is more to them than that. I would go with his own view, that Western critics responded better to his films than Indians, although they could also be wrong.

Ray himself had been known to not react too kindly to adverse criticism of his cinema. In fact, he used to respond to such criticisms through his writings as well. A classic example was the way he responded to the *New York Times*' iconic film critic Bosley Crowther, who predicted that *Pather Panchali* would fail and *Aparajito* would do well in New York, whereas, in reality, the reverse happened. As a

film critic yourself, what is your reaction to filmmakers who hit back at critics?

I don't think any artist would be happy with hostile criticism. But Ray himself was a very good critic, though he didn't write much criticism. He was better than any other in his own time, including the redoubtable Chidananda Dasgupta. He dared to say things about world cinema while Indian critics were notoriously timid. For instance, he explains [Jean-Luc] Godard lucidly in *Our Films, Their Films*. But Ray also became such a haloed figure in India in his last years that he lost the sense of being one artist among many and began to see himself as a seer or an oracle pronouncing upon the world. That attitude is evident in his later films, such as *Agantuk*.

Among the ones you have seen, which are your favourite and least favourite Ray films and why?

My favourites are *Pather Panchali, Goopy Gyne Bagha Byne, Jalsaghar, Charulata, Jana Aranya* and *Shatranj Ke Khilari*, and my least favourites are *Sadgati, Pratidwandi, Seemabaddha, Agantuk, Shakha Proshaka, Ganashatru* and *Hirak Rajar Deshe*. On examining the list, I think that Ray's best films are those where he observes with minimum intervention, while the worst are those where he is making grand statements—social, political, moral. I think his statements were always dubious, while he had a sharper observational eye than any other in Indian cinema.

In one of his essays, Ray said that where the requisite knowledge and perception to understand and appreciate a film is missing in an audience, it is the responsibility of a film critic to help the audience understand the film. What do you have to say about that?

Yes, but that presumes that the critic is above the audience, which has not been generally true in India. A critic must have language skills but that also presumes that his readership will recognise the skills when it sees them. The critic must be authoritative, which implies not only knowledge of the field but also clarity and lucidity—saying things the audience hadn't suspected. Today, everybody has opinions, including members of the public, and all opinions are equal—there is no such thing as informed opinion. The public lacks judgement and would want to know who you are before responding to your work. As an instance, book reviews have ended. When books are reviewed, only the easy, trashy writing gets attention and not the ambitious, difficult books. I would say that before someone starts writing criticism, he or she should test himself by writing on the most difficult international cinema, such as that of David Lynch or Robert Bresson.

Madhabi Mukherjee

'In his films, Satyajit Ray has never shown any ugliness'

If there is one Ray actress who has stood out over the years, and one character that highlights his filmmaking genius, it is Madhabi Mukherjee's portrayal of Charulata. Mukherjee acted in only three films by Satyajit Ray—*Mahanagar*, *Charulata* and *Kapurush*. And yet, in all three films, she played strong characters—women with enough agency and grit to make each film their own. These are not films about the heroes any more. These are stories about exemplary courage, determination and impeccable self-worth. In many ways, Mukherjee is the greatest highlight of Ray's career, because she represents the women of Ray's cinema.

You have acted in the films of the three most celebrated filmmakers of Bengal—the triumvirate of Mrinal Sen, Ritwik Ghatak and Satyajit Ray. What was the difference in the filmmaking styles of these three directors?

Manik-da used to give me a script and insisted that I go through it carefully. Those were the days when there were no photocopies. Manik-da would write the entire script in longhand and give it to me. Mrinal Babu used to do that too. His scripts also used to be handwritten. As were Purnendu Patri's. There were a lot of remarkable similarities between the writing of Purnendu Patri and Satyajit Ray. Unfortunately, these priceless scripts are mostly lost now. I lost some of them myself when my mother passed away and I had to shift from one house to another. The value of these scripts was known only to me. It is very unfortunate that I lost them.

Nowadays, many people say that Ritwik Ghatak never had a formal script. That claim is, of course, false. Ritwik Babu used to have a detailed script. The only difference between him and the other filmmakers was that he never gave the script to anyone. For some reason, he used to keep it close to his chest. However, he used to read out the entire script to us and explain each scene—what it meant for the overall film, what it meant for the characters and how we were supposed to execute it. And in order to narrate the script to us, he never had to look at it. It was all in his head, and he used to narrate the entire thing to us from memory.

Mrinal Sen used to give us a lot of freedom to do a scene in our own way. For instance, in *Calcutta 71*, there was a scene in which I was supposed to have a big quarrel with my mother, who was played by an actress named Binota Ray. I went to Mrinal Babu and asked him, 'Can I bring in some of the elements of my personal life into this scene? I think it will help me do the scene better.' And he immediately agreed and encouraged me to go ahead. Not once did he ask me to stick to what was written in the script. Yet, with Manik-da, it was all planned—he had everything chalked out, from the shot division down to the minutest detail—and he preferred his actors to do a scene the way he wanted. He used to make his actors very comfortable but insisted that we do things his way, not ours.

Ritwik Babu's process was entirely different. Let's say we are supposed to shoot a serious scene. The first thing he would do on coming to the shoot was yell and shout at his assistants and technicians, making the entire atmosphere rather sombre. No one would dare smile or whisper any more. Then he would explain the scene to his actors and say rather sardonically, 'Have you understood? Will you be able to do it? I don't think you'll be able to pull it off!' Under such circumstances, hearing those words, the actors would take it up as a challenge. And their best performances would come from there.

Each of them had their own style of working. For instance, Mrinal Babu never used to call me by my name. He always called me by the name of the character I play in the film. Back then, I used to find it strange. But now that I think about it, I realise why he used to do it and how much it contributed to my performance.

In *Kapurush*, your character Karuna comes to the railway station at the end of the film. And yet, her former lover cannot gather the courage to take her away. Do you think Karuna was sure that Amitabha wouldn't be able to take her away?

Yes, because she has had years to think about him, you see. Karuna knew that Amitabha was a coward. And she had proof of it time and again. On one occasion, she had gone to his hostel, telling him clearly that she was ready and willing to go away with him. But he could never gather the courage. For a woman, that is quite a sad moment. And then many years later, when Amitabha landed up at her home by a stroke of luck, he claimed that he had realised his mistake, that he had worked up the courage to take the step that she had wanted him to then. But by then, Karuna knew Amitabha all too well. She was sure that though he didn't quite realise it, he would not be able to take her away. It was his cowardice that she wanted to prove one final time. That's why she came to the station. The sleeping pills were just an excuse.

How beautifully it has been shown in the film, hasn't it?

That's who Satyajit Ray was. I will give you another example and you will see how simple and yet how powerful his cinematic language was. In the film *Mahanagar*, my character's father-in-law is a retired schoolmaster. He has taught many students, quite a few of whom have become successful in their own lives. Yet, he lives in penury. One day, he laments, saying, 'When we used to be there, we had so much respect ...' What do you think Ray meant when he used that word—'*there*'?

He was referring to East Bengal, wasn't he? Bangladesh?

Exactly! But did he say as much? No, he didn't. And why didn't he? Because, in that scene, in that set-up, that particular character would not have used that term. He would have used that particular word—'*there*'. You may say that it's just a harmless word—what is the big deal about using this or that? But no, every single word, every single expression, every single gesture, or pause, or voice modulation had a meaning. That is why Satyajit Ray was who he was. It is impossible to appreciate his films in a single viewing.

In one of my speeches at Kalyani University, I had made a comment that had taken everyone by surprise. I had said that as a filmmaker, Satyajit Ray was a total flop. Naturally, everyone present there was quite shocked. I went on to explain that while his films are classics, while his legacy is one to be proud of, it is unfortunate that I do not see any filmmaker after him having learnt anything from his style of filmmaking. And it is in that sense that he was unsuccessful. He couldn't leave an impression on future filmmakers. At least not one that I have seen.

In his films, Satyajit Ray has never shown any ugliness. Everything in his cinema, even the most heinous things, has been shown with a certain grace and elegance. Look at his antagonists, for instance. Even they have been shown as interesting characters. Characters that we want to invest in, that we want to see more of. They are not your typical villains. They have their reasons to do what they are doing, and we cannot simply ignore those reasons, nor can we wish them away.

I always say that there are two kinds of teachers in the world. The first kind is full of knowledge, but when they teach, they can't really reach their students. Their students have to flock around them after class to clear their doubts. But the second kind, full of knowledge, is remarkable. Because once they have taught something in class, you would never have to turn the pages of your books again. Their teachings will remain with you for the rest of your life. Satyajit Ray belonged to this second kind.

It is really sad, then, that none of the filmmakers of the current generation have learnt Ray's sensibilities from his cinema. He did his best to teach them, to leave valuable lessons in his films, but it was all in vain.

You mentioned Ray's sensibilities. How do you think he must have acquired these sensibilities? And why is it so difficult for modern filmmakers to acquire them?

Well, for one, he used to keep his mind fresh and open to all kinds of ideas. Much of that happens when you read. I have seen him, I know what a voracious reader he was. Him, and another man—Utpal Dutt. I had to go out of Calcutta with him for shooting on a few occasions. Wherever he went, he would disappear after the day's shoot. When we went looking for him, he would be found in some obscure bookstore, engrossed in books.

The other habit that Manik-da and Ritwik Babu had was that they never used to confine themselves to one art form. Ritwik Babu himself used to write poetry, and it would be such a pleasure to hear him recite! He had acted in many plays too. He did everything with such conviction— that itself was such a lesson. There was no half-heartedness about him. I don't see such convictions in people of the present generation anymore.

Ray has said that *Charulata* is the one film in his filmography that has the least number of flaws. When you think about it, this is quite remarkable, because Charu herself is such a complex character. How did you prepare for what is perhaps the most important role in Ray's entire filmography?

I was six or seven years old when I started acting on stage. I have had such teachers as Shishir Bhaduri and Chhabi Biswas. They had taught me how to think, how to read a character, how to understand what she must be going through, how to present her joys and sorrows before an audience. This was perhaps why Satyajit Ray didn't have to explain Charu's character to me. At least not to the extent of having to explain her thoughts to me. I understood Charu. So I played Charu.

When the film was sent to Cannes, Manik-da told me that they were considering giving an award to me for my performance, but that I would have to be present in person to accept the award. The festival had a rule, that all awards were to be accepted in person, or something of that sort. But unfortunately, in those days, my financial condition wasn't very good. A ticket would have cost a lot of money back in the day and I couldn't afford to buy one. I couldn't go, nor did I win the award.

I don't have any regrets, though. They say when it was played at the festival, people loved it, applauded it, praised my performance profusely. That's more important than an award, which would perhaps have been gathering dust in some corner of a cabinet in my home by now.

What was the experience of working with Soumitra Chattopadhyay like?

Nothing out of the ordinary, you know. When you work with a person for a long time, there is a respectful friendship that develops between the two of you. Both he and I used to have a lot of mutual respect. He used to address me by the Bengali honorific '*aapni*', which marked a sense of respect for me. I used to address him by the same term. Those who belonged to the subsequent generation used to be surprised by this. They used to ask me, 'You speak so formally to each other. How on earth are you going to do a romantic scene together?' And I used to explain to them that both he and I were professional actors and that our work and real lives were entirely separate from each other.

You mentioned theatre. How important do you think the stage is in the life of an actor, especially a film actor?

A stage is a place where an actor is born. It is a place where all great actors are made. And I will tell you why. Acting is an instinctive art form. You are constantly learning from your performances, and in doing so, the feedback from the space around you is of paramount importance. When you are on stage, this feedback is instantaneous. Your audience is there right in front of you. You say a line of dialogue a certain way and realise that the audience hasn't taken it well. So what do you do? In the next show, you change it a bit, try something new, see what the audience's reaction is. In a film, this collective feedback is reduced to just one person—the director, saying 'okay' or 'not okay'. How can that possibly be enough? And by the time your performance has reached your audience, it is too late. There is no way to change it anymore.

You acted in three films by Satyajit Ray. Which among these performances do you consider your best?

You see, whether we are walking or running, we all take only one step at a time. It's the same with each of us, anywhere in the world. Whenever I have gone back to watch a film I have done, it has seemed to me that perhaps I could have done some bit somewhat differently. Perhaps that would have made the scene better. A different gesture, a different way of saying the same words, a different expression. This is why every revisit of a film is a learning experience. To note and promise to rectify small errors—errors that others will not even notice. But as an actress, I know what I have done. So instead of considering one film better than the other, I look at each film as a lesson.

Mamata Shankar

'*Agantuk* was the culmination of one of the most illustrious careers in cinema history'

In 1990, when Satyajit Ray returned to filmmaking after a long break owing to his failing health, he made three films in quick succession—*Ganashatru*, *Shakha Proshakha* and *Agantuk*. All three films starred Mamata Shankar in important roles. Shankar, who was the daughter of renowned dancer couple Uday Shankar and Amala Shankar, and who had already acted in several films by such established filmmakers as Mrinal Sen, Buddhadev Dasgupta and Gautam Ghose by then, made a mark for herself in Ray's final films too, by playing strong, principled characters with an endearing sense of empathy.

What was the beginning of your association with Satyajit Ray?

I have always called him Manik Kaka. He was extremely close to our family and used to come to our house on many occasions. I think it all began when he attended one of my father's shows. After that, Manik Kaka drew a sketch for the brochure that was made for my father's foreign tour. It was a sketch of Shiva with a temple in the background. He hadn't become 'the' Satyajit Ray yet. There was this one time my parents were returning from their show at New Empire, when they saw Monku Kakima [Bijoya Ray] standing in a corner outside the theatre. They picked her up and dropped her off near the Grand Hotel, just as she requested. It was there that they saw a tall, young man waiting for her. Monku Kakima and Manik Kaka were in a relationship back then. Many years later—I had done a few films by then—my husband read in the papers one morning that Satyajit Ray was making a comeback after a long medical leave to adapt Ibsen's play. It was early in the morning and I was still in bed. When he read out the news to me, I must have muttered in my sleep that it would be so lovely if he would cast me too! Little did I know that my husband would call him up right then and hand over the phone to me. I was still half asleep, and here was this famous baritone on the other side of the phone going, 'Hello! Who is this?' Scared to death, I somehow responded to him and said that I would love to get a role in his new film. 'Not that I haven't thought of you, you know?' came the response. He said he would call me back after a few days, and he did. That's how I got the role in *Ganashatru*.

So, it would seem that he had watched some of the other films you had done?

Oh yes! I would bump into him on various occasions and he would tell me in that grave, heavy voice of his, 'Listen Momo, I have seen that new film of yours. I didn't like the film, but you were very good in it!'

One of the complaints that readers of Satyajit Ray's literature have had of him is that there is an inexplicable dearth of female characters in his stories. Ray has, of course, responded to the criticism in his own way. However, he had written and imagined several strong female characters in his cinema—starting from Karuna in *Kapurush* and Mrinmoyi in *Samapti* to Aparna in *Aranyer Din Ratri* and Anila in *Agantuk*. As a woman, do you feel Ray understood women?

Whether it was Feluda, Shonku or Tarinikhuro, or even the short stories that he used to write for *Sandesh*, when I read his fascinating stories, I indeed felt very bad that there were no prominent female characters in them. But as you rightly said, his films more than made up for that. The most interesting thing that I have found by studying his films is that there are two types of women in them. The first is down-to-earth, very chirpy, extremely warm, sort of happy-go-lucky and with most of the qualities that can be found in an average ordinary middle-class Bengali woman. And the other is a complete contrast to the former. This other type of woman has a different intellect altogether—a clear and demonstrated sense of dignity, not to mention an enviable maturity and understanding of the world. She stands out from all the other characters in the film— male or female. For instance, you have Madhabi-di's character, Karuna, in *Kapurush* and Sharmila-di's character, Aparna, in *Aranyer Din Ratri*. You find this contrast in *Shakha Proshakha* too, between Lily-di's [Lily Chakraborty] character and mine. Even in *Agantuk*, the way I come across to the audience is a far cry from Subrata-di's character, Chhanda. Then again, in *Charulata*, you have Charu and Manda—two entirely different personalities. In *Nayak*, there is Sharmila-di's character, Aditi, on the one hand, and all the other female characters of the film on the other. There is a difference between them, and that difference is for everyone to see. One must understand, though, that neither of these two types of characters is better or worse than the other. They simply have their own shades.

In *Shakha Proshakha*, your character has a beautiful relationship with her brother-in-law, who is roughly the same age as she is. The relationship is almost symbiotic and is reminiscent of similar relationships in films such as *Charulata* and *Jana Aranya*. And yet, when Tapati learns that her brother-in-law is in a relationship, there is a clear sense of disappointment and disillusionment in her, albeit momentary. What was Ray's brief to you on this aspect of your character?

In that scene, she starts praising her husband from a certain sense of dignity that's still there within her, despite her somewhat troubled relationship with him. She tries her best to hide any signs of discord that might be showing. It was a powerful scene, and I still have fond memories of it. Let me tell you an interesting story behind the shooting of that scene.

Manik Kaka used to follow a certain process for the narration of his scripts. It used to be like a large gathering, where everyone involved in the film would be present, and he would read out the script. For my first film with him—*Ganashatru*—I had heard the script on a recorded cassette in a Walkman, as the script-reading session had already happened by then. But in *Shakha Proshakha*, we all sat together, and he narrated the entire script to us on a Sunday morning. After that, he gave us the bound script. But after two or three days of shooting, he suddenly said to me, 'Momo, don't read that scene now because I haven't finalised it yet. Give me some time.' This was the scene in which Tapati learns that Pratap is in a relationship. I was quite baffled and a bit frightened as well. Because I have always felt that homework is important for an actress. A couple of days later, he asked me again, 'You haven't read that scene, have you?' With a bit of confusion and fear, I told him that I hadn't. After quite a few days, he wrote something down and gave me the pages and said, 'Now read it.' On reading the scene, I realised why he had spent so much time perfecting it. It was the one scene in the film that showed the relationship between Tapati and her brother-in-law, and he wanted it to be perfect.

On the day of shooting, we were all ready and he said, 'I want to take Ranjit's [Ranjit Mullick] shots first.' I was behind the camera to give the cue. Manik Kaka had three ways of saying the word 'cut'. He used to say 'cut' and then 'excellent' either in a high or a soft tone, depending on whether he had liked the shot. And he had a third way of saying the same words, where he used to shut his eyes and utter those words in a very low tone, because he didn't want to break the spell of the scene. He wanted the moment to linger. When this scene was shot, he shut his eyes, said 'cut', followed by an ever softer 'excellent'. And the entire studio was silent for the longest time. I was shivering.

But as luck would have it, after a week or so, Manik Kaka rang me up and said, 'Momo, there is some bad news for you.' I was shocked. He said, 'There is a problem with the negative of a particular scene. And we have to reshoot.' I asked him, 'Manik Kaka, it's not that scene with Ranjit-da and me, is it?' He said, 'Yes, unfortunately, it is.' I went numb. When a scene is done beautifully and performed spontaneously, a lot of genuine emotions go into it. And when one has to reshoot a scene, it becomes mechanical and somehow doesn't seem to work. Naturally, I was very upset. Anyway, what had to be done had to be done. Before we started shooting the scene again, he asked me to sit down beside him on a vacant chair. Out of respect for him, I dragged the chair behind his by a couple of inches and sat down.

Manik Kaka was not allowed to smoke at that time but he had this habit of biting his pipe. Ranjit-da had a line of dialogue in this particular scene, '*Bou bondhu hole ki boudir shongey bondhutto phuriye jai* (What makes you think that if I marry her, I won't be friends with you any longer)?' To this, my response was supposed to be, 'Three is a crowd, Pratap.' Biting hard on his pipe, Manik Kaka said to me, 'Momo, I don't think small-town audiences will understand the meaning of those words. Since we are reshooting it, can you think of something else? Something that will be easier to understand but will carry the same message?'

Can you believe that? A man of that grand stature, who had such immense grip on both the English and the Bengali languages, was asking an absolute nobody like me, who had neither any knowledge of language nor any sense of writing dialogue, to find a suitable phrase for that translation! I was speechless. And I nervously said to him, 'Manik Kaka, what if I say, "*Oshob katha akhon thak, Pratap*" (Let's not talk about that, Pratap)?' His immediate reaction was, 'Exactly! Say that!' Even today, I sometimes wonder how devoid of ego a man of his stature has to be to say those words to someone like me! Filmmakers these days come to me and say that they are making films for the festivals—and here was a man whose films had travelled to all the festivals of the world, and he was thinking if small-town audiences would be able to understand a line of dialogue in his film! That's who Manik Kaka was, you know? If you see the film today, you will see that he kept the words I had suggested.

As someone writing a book on Satyajit Ray in 2021, one of the problems that I face is that an unfortunately large number of people who have worked with him and could have given me great insights into his style of filmmaking are not alive any more. For instance, I am very keen to understand the working relationship between Satyajit Ray and Utpal Dutt.

I believe they shared mutual respect. I had seen them work together in only one film—*Agantuk*. Manik Kaka knew that Utpal Dutt was a fantastic actor both on stage and on screen. So, whenever Utpal Babu would give a shot, if Manik Kaka did not like it, he would simply say, 'Can we go for another take?' When he would see that even the second take wasn't up to his expectations, he would pretend as if everything was fine in the shot and that some technical glitch had happened. He would apologise and say, 'Sorry, sorry, sorry, but we have to go for another take.' And then he would walk up to the actor and say, 'All right, Utpal. Can we do it in a slightly different way?'

Everyone knows that in *Agantuk*, it was Satyajit Ray speaking through the character of Manomohan Mitra. In other words, Utpal Dutt was playing Manik Kaka. When Manik Kaka was reading out the script of the film to me, it was just him and me in the room, with only a table lamp burning. I cannot even begin to explain to you how beautifully he narrated the script that night. His gestures, his voice modulation, his enunciation, his pauses, the way he raised his hand to stop Dipankar-da's character from saying anything by way of an apology—everything was perfect. Even after all these years, it gives me goosebumps to even think about it. Utpal Babu gave a remarkable performance in the film. But I will never forget what I saw in that dimly lit study of Manik Kaka that night. That was the performance of a lifetime.

Have you ever seen him losing his temper?

No, I haven't. I have done three films with him but have never ever seen him lose his temper. He used to say 'Silence!' out quite loud and his voice would ring through the sets. And once it did, there would be pin-drop silence. When we would rehearse our scenes, he would look through the camera to observe every single minute and intricate movement in our performances. If he felt everything was fine, he would never say a word. On the other hand, if he felt that there was a need for change or some room for improvement and it would make the scene better, only then would he give suggestions. He would do this politely and sensitively. But at the same time, he was very particular about those suggestions. He was very sure about what he wanted and he never compromised on the quality of his work.

Another trait of Manik Kaka's personality that I really admired was his simplicity. We were shooting for *Agantuk*, and Manik Kaka and Monku Kakima came to the sets one day. We were shooting a scene inside a bedroom and both of them were rather displeased with a bedsheet that someone had put on the bed. When the question of getting a new one came up, I stepped forward and said, 'Manik Kaka, I have a beautiful Rajasthani quilt at home, we could use that.' Manik Kaka said, 'Of course, but how do we get it here?' I said, 'I could write down my residence address and someone could go pick it up.' Manik Kaka immediately pulled out his Sheaffer pen and handed it to me. The moment I held that pen in my hand, I froze. How many world-renowned films, how many beautiful stories, how many knowledgeable essays, articles, speeches and letters must have been written with that pen! And moreover, anyone who has used a fountain pen on a regular basis will know that the nib wears off at a particular angle, depending on how the user holds the pen. It's almost like a unique one-on-one relationship that one has with his or her pen. Which is why no one likes handing over their pen to someone else. And here was a man of Manik Kaka's stature, who had offered his pen to me! With trembling fingers, I returned the pen to him, saying, 'I'm sorry, I can't write with this pen!' From the smile on his face, I could see that he had realised that I had done so out of respect.

During the shooting of *Shakha Proshakha*, I could hear him say from another room, 'Has anyone given a chair to Momo?' I was suffering from an excruciating lower-back pain during that time, and although I tried never to show it, not only did he realise that I was in pain, but he constantly took care to see that I was comfortable. And he used to do this with all members of the cast and crew. He was a very humane person.

You have worked with Ray in the final phase of his filmmaking career. Your first film with him—*Ganashatru*—flopped and is often considered by even the most die-hard Ray fans as one of his weakest. What was your reaction to the critical and commercial failure of the film?

He was under too much pressure when that film was made. His health had suffered, he had become frail and he was returning to the sets after a long gap of five years. Dr K.P. Bakshi was always present on the sets, as was an ambulance. His blood pressure had to be monitored every fifteen to twenty minutes. Manik Kaka used to walk like a child, taking only one step at a time. Anything more than that was simply not possible for him. Imagine having to shoot an entire film under such circumstances! Moreover, Dr Bakshi had strictly prohibited him from doing any kind of outdoor shooting whatsoever.

From this situation, he recovered somewhat and became a bit more fit during *Shakha Proshakha*. And then even better during *Aguntuk*. I still remember, one day, he was showing camera movements to Dipankar-da and me for a scene. He was running and showing Babu-da [Sandip Ray] how the camera would move and he was doing this so enthusiastically that he was completely lost in his own world. Suddenly, someone noticed that there was blood gushing out from his feet. Everyone jumped forward to help him, and he looked down at a deep cut on his foot and smiled, 'Oh! When did this happen?' We realised he must have cut himself on the sharp corner of the bed, and from the size of the wound, it was quite clear that it must have hurt. But he was so lost in his work that he did not even realise it.

The one aspect of Manik Kaka that always captivated me was how down-to-earth he was, despite being such an erudite person. His language was so beautiful and clear, and yet so simple that it could be read and understood by everyone. Be it his cinema or his literature, his language had several layers and persons from different ages would connect with it and derive meaning from it, according to their ages. This is quite evident from his films such as *Hirak Rajar Deshe*, which can be considered an adventure fantasy for children but also a political satire for adults.

Ray has used his own voice in singing some songs for his two final films—*Shakha Proshakha* and *Agantuk*. Why do you think he must have done that?

In *Shakha Proshakha*, it was just a hum. In *Agantuk*, yes, he sang as many as three songs in his own voice. I have a feeling he must have done so because it was a film about his thoughts, his consciousness, things that *he* wanted to say. He must have wanted to leave a signature on the film somehow—a distinct, unique thumbprint of sorts. After all, it was the culmination of one of the most illustrious careers in cinema history! There's also a beautiful incident that I just recalled. One of the songs that Manik Kaka sang for *Agantuk* was *Rai Dhoirjong*. On the day of the shoot, the shot was being set up. Manik Kaka was sitting in one corner with Monku Kakima and singing the song, '*Rai dhoirjong, raho dhoirjong, momo gaccham, Mathuraye.*' And from the adjacent chair, Monku Kakima was saying, 'No Manik, it's not like that.' And she was singing it out for him. After three or four times of getting corrected, Manik Kaka finally gave up and said, 'Oh, I am going to fix it during dubbing.' Monku Kakima struggled to rise from her chair, but rise she did. She walked up to Manik Kaka's chair and slapped him on his thigh, saying, 'No! You are going to get it right. Right now!' Oh, you should have seen the smile on Manik Kaka's face, and the love in his eyes for his wife! Like an obedient child, he continued to sit in his chair and hum that tune.

What do you think present-day filmmakers can learn from Ray's cinema?

The other day I was watching *Pather Panchali*, and I was suddenly struck by a thought. We try to make people understand the meaning of a certain thing in such difficult and complex ways. Maybe our lack of knowledge and confidence forces us to present things in such a convoluted manner. Whereas truly great artists have always tried to convey difficult notions and concepts of life in a simple way and with humility. One of my favourite dialogues from *Aguntuk* is when Manomohan Mitra says, 'I'm used to living amid simple people, so I can't tolerate it when I see someone trying to show off.' Nowadays, everyone seems to know everything about everything. We seem to be in this constant rush to tell everyone how much we know. This is true about the current generation of directors too. They seem to say, 'If you want to understand my films, you have to come up to my level first.' Whereas Manik Kaka used to extend his hand to try and reach out to everyone. That's something that the filmmakers of today can perhaps learn from his cinema.

Neeraj Ghaywan

'Ray never compromised his narrative for the sake of his politics'

Not very long ago, Neeraj Ghaywan entered the Indian film scene like a breath of fresh air and swept audiences off their feet with his bold and honest take on one of the most vicious problems to have afflicted our society since ancient times—the problem of caste. In his final film, Satyajit Ray had said through his protagonist, 'I do not believe in anything that divides people', and had gone on to mention that caste does that. Ghaywan is one of the few rare filmmakers in India who have not only raised the issue of caste discrimination in their cinema but also taken care to ensure true representation in the making of their films. It is refreshing to see a young filmmaker in India take on such an age-old issue by its horns. In this interview, Ghaywan speaks of how he has been influenced by Ray's cinema and what he finds the most appealing about his films.

When and how were you introduced to the cinema of Satyajit Ray?

I might have watched a Ray [film] when I was in school. The Sunday afternoon slot of Doordarshan used to play regional films and our family would watch with a lot of excitement. But I have no recollection of which films I might have watched. To tell you the truth, Ray was never a big part of my childhood. My real introduction to a Ray film happened years later, when I was doing my MBA in marketing communications at Symbiosis Institute of Business Management, Pune. We listened to a lecture on cinema by the dean of FTII [Film and Television Institute of India], Mr Samar Nakhate. He would talk about films but none of the students in our batch would pay attention in his class. It was mostly assumed to be one of those 'leisure' classes. I, on the other hand, used to find this particular class fascinating. In fact, almost all my attempts to ask questions would be booed by the other students. Nobody wanted the recess to be delayed, after all! Anyway, there was this one session, in which Mr Nakhate had shown us a small clip from *Aparajito* and spoken about the notion of spatio-temporal dislocation in cinema—the movement of space and time. It stirred something inside me. I would hound the professor in the canteen and ask him questions related to cinema. From that point on, I started seeing cinema as an art form, as opposed to a means of entertainment.

Then, of course, I discovered *Pather Panchali*. I remember having watched it and also distinctively remember that, for quite a long time, it simply made me numb. I think a lot of people relate their familial childhood to Satyajit Ray's works, as they feel a certain kind of nostalgia when they watch his films. *Pather Panchali* made me remember the days I had spent exploring little things in my childhood—plucking tamarind leaves with my sister, my grandmother's loving hands. I had once tweeted in jest that Ray made the Apu trilogy years before Richard Linklater made *Boyhood*. It's quite elaborate, and it really moves you.

What is it about the cinema of Ray that you find special?

I think a salient feature of Ray's cinema is that his narrative is always at the foreground. He never compromises the narrative for the sake of the politics that he is eager to talk about. And he never sacrifices a character's world at the altar of wanting to make a poignant point. So, one never sees the writer speaking through a character. A character belongs to its own world and the politics is always secondary. I have always been heavily inspired by this treatment of Ray. Personally, I would fail if my politics is at the fore and it supersedes the narrative, or if it doesn't have a cinematic language to it. It then becomes news or propaganda, no matter how well intentioned.

After *Masaan*, I had an idea for a film that was very close to my heart. It was about the farmer suicides, an issue that had affected me deeply. But even after two–three years of going around India for my research, spending time with farmers, speaking to them, it didn't shape up as a good narrative. I was passionate about the subject, but I was trying to weave it into a narrative that was simply not adding up. It took me three long years to realise that I was trying to force-fit my passion into a narrative that was just not holding together. So I abandoned the idea. I would rather be happy that people are talking about my characters themselves, instead of heaping hollow praises on me simply because I made a film on an important social issue. That's one thing I have learnt from Ray.

I see what you mean. In fact, Ray did believe that film is primarily a medium of storytelling and not so much a medium of propaganda— be it political or social or anything else.

I will agree and disagree with that statement. I agree with what he said about propaganda. But I feel that the allusion to storytelling by way of plot and narrative being the core of a film may not be entirely true. There are avant-garde films where the plot isn't very important. There may be visual poetry in the scenes that does not add up to anything, and yet may seem more powerful than pure narrative. Although he was a socio-realist filmmaker, he celebrated all forms of storytelling and not just the traditional ones.

You have done so much to raise awareness about the social evil of caste discrimination. What is your opinion of Ray's adaptation of Premchand's *Sadgati*?

I think I had watched the film after I made *Masaan*. When I watched *Sadgati*, I was quite moved by what I saw. Like all his films, it has a very strong message, but not once does he stray from the narrative to deliver that message. The film can teach us a lot of things, including the time he takes to establish his characters and then the way he seamlessly talks about the politics through the characters. Also, I think he was paying homage to Bergman in *Sadgati*. In a scene from the film, Mohan Agashe's character carries Om Puri's corpse and goes over a cliff. And in Bergman's film *The Seventh Seal*, there is a similar scene, where death has come and the people are holding on to a rope that death is carrying across. Bergman's film has this sound of a gong. Ray has also used a similar sound in his film.

Today we only make films about urban and small-town India. Even when we are telling stories from small towns, it is through an outsider's gaze. We make fun of them—about how they speak English, their habits, their foolishness. We don't talk about how they relate to the state, their existential problems or try and gauge their point of view—and not simply reduce them to a trope. Small towns are a fad now in cinema but we have absolutely forgotten rural India. We have excluded a large set of the population by way of ignorance, commercial disinterest and the ubiquity of caste. Most of the people who are working in Hindi cinema are Savarnas. They belong to the upper class of society, which is why it is only natural that we are making films about them. As a direct outcome of that, 90 per cent of our cinema is only about 15 per cent of the population. This can only change when you bring in people from the remaining 85 per cent, who are never represented. From the dawn of Hindi cinema, there has never been a single acknowledged Dalit in the industry. Even the handful of films that we have made on the Dalit discourse have all been about how an upper-class Savarna protagonist saves the day. As a result, either it is coming from the perspective of a saviour or from that of atrocity. We show the pain, the poverty of the Dalit. But no one has spoken about assertion, no one has taken care to humanise the characters. The characters have been reduced to tropes.

How will this change? It will only change if we bring in people from the communities to share their stories or have well-meaning allies who learn and incorporate lived experiences from these communities. Mere tokenism will not suffice. We need people to tell *their* stories. Because you can never, ever replicate a lived experience.

Premchand's short story *Sadgati* was published in 1931. Fifty years later, in 1981, Ray adapted it for the screen. Forty years after Ray made *Sadgati*, you are still making films on casteism, in 2021. What has changed in India in all these years?

There is more of a discourse happening at the urban level, where the problem of untouchability has become neutral to some extent. But now there is huge resentment towards reservation. And that has become the main reason behind urban hatred towards Dalits. I consider reservation as an incorrect term, because it's about reparation to those who have been underprivileged for so many years. And it's such a misnomer, when you think about it. The word 'reservation' denotes something like a cushion or a favour given to someone. That is completely wrong. I think the correct term we should be using is 'representation'. Even in cinema, the dominance of the Savarnas is still persistent.

Ray was a Savarna. He made *Sadgati*. But notice how Om Puri was his protagonist, not Mohan Agashe. It was not that he had made Mohan Agashe the hero of his story by giving him a change of heart about what he was doing and granting Om Puri's character the deliverance he deserved. No, he does not get to play the protagonist in the film. The film was about the untouchable, and rightfully so. If we really want to make something subaltern, we have to bring them in and listen to them. The only other film that I feel has this amount of honesty is *Bandit Queen*. Because it puts its central character on a pedestal—it chooses her as a hero. Almost all other films about the Dalit is based on the saviour-complex depiction. And, of course, when I say all this, I am speaking in the periphery of Hindi cinema, because regional cinema in India cannot be compared to

Hindi cinema at all. They are far ahead of the rest of us—be it in craft or representation.

But coming back to your question, many decades ago, there was this whole revolution against temple entry down south in the country. But even today, some people are not allowed to enter temple premises, they are not allowed to ride a horse, they are not allowed to wear jeans, they are not even allowed to drink water freely. India is still the same. I think it's so ironical. Caste is ubiquitous—it is in every small corner of the country. Our lives and careers are shaped through this, regardless of religion, language or state. And yet, unlike race, caste is invisible. Cinema has changed considerably from the time of Ray but, sadly, the oppression of caste has remained the same.

What is the contemporary reaction to the cinema of Ray outside India?

If there is one name that is most mentioned by Westerners, it is that of Satyajit Ray. And it's really a matter of great pride for someone like me. When *Masaan* was travelling, they wanted to edit it in a certain way, so as to cater to the sensibilities of the European audience. I retained a cut that was for India while agreeing to an international cut for Europe and the rest of the world. They said, 'Ray never needed two versions for any of his films!' More than anything else, that was a matter of great pride for me. But I also believed Ray never needed to make two versions of his films because he had complete control over his films, not to mention complete independence to make his films the way he wanted to.

Would you say that the cinema of Ray has influenced your own cinema?

One of the biggest inspirations for *Masaan* was *Pratidwandi*. I was deeply moved by that film. The problem of unemployment hasn't been explored in Indian cinema before. Indian films were always about this hero who fights zamindars, falls in love or falls out of love. But that film actually showed the importance of career in our lives. Deepak's narrative in *Masaan* is also the same, as he also faces an interview like the protagonist in *Pratidwandi*. In that interview scene, Ray also uses this amazing technique of establishing a lot of things about his characters without verbalising their politics. He does it simply through the smart presentation of the characters. I remember when Siddhartha is asked what the most remarkable thing about the last decade is, he says the war in Vietnam. When he is asked if the war is even more significant than the landing on the moon, his explanation says a lot about him as a person. The sequence on the terrace has also had a deep impact on me. Subconsciously, it is reflected in the climax of *Masaan*, where there are two lonely people against the rest of the world.

Again, when I made my short film, *Shor*, I was subconsciously inspired by *Mahanagar*. My film was about a woman who has to go to work because her husband is out of work. And how, despite having to do so, she has to hear complaints from her family about the fact that she is stepping out of home to earn their daily bread. That's the central theme of *Mahanagar* too. I strongly believe that our entire generation of filmmakers is either consciously or subconsciously inspired by the works of Ray.

You are a young, present-day filmmaker. What do you think filmmakers of this generation can learn from Ray?

Ray made films with such restricted resources, but they cut across time and really move you, even today, no matter which part of the world you are from. His films have a universal appeal in the truest sense of the term. Ray will continue to inspire generations with his cinema. His adherence to his narrative truth was his sole guiding force. That is the most honest form of storytelling. He was an avid reader, had a keen eye for art and a life full of experiences. These things have enriched his worldview. Our worldview and experiences guide our cinema, and it is our responsibility to stay true to it. That is the lesson I learn every day from Ray

Oliver Craske

'Satyajit Ray was a polymath talent, but the flip side of that is being a bit of a control freak'

Oliver Craske is the official biographer of sitar maestro Pandit Ravi Shankar, who composed the music for four Satyajit Ray films—the Apu trilogy and *Parash Pathar*. Craske is the author of *Indian Sun: The Life and Music of Ravi Shankar*, published by Faber & Faber (2020), which is the first full biography of his subject; and *Rock Faces*, a survey of music photographers. During a career in book publishing, he also collaborated with Ravi Shankar on his autobiography *Raga Mala* (1997) and has edited books on numerous subjects, from Einstein to the Beatles, and from cricket to art collecting. In this interview, Craske talks about the personal and professional relationship between Ravi Shankar and Satyajit Ray.

Would it be accurate to say that Ravi Shankar and Satyajit Ray were friends before they started collaborating on the Apu trilogy?

Yes—perhaps not close friends, but definitely friends. Funnily enough, as children, they had both been in the audience at the first All Bengal Music Conference at Calcutta University in 1934, the occasion when

Ravi Shankar first saw his future guru Allauddin Khan performing and was mesmerised. Yet, they did not meet then. When at last they did, in 1944, Ravi was twenty-four and Satyajit twenty-three. (I'll use 'Ravi' here, although I always called him 'Ravi-ji'.) Ravi had recently moved from Maihar after his years of intensive study with Allauddin Khan and was staying with his older brother Rajendra in Malad, in northern Bombay. Satyajit came to visit a relative who lived nearby and who was known to the Shankars, and that's how they were introduced. At the time, Satyajit was working as an art director in advertising and was yet to embark on his film career, but I have a theory that the Shankar he most wanted to meet that day was Rajendra, who was a scriptwriter for Bombay Talkies. Either way, the meeting with Ravi was a blessing for both of them. By then, Ravi was gaining some renown for his concerts and radio recitals. When Ravi played his breakthrough concert in Calcutta a year later, Satyajit was present. Thereafter, whenever Ravi came to the city to perform, he would stay at the Great Eastern Hotel, close to Satyajit's office, and they got to know each other over coffee and 'adda'. Satyajit regularly attended his recitals and was impressed by a theatrical production of Nehru's *Discovery of India*, for which Ravi had composed the music, when it came to Calcutta in 1948. The same year he also watched and adored the film *Kalpana*, directed by Ravi's eldest brother Uday, which featured Ravi on the soundtrack. Although Ravi wasn't the music director of that film, he had by then already composed two film scores, for *Neecha Nagar* and *Dharti Ke Lal*.

Ravi's profile really started taking off after he became director of music of All India Radio in 1949 and began to be heard more on the airwaves nationwide. We can tell how fascinated Satyajit was in this period by Indian classical music, and by Ravi in particular, because as he became serious about becoming a filmmaker, one of his earliest ideas was to make a short film of Ravi playing a raga on the sitar. According to Ravi, this was conceived as one in a series of short films on Indian classical ragas. In 1951, Satyajit even sketched out a thirty-one-page storyboard for it, which still exists, but the film was never made. It probably fell by the wayside as Satyajit became focused on making *Pather Panchali*, which he began filming in October 1952.

You have said in your biography of Ravi Shankar that he was the sort of artist who thrived under the pressure of deadlines and depended on last-minute inspirations to create his best work. Satyajit Ray, on the other hand, was known for his meticulous and detailed planning of every single aspect of the filmmaking process—a trait that allowed him to make the best of cinema despite tight budgets and tighter schedules. There seems to be a contrast in the way the two of them worked, don't you think?

Yes, there clearly was, and this contrast was important. Sometimes pairings of creative opposites can result in greater art. If the talents they bring dovetail with each other and the personalities can work together, one enables and inspires the other. As Nitin Sawhney once told me, Ravi and Satyajit complemented each other the same way Bernard Herrmann and Alfred Hitchcock did, or Ennio Morricone and Sergio Leone did.

Ravi once said that a film director should either tell him exactly the mood he wanted to convey in a scene or leave it up to Ravi. Satyajit always knew his mind, so this meticulousness played to Ravi's strengths. Satyajit defined what Ravi needed to achieve, and within these limitations, he was free to create. That gave him an ideal combination of constraints and freedom. If you think about it, this is what Indian classical music itself is about: within the framework of a raga, which narrows down the options of what you may play but suggests all these routes to explore, you improvise and soar free. The constraints themselves serve to make you more creative.

It's not that Ravi couldn't work in a meticulous way—after all, he composed many major works for Indian and Western orchestras, and they could not all be improvised on the spot—but even in these complex works, he relied on moments of inspiration to produce material that he would then rework and arrange. That's how he felt he came up with his best music. He was incredibly creative. All his life the music just seemed to flow—he kept going to the well, and the well never dried up. So he loved working like this.

Creative tension can be unstable too, and maybe that's why their partnership didn't last. But while it did, they made four films together in four years, each of which has a brilliant soundtrack. At the end of his life, in 2010, Ravi wrote that Satyajit was 'undoubtedly the greatest director I worked with—meticulous, disciplined and an expert in every aspect of filmmaking'.

Please tell us about the process of composition of the soundtrack of the three films of the trilogy.

Satyajit wrote to Ravi in late 1954, inviting him to compose the score for *Pather Panchali*. At the time, orchestral music—with or without songs—but with Western instruments predominant, was the normal soundtrack for Bengali films, as in Hollywood. But Satyajit wanted a fresh approach. He felt Ravi could provide something different, and Ravi accepted the challenge. He was in much demand by that time and he proposed recording it the next time he came to Calcutta, when he had one day to spare after a recital he was due to give there. Satyajit knew the film had to be edited and packed off to New York in time for its world premiere there in May 1955.

The exact date of the session has been lost, but I believe it may have been the night of 3rd/4th January 1955, because Ravi played at Dover Lane on the 2nd. If so, during the daytime on the 3rd he watched a rough cut of the film at Bhavani cinema. Ravi was so moved by the film that his memorable folk-like main theme came to him there in the cinema itself. That evening, he assembled a small musical ensemble in the recording studios. Ray screened the scenes that he wanted music for, Ravi composed and arranged each piece on the spot, and they recorded them straightaway. Ravi also recorded a few extra short pieces on solo sitar, which Ray could place wherever he wanted during the edit. This process was an ideal outlet for Ravi's spontaneous creativity. They worked through the night in a single eleven-hour session. The next day, Ravi returned to Delhi and Satyajit was left to carry out the edit at his leisure. This was a typical pattern for how they collaborated.

Three things made Ravi's film scores in that period really distinctive. First, the use of Indian instruments rather than Western. At the time, some people argued that Indian instruments could not render every shade of mood required of a film score, yet Ravi firmly believed otherwise. His ensemble consisted of a dilruba player (who also played the tar-shehnai), a flautist and a pakhawaj player, as well as his own sitar, which he played exquisitely on the soundtrack. And one of the marks of his genius is how he reworked his main theme music in different arrangements to suit the mood on screen, from wistful to playful to melancholy. Secondly, the use of classical ragas: these are important to the mood of the film, though there are a lot of semi-classical and folk forms too. One of those extra pieces he recorded, in the rainy-season raga Desh, even inspired Satyajit to add an extra scene to the film, matching this music with some spare footage he had shot of waterbugs skating on a pond to create a sublime sequence. Thirdly, the emphasis on incidental music. In Ravi's opinion, the Apu trilogy allowed him 'to break away from the age-old theory that there can be no films without film songs. Satyajit's films have falsified for good this rotten, crusty theory.'

But setting aside these technical aspects, the music of the trilogy gives me, as it has so many other people over the years, the sense that Ravi had somehow bottled magic. He spoke of how the films had touched his heart and that's where the music came from. That's not a throwaway comment. I think he really identified with the protagonist: like Apu, Ravi was an intensely curious Bengali Brahmin boy growing up in Varanasi in the 1920s, who suffered the premature deaths of an older sibling and both his parents, and later struggled to relate to his own son. So, in the famous scene when Sarbajaya reveals to Harihar that their daughter Durga has died—when, in a moment of genius, we hear only the high wail of the tar-shehnai—we are really feeling Ravi's own grief at his brother Bhupendra's death.

The music for *Aparajito* was also recorded in Ravi's hit-and-run style, squeezed into a visit to Calcutta in August 1956. Both the instrumentation and approach echo those used in *Pather Panchali.* He came up with another lyrical main theme in advance, and then improvised and composed in the studio. It's wonderful music again, and Ravi develops his style a little further—it's like the progression of a raga. But it's the third film that shows another quantum leap: *The World of Apu* is not only my favourite of the trilogy, but I also feel that Ravi's music—recorded in early 1959, this time in less of a rush, across three days—has pushed on in interesting ways. As the story has progressed from youth to adulthood, and from village to city and then to the multiple locations of the third instalment, the music has become more sophisticated, with more serious ragas displacing the folkish tunes, and the addition of strings and even a piano introducing a bigger, wider sound. At the film's conclusion, there is the reappearance of the tar-shehnai theme from *Pather Panchali* that has haunted the trilogy. But what has, until now, been a recurrent reminder of unbearable grief is now transformed by Apu's redemption. This is superb filmmaking as well as music-making.

Although it was a comedy that very few people in the world have watched, I have always found *Parash Pathar* to be (a) a very philosophical film and (b) extremely rich in visuals. It is, to my mind, one of the most criminally underrated films in Ray's filmography. It raises several profound questions about human desires and wishes. The art direction is impeccable, the performances are marvellous, the cinematography is remarkable and the writing is superlative. But hardly anything is said about the extraordinary experimentations with its score, composed by Ravi Shankar. Had Shankar ever spoken to you about this film's music?

It's interesting you say this. It is a very unusual soundtrack for that time. Rather than memorable tunes, it is all about experimentation and effect—portentous strings, iridescent percussion, other-worldly drones. Satyajit had told him he wanted to create a sense of fantasy and the supernatural, and Ravi loved being given the freedom to deliver to that clear brief.

Perhaps Ravi felt emboldened by his successes. He recorded this soundtrack in September 1957, a month after returning from a long, groundbreaking tour of Europe and America, which kick-started his prolific solo touring abroad that would culminate in his global fame a decade later. But the more immediate impact of this tour was back in India, where it raised his profile into the stratosphere— the newspapers went wild at this returning hero, this new music ambassador for India.

The *Parash Pathar* session was also taking place shortly after two films he'd scored had won awards at the Venice Film Festival: Satyajit's *Aparajito*, which won the top prize, the Golden Lion, and Norman McLaren's delightful short film *A Chairy Tale*, which won first prize in the category of avant-garde and experimental films. Satyajit himself was in Venice. So Ravi was in hot demand as a film composer.

Ravi didn't speak about *Parash Pathar* with me, except in passing— it was the 'other' film score he recorded for Ray, the one outside of the trilogy. It was only while researching my biography of Ravi that I eventually got hold of a copy of the film. As you say, it is little known, although I see it has now appeared on YouTube. So I did not have the chance to quiz him on it after hearing its music. But I came across an article in *Filmfare* in 1958, which he had written shortly after *Parash Pathar* was released, in which he talked about how he had used 'weird and musically fantastic sound effects to bring out the moods and emotions'. And, fascinatingly, he added that he believed this was his best film score to date—even after making the timeless music for *Pather Panchali*. That was, admittedly, the instant reaction of a composer to his latest release, to the excitement of being able to work in an unusual way and to delivering on his brief, rather than being his lasting lifelong judgement. Other film scores of his are greater and more durable achievements, but it gives you an insight into his approach to film music. He had the mindset not only of a classical musician but of a true film composer, who wanted to deliver a sound world that enhanced the action and the mood on screen.

Why do you think Ray started composing his own music for his films, rather than working with professionals?

There is no great mystery about this. Satyajit took being an auteur director to the extreme. He did almost everything for his films—apart from acting—to the extent that he eventually decided to make his own music for them. That's rare in the world of movies, which is a collaborative medium. Chaplin did it, but not many other directors have the necessary musical gift, energy and, it has to be said, self-belief. Satyajit was a polymath talent, but the flip side of that is being a bit of a control freak.

He loved the music that Ravi had written, but he felt there were limitations to the process. He wanted more control over the soundtrack, including the ability to create and refine it over a longer period of time, rather than having it emerge in a single intense burst of creativity. Also, although Satyajit appreciated Indian raga music, his tastes were more for Rabindra Sangeet and even more so for Western classical. He wanted to bring these and other influences in, and blend them in ways that just wouldn't be possible if he were deferring to an Indian classical maestro.

As well as working with Ravi, Satyajit made films with two other great Indian classical musicians in those early years, Vilayat Khan and Ali Akbar Khan, who provided the soundtracks to *Jalsaghar* (1958) and *Devi* (1960), respectively. In fact, Satyajit was even more frustrated by working with Ali Akbar Khan than he was with Ravi. To be fair, Ali Akbar was also less than enamoured of the experience—later he cuttingly described Satyajit as 'not a connoisseur of Indian classical music'. *Devi* was the final straw for Satyajit, the prompt for him to be his own music director thereafter.

Much has been speculated about the friction between Ravi Shankar and Satyajit Ray—two stalwarts of the arts. As the biographer of Shankar, would you like to comment on this?

Satyajit was frustrated that Ravi hadn't provided enough music for *Aparajito* on his flying visit to Calcutta, and he felt there were some patches of the film that had too much silence. That caused a bit of tension, but it didn't stop them from working again on two more films, including *The World of Apu*, which has wondrous music with which Sayajit was very happy. Anyway, some element of artistic tension can be beneficial. They inspired each other.

In later years, after they had stopped working together, there was what Ravi called 'a slight misunderstanding' between them. Satyajit once made a public comment to the effect that Ravi was unique as a composer for dance or the theatre, but not so ideal for film, because of his hit-and-run way of working. This comment hurt Ravi. He was a tremendously generous person, but also, like many artists, sensitive to slights. I recall him telling me once that he felt he'd said enough publicly about his relationship with Satyajit. This was after Satyajit had died. It could well have been a reflection of how often he was asked about the subject—he just didn't have anything left to add. But I sensed that it also spoke to some residual level of discomfort.

However, I'm sure whatever misunderstanding remained was on a superficial level and would have died away soon enough had theirs not been the sort of public friendship that invited fascination and speculation. The dying embers of any mistrust were periodically fanned by critics and reporters who sensed a story—which, in a way, is what you and I are doing right now. That's the problem with friendships in the public eye. But in private there wasn't a problem—the friendship and the mutual admiration went deeper than that. There were striking gestures of private warmth from both of them over the years. They saw each other socially—for example, Satyajit visited Ravi's home in Los Angeles in 1967 and in Varanasi in 1977. After Satyajit had his first heart attack in 1983, Ravi paid him a visit in Calcutta during his convalescence. Similarly, when Ravi was waiting for his heart bypass in New York three years later, Satyajit, who had been through the same operation, rang to wish him well. And after Satyajit died in 1992, Ravi recorded a beautiful tribute to him, weaving together his *PatherPanchali* theme with Raga Ahir Bhairav, and released it as *Farewell, My Friend*—a title that says it all, really.

What was Ravi Shankar's opinion of Satyajit Ray as a composer? How did he react to Ray's own film music in the years following *Devi*?

He never discussed this subject with me, except to say that Satyajit had every right, as a director of such stature, to make whatever music he wanted for his films. Ravi was not dogmatic about Indian classical music being the ideal style for films. As he put it, 'There are many roads to Rome'. The same film could be adorned equally well with very different scores by different film composers. But that's not exactly a ringing endorsement. Similarly, in 1965, he had described Satyajit's music as 'competent', nothing more. But his view evolved. In 2009, he told the *Times of India* that Satyajit had been 'an outstanding composer'. While Ravi loved the Apu trilogy and always considered *Pather Panchali* to be Satyajit's finest film, he also rated very highly some of the films he didn't score himself. Writing in *Raga Mala*, he singled out *Jalsaghar*, which has Ustad Vilayat Khan's soundtrack; *Charulata*, for which Satyajit had arranged Rabindra Sangeet and some of his own original compositions; and *Kanchenjungha*, which features Satyajit's own score.

Pradip Mukherjee

'Even on the first day of the shoot, every single person in the unit knew that the whole film had already been made in his head'

Pradip Mukherjee was cast as the somewhat timid and out-of-his-depth Somnath in Satyajit Ray's *Jana Aranya* (1976). The final addition to his famous City trilogy, the film was by far the darkest in Ray's filmography and dealt with the struggles of the Bengali middle-class educated yet jobless youth and the slippery slopes they were often forced to tread. As revealed in this interview, it changed the fortunes of its lead actor forever.

You had had several years of experience in theatre before you joined films. How did you happen to land the role of Somnath in Satyajit Ray's *Jana Aranya*?

I used to work in commercial theatre, but I must admit to you that I was not a very good actor. In fact, to begin with, I never quite enjoyed the atmosphere of group theatre. I found it quite toxic. Then I came to the commercial stage. Although I started by playing small roles, I became quite popular quite quickly. There was a time when audiences would wait for me to come on stage. But it is Ray who took me to the heights of real success. Way back in 1972, my friends and I used to go to Manik-da's house on Bishop Lefroy Road. He saw a very short bit of my acting performance on stage in *Lamba Karna Pala*. Perhaps it was then that he had thought that if he would make a film on a middle-class subject, he would cast this young man who was running around in half-shirts with thick-rimmed spectacles on his eyes. Manik-da had a propensity for casting middle-class intellectual characters as the protagonists in his films. He also had a hidden belief that the hero had to be fair-skinned and good-looking. Anyway, when he actually thought of making the film, he started looking for me. But by then, I had stopped visiting his home and gotten busy with my theatre. Then one day, he asked me to see him and told me he had selected me to play the role of Somnath.

Did he ever ask you to read the novel on which *Jana Aranya* was based?

Yes, he did. On the very second day. As far as I can remember, the date was 24 December 1974. I was returning from work, trying to make my way to his home on Bishop Lefroy Road. It was raining heavily and traffic was a mess, so I reached half an hour late. When I knocked on his door, he opened the door himself, as was his custom. Then he said, 'Some people have dropped by and I am a bit busy right now. I am making Shankar's *Jana Aranya*. Pick up the novel and read it thoroughly, because I am planning to portray the main character through you. You are going to be the hero in my film.' Having said this much, he shut the door.

What was your reaction?

What can I say? When one's long-standing wish gets fulfilled, the immediate next moments are of disbelief and then of immense joy. And my situation was quite similar. For a minute or two, I couldn't believe what I had heard. And then, when it sank in, I was on top of the world. I had read the novel already but I went home and read it again. It was an entirely different experience this time. This time, I knew I was playing the hero! But there is something that I have always believed—I was always destined to be in cinema. Cinema was my destiny and Satyajit Ray helped me fulfil my destiny. At the age of seventeen, after writing only three papers of my Higher Secondary exams, I had run away from home, bought a ticket and hopped onto the *Bombay Mail*. I wanted to act in films. Had I not met a boy of my age who asked me to go and see one of his friends in Borivali, I would have died on the streets of Bombay. That man used to give me one meal a day and I used to sleep on the street right at his doorway. From those days of struggle to being the hero of a Satyajit Ray film—an invisible hand seemed to have always guided me, saving me from falling face-first. What would you call that, tell me? I'll tell you what. Destiny.

What did Ray tell you about the differences between acting on stage and acting for the screen?

First, he asked me to forget all the methods of theatre-acting. He used to say that there is a huge difference between stage acting and film acting. He spoke about this in his film *Nayak* too. He asked me to be my natural self, to act and behave normally. And the interesting part was that he never, ever interrupted the process of spontaneous performance. Even if he didn't like a shot, he would say, 'This was good, let's take another one.' He used to give these seemingly trivial inputs, which didn't mean much at the time of taking the shot but which used to completely change the meaning of the frame altogether. For instance—use the handkerchief to wipe your face. He asked us to perform bits and pieces of daily activities of real life in front of the camera. And he never provided any elaborate explanation as to why we should do it, as any such explanation would have turned out to be a burden on the actor and affected his or her performance. It was all in his head, although we couldn't see it.

As a person, what was Ray like on the sets and on location?

He was totally normal. Though he was making all these masterpieces, he never had any pomp and show. Even on the first day of the shoot, every single person in the unit knew that the whole film had already been made in his head. And all that we needed to do was execute it. It was fascinating, when I think about it now. It almost seemed like he was simply playing the reel in his head backward to take a glimpse or two from time to time, and check whether he had done everything that was in his head or not. But there was no manifestation of ostentation in him. Nor any sign of pride. As far as I can remember, I have never seen him wearing any kind of luxurious attire. He was very neat and clean, but was not fond of expensive clothes or accessories. He was a big foodie, though. But there was something very strange about him that I must tell you about. You couldn't stare into his eyes for too long. I know it sounds very strange, but it's true. You would be forced to lower your gaze after sometime. It's not that he was trying to make you feel uncomfortable or anything of that sort, nor was he trying to establish his dominance. But when you looked into his eyes, you could make out that he was reading you. Like a book. He was trying to understand you as a human being. And you had no option but to look away, if not down.

If anything went wrong, did he get angry or irritated?

If I did anything wrong, he would ask his assistant, 'Punu [Ramesh Sen], haven't you explained this to him?' One day, after much hesitation, I asked him if he was indirectly reprimanding me. He laughed out loud and said, 'How can I scold you? You are my hero!' That was the sort of man he was. Always quick to diffuse a tense situation. We used to have a lot of fun during shooting. There was never any atmosphere of fear or apprehension. Everyone was relaxed but dedicated to the job at hand. His narration of the screenplay used to be another remarkable affair—an event in itself. He gathered all his principal artists and chief technicians and narrated the entire script without a break. It was like listening to a radio play.

What was the experience like of working with Utpal Dutt? Both of you were stage actors. Was this the first time you were working with him?

Yes, because I hadn't got the opportunity to work with him on stage. I did my screen test with another great actor, Rabi Ghosh. And right from then, I knew that I would be working with the great Utpal Dutt in this film. And I was looking forward to it. On the second day of shooting the office sequence, I saw him quietly sitting on a chair in a corner. As soon as he saw me, he waved at me and said, 'Come here. I have been waiting for you.' And we chatted for quite some time. He was an extraordinary actor. He could portray any character on any stage, on any platform. He could be in any kind of cinema and he would still make it shine.

When one watches *Jana Aranya*, one almost gets the feeling that Ray is making a case for entrepreneurship among the Bengali middle-class youth. Why, then, do you think he goes on to show the dark side of entrepreneurship? Why this duality?

Well, if you think about it, Ray had shown that the girl—Kauna, who was the sister of Somnath's friend—had already come into this business. Somnath himself had nothing to do with that. That night, if it had been someone else but Somnath, Kauna would still have gone with him. And that's why, in a subsequent scene, Somnath says, 'You don't have to do this, let's go back.' To which, Kauna responds, 'No, you're acting like a child. Doing so won't help anyone.' And this is exactly where the film becomes a black comedy. Manik-da was a very conservative man when it came to these matters and he considered this scene to be a proper ending to the film. And to be honest, this led to a cold conflict between him and Shankar-da, the author of the novel.

In the film, Somnath has been shown to have a beautiful relationship with his sister-in-law, Kamala, played by Lily Chakravarty. In one scene, when Somnath is feeling rather bitter about women after a break-up, Kamala is trying to cheer him up. In response, Somnath tells Kamala that he remembers her weeping profusely from the night of her wedding. That one scene is so loaded, so rich in meaning and suggestion! What was Ray's brief to you for that particular scene?

Believe it or not—nothing!

Nothing?

Nothing! Not a single word. You are right, it's a beautiful scene. But on the day of the shoot, he explained our positions and reactions to us, and we took the shot. That's all. He understood that I had already got the essence of the scene. There was no explanation, no analysis, no grand speech. Absolutely nothing! *That* was the nature of the man we are talking about.

You also acted in *Shakha Proshakha*, didn't you?

Yes, I did. But it was a small role, that of a journalist. Just one scene. Right from the days when I was a young man, I had always wanted to act in films. And I had always wanted to act in a Satyajit Ray film. My first film was a Satyajit Ray film, so I consider myself immensely fortunate. I did end up acting in many films after that. It was Ray who is responsible for my success. But I never got a big role in another Ray film again. I still consider myself fortunate, though. I still count my blessings. You never get roles according to your wishes, you know? As I said before, it's all destiny. It's all written beforehand. Predestined.

Sharmila Tagore

'Whenever I travel abroad, wherever there is good cinema, people know me because of *Devi*'

There are many iconic director–actor frequent collaborations in the world of cinema. Many filmmakers have been known to go back to a particular actor over and over again and cast them in leading roles. This can perhaps be attributed to the fact that at its very core, cinema is a collaborative art form. More often than not, it takes more than one person to give it its final shape. The fact that an actor can easily understand what a filmmaker is trying to say through his or her film is not one that can be taken lightly. It makes the filmmaker's job simpler and helps give birth to a beautiful film. Satyajit Ray, too, had frequent collaborations with many actors, chief among them being Soumitra Chattopadhyay. But among the leading actresses, Ray had worked the greatest number of times with Sharmila Tagore, whose naturalistic performances, dignified grace and the ability to fit into any role has given us five remarkable films—*Apur Sansar* (1959), *Devi* (1960), *Nayak* (1966), *Aranyer Din Ratri* (1970) and *Seemabaddha* (1971).

There had been several stalwarts and veterans from the Hindi film industry in Bombay who had expressed their keen desire to work with Satyajit Ray. And yet, it was you he kept casting in his films over and over again. In fact, among the 'lead' actresses, you have appeared in the maximum number of roles in a Satyajit Ray film, that, too, at a time when you were a busy actress in Bombay. Clearly, you must have had a wonderful working relationship with him. Has there ever been a time when you were forced—either by circumstances or by choice—to say no to Satyajit Ray?

Never. He was the one who introduced me to cinema. And he was very fond of me. I was very young when I first met him. He was always 'Manik-da' to me. In a way, he felt responsible for me. At the same time, he had immense faith in me. Throughout my career, I have always remained 'Rinku' to him—the same little girl he had first met and seen the potential I had, even more than I did. So the question of saying no to him did not arise. The only time I was unable to collaborate with him was for *Kanchenjungha*, as my senior Cambridge exams clashed with the shooting schedule of the film and my father was hesitant to say yes. By choice, I would never turn down an offer made by Manik-da.

Has there ever have been a time when you had to do the reverse? When you had to reschedule or cancel a shoot for a Hindi film to accommodate a shoot for Ray?

When Manik-da asked me to play the lead role in *Aranyer Din Ratri*, I had already given those dates to Shakti Samanta for his film *Aradhana*. In fact, Rajesh Khanna's dates were fixed too. Shakti-ji had to finish the shooting of a song featuring Rajesh and I in Darjeeling before the rains came. And Manik-da also had to complete his shoot within a specific time, because he needed a certain seasonal look and feel for his film— something that would not have been possible once the rains set in. So there was a conflict in my schedule. But there was not even a moment's doubt or hesitation in my mind. I spoke to Shakti-ji and explained the situation to him and he accommodated duly as he knew what Manik-da meant to me—and as a filmmaker he had tremendous respect for Satyajit Ray.

In an essay you wrote for one of my books, you said that *Devi* is your favourite, among all the films you have done in your career. That story was written by Prabhat Kumar Mukhopadhyay a century ago. The film itself was made way back in 1960. In principle, do you think anything has changed in our country since the film was made?

On paper, it ostensibly has. Today, several laws forbid things such as sati, superstition, etc. There are laws to protect women. But when it comes to practice, and depending on how far you are from a city, from the media, things carry on. Perhaps not exactly what happened in *Devi*, but by and large, in a male-dominated society, women still continue to suffer injustice—in the name of religion, tradition, family and honour. When it comes to nutrition, the male child is given preference; when it comes to medication, the male members of the family are always given the required attention, leaving the women to suffer in silence; when it comes to education, the boys of the family are sent to school and the girls assigned household chores, right from their childhood.

Until not very long ago, in several states of India, women didn't even have right to their parents' property. And when they made a law to change that, the father would force his daughter to sign away those rights. If she didn't, she was ostracised in the village. So some things may have changed—at least people are talking about the issues—but there's still so much that remains to be done. Especially in practice. I have recently employed a young girl—around twenty—to help me with household work. I was chatting with her the other day and she told me that her mother had passed away when she was very young and that she was brought up by her aunt. Her male cousins were all sent to school, whereas this girl doesn't even know how to read and write. Can you imagine that, in today's day and age? She can't even read the name of the medicine she's been prescribed. This is what Manik-da tried to talk about in his films. His films are considered the greatest because they are so relevant. That's what great filmmakers do, you know. They talk about things that will remain relevant even if they are not around to see it.

The famous Austrian composer and pianist Artur Schnabel once said, 'The notes I handle no better than many pianists. But the pauses between the notes—ah, that is where the art resides!' When we watch one of your memorable scenes in *Nayak*, we know exactly what Schnabel was talking about. Your character, Aditi, has been trying every trick in her bag to dissect and unravel the man behind the superstar, Uttam Kumar's Arindam Mukherjee. And yet, when she finally manages to do so, she does not want to publish his interview. By the end of the film, when Arindam asks her, 'Why did you tear it up? Are you going to write it by heart?', she responds, 'I'll … keep it in my heart!' That iconic pause makes so much difference to the entire scene—in fact, the entire film. As an actor, what is your interpretation of that pause?

Manik-da always used to say that the most important scene of the film should have no spoken words in it. And he has done that throughout his career. You've mentioned this pause, for instance, in my lines from *Nayak*. To fully understand the pause, we must first understand who Arindam Mukherjee is. He is essentially a puppet, a doll, who can laugh and cry and sing on cue. He is immensely popular. But he is constantly surrounded by his fans. And fans always have a very complex relationship with their stars. They adore them, even worship them, but the moment someone says anything bad about them, they are quick to believe those words. There is no real connection with them, certainly not on a humane level. Aditi is not a fan of Arindam Mukherjee—she just wants to interview him for her magazine. And over time, Arindam pours his heart out to her. But she does not make a scandal or scoop out of it. She does not take advantage of him. On the contrary, she protects him. Because she realises how brittle, how miserable a life this man is leading. She sees him in a new light. Not as a star, but as a human being. And all of this is fed into that one pause. That pause is so symbolic. It tells us how we are quick to judge people, to form opinions about them without thinking, without any hesitation. It's just so beautiful, if you think about it. In cinema, you can achieve so much, with so little! But, of course, you have to have a mind like that of Satyajit Ray to do so.

Another iconic scene from a Satyajit Ray film also features you, among others. This is the memory-game sequence from *Aranyer Din Ratri*.

If my memory serves me right, that scene was shot in a single day. We sat in a circle—the six of us. Manik-da was on the camera. His hands were steady, the frames were perfect. There was a sense of rhythm in his camera movements. And even the words that he had given us were perfect. In any case, whatever little words Manik-da used to give his actors—it would be such a delightful experience to speak them. In this scene, too, even the names of the famous people each of us were taking in the memory game gave each of us our personalities—who we were, how we thought. And the little gestures. As the game goes on, Soumitra is getting fed up—he wants to win. Rabi-da is bored—he is humming a tune. Soumitra asks him to shut up. And then, there's an interlude, in which Subhendu goes inside and fetches pillows for Kaberi-di. And Kaberi-di played her role so beautifully! She was absolutely superb in the film.

You have been the chairperson of the Central Board of Film Certification for more than six years. When one looks at films such as *Devi*, *Ghare Baire*, *Mahapurush* and *Hirak Rajar Deshe*, one can't help but wonder if these films would have seen the light of day had they been made today. In your opinion, should films in India be censored or certified?

Yes, of course, these films would have run into trouble today. *Devi* did run into trouble back then too. There were huge protests. Manik-da was accused of hurting the religious sentiments of the Hindus and accused of doing so because he was a Brahmo himself. And he had to defend himself by saying that he was only against religious orthodoxy and superstitions. *Ghare Baire* showed the other side of Swadeshi and I suppose there might have been trouble with that too.

I agree with you, but the question remains. These films may have run into trouble with the people back in the day, but not with the Board of Film Certification. Do you think the board would allow such films to be screened today?

Well, we are still an industry whose fortunes are decided by the people, aren't we? Even if the board were to pass these films today, there would inevitably be a PIL or a legal proceeding against them. But I must say that whenever I travel abroad, wherever there is good cinema, people know me because of *Devi*. And they think the world of me because of *Devi*. That's how popular the film was, and still is, outside India. Whereas in India, when the film was released, the government did nothing to stop the protests against Manik-da.

Which is the one role in a Satyajit Ray film not featuring you that you wished you had done?

Obviously, *Charulata*. In fact, he had given me Rabindranath Tagore's short story to read. I loved it and I was very excited. But a few days later, he called me and said, 'No Rinku, you are not in the film. You would be too young to play Charu.' But I thought Madhabi was perfect as Charu. Spot on. I wouldn't say it unless I really meant it, you know.

Shyam Benegal

'If Satyajit Ray would have made a film today, the state wouldn't dare to interfere with it in any way'

Shyam Benegal is one of the finest filmmakers Indian cinema has ever had, and one of the pioneers in the parallel cinema movement in our country. The list of his awards and nominations—both national and international—is understandably longer than his filmography itself. This is why when he made a documentary on Satyajit Ray, it was like the coming together of two great filmmakers with immense regard for each other's cinema. In this interview, Shyam Benegal talks about Ray as his mentor and about a certain section of Ray's filmography that is hardly spoken or written about—his documentaries.

Your biographical documentary on Satyajit Ray won a National Award in 1982. It is one of the most detailed and incisive films I have watched on Ray, which analyses his cinema and deep-dives into his process—and often into his mind. When and how did you first meet Ray? And when did you decide to make a film on him?

I was a college student when I met Satyajit Ray for the first time. I'm talking about the late 1950s. I was the captain of my university swimming team at the time. The national swimming championships were held in Calcutta in 1957. I was very keen to meet Mr Ray because I had discovered *Pather Panchali* and a couple of his other films by then. Soon after, I got his trilogy for our film society screenings in Hyderabad.

Many years later, when he was shooting *Nayak*, I happened to be in Calcutta and met him fairly frequently. He was very considerate, in the sense that when he didn't have time to meet me because of his shootings during the day, he would say, 'Why don't you come to see me at my home?' So I would go in the evening, usually around teatime. He was a typical Calcutta person. He had an adda in the evening. But in his case, these addas were at his home. He didn't go out. People came to visit him between 5 and 5.30 p.m. or so, and stayed till about 7.30 p.m., which was curfew time. All it needed was for his wife to look at him from the door to the dining room. This meant that he had to wrap things up and keep the rest of the evening free for family. The quintessential Bengali lifestyle! There are some unsaid and unspoken rules. Visitors are allowed up to a certain time and not allowed to sit around forever, as is often the case in middle-class Indian homes. This was necessary because he found it difficult to send his friends and hangers-on away. He had to have his family around him to protect him, which they did. He needed to conserve his time for his work. He was hugely prolific. He would be editing *Sandesh*, writing for it, giving interviews to people from all over the world, frequently travelling and, of course, writing scripts and making films. He was very, very busy. Naturally, his time had to be rationed.

When I met him, I was very conscious about the fact that I couldn't possibly take up more time than was necessary. I would telephone and find out when he would be free and then go and meet him.

Eventually, I got the opportunity to make a film on him, because I had seen all the films he had made more than a dozen times. In some ways, I saw him as a mentor figure, because I felt no one in our country understood the language of cinema as well as he did. I mean nobody among Indian filmmakers, at least. He understood the grammar of film, different narrative styles of cinema, the way of telling a story through the film medium—the art of adapting literature to the medium of cinema. There was hardly anyone in India who had such a deep understanding and profound knowledge of cinematic art as he did. At the first opportunity I got, I decided to make a film about him. I was already making features by that time and I would arrange for a screening for him whenever he came to Bombay. In those days, Calcutta didn't have the latest equipment for mixing and re-recording his films. He would have to come to Bombay to do all that.

I think it must have been in the early or mid-1980s when the Films Division decided that they would get some films made about eminent Indians. By 'eminent' I mean those who had been honoured by the State with a Padma Bhushan or Bharat Ratna, and so on. In that connection, there was a film to be made on Satyajit Ray. Knowing that I was a great admirer of his work, the Films Division asked me if I would like to make the film. It was to be a twenty-minute film, because that was the format of the Films Division. With the amount of money I received from them to make a twenty-minute film, I made a film that was two and a half hours long!

Ray was very cooperative. However, it took me some time to complete the film, because I had to catch him at work without bothering him and taking up too much of his time. Moreover, it took me some time to put together the money, to get the raw stock, etc., because what was given from the Films Divisions was enough only for a short film. But by then, I was making feature films, so I could hustle my way through. When I finally made that film, it was called *Ray by Benegal*. Very pretentious! Because it was in the form of an interview, and although I was asking him questions and he was giving answers, I was hardly seen in the film. Ray had a great sense of humour. He watched the film and said, 'Yeah, it's good. Wonderful, in fact! But where is Benegal? This is more Ray than Benegal!'

Ray made five documentary films—*Rabindranath Tagore*, *Sikkim*, *The Inner Eye*, *Bala* and *Sukumar Ray*. In your career, you have been a

prolific documentary filmmaker yourself. Much has been said about Ray's feature films. I would like to ask you—what did you think of Ray as a documentary filmmaker?

The film on Tagore is very good—it is a fine documentary. The few documentaries he made were quite exceptional, although he was not a documentarist by choice. He was essentially a person who loved to tell stories through cinema. And the stories that he had to tell were often great works of literature. After all, he took some great works of Bengali literature, from which he made exceptional films. They were not at all literal and stood out as films on their own. Take *Pather Panchali*, for instance. It's a great novel but Ray's film is outstanding and has an identity of its own. The entire trilogy is outstanding. You don't refer back at all to the book from which it has been sourced. He had the ability to transform a work of literature and make of it an entirely independent work of art. It's like what the painters of the European Renaissance did. You look at Michelangelo or any of the other artists—they learnt from different masters but what they produced was nothing like the masters from whom they learnt. Instead, they created original masterpieces. Satyajit Ray did the same.

You spoke about Ray's penchant for storytelling. Do you think Ray had tried to weave in a 'story' into *The Inner Eye*?

That film was one his best. And the reason was that he knew the painter Benode Behari Mukhopadhyay very well. Ray was a student at Shantiniketan and Benode Behari was his teacher there. Quite naturally, Ray's understanding of this blind painter was extraordinary. But I couldn't say the same about his film on Balasaraswati. It wasn't anywhere close to who she shyas and the type of work she had done. Balasaraswati was one of the best Bharatanatyam dancers our country has ever produced. The film was more on the art than on the artist—unlike *The Inner Eye*, in which he understood the artist almost intuitively.

In your film on Ray, he says filmmaking is a difficult job, at least in India. And yet, he always seemed to work with what can be best described as an astonishing and almost enviable amount of efficiency. Anyone who has seen him work has said this about him, without exception. As a filmmaker yourself, how do you think he managed to be so lean and efficient in his craft? And what can filmmakers of the present generation learn from him?

Indeed, he used to work under very difficult circumstances. The camera equipment and lights, etc., he had were nowhere close to the sophisticated equipment available in other parts of the world.

In the 1930s, Calcutta was an important centre of filmmaking and had a flourishing industry. But by the time Ray started making films, it was already in a state of decline. Most of the great technicians had moved out and come to Bombay. Despite that, Ray managed to make some exceptional films with whatever little he had at his disposal. And he had some exceptionally talented people around him to share his vision. Subrata Mitra, for instance, was a great strength for him, because they shared this wonderful sensibility between the two of them. In terms of lighting, Subrata Mitra's contribution to Ray's cinema is outstanding. The sense of naturalness that they managed to capture in their films could never be achieved by anyone else in Indian cinema at that time. Of course, there were instances such as that in some of the neo-realist films of Italy and in some of the films made by the great French masters of that time. In India, there was this great triumvirate—Satyajit Ray, his cameraman Subrata Mitra and his art director Bansi Chandragupta. Theirs was the best combination.

You have worked with both Bansi Chandragupta and Subrata Mitra. How was the experience of working with them?

Subrata shot my film on Nehru. He was immensely talented, but he often behaved like a spoilt child. He would look at things in certain ways and would insist that I look at those things in the same way. I used to have huge fights with him and I would tell him, 'Subrata, this is *my* film. You are my cameraman. So you have to see it from my eye, and not expect me to see from yours.' We used to have some massive quarrels! He was crazy, as most geniuses are! He would set up a shot and I would say, 'Subrata, this is not the shot I want. This is the way I want it and this is the lens I want to use.' And he would sulk and sit in a corner and say, 'Go ahead, shoot your film the way you like!' There was something very exasperating and endearing about him at the same time.

What about Bansi Chandragupta?

Bansi was absolutely marvellous. He was my art director for *Kalyug*. If I were to be perfectly honest with you, I haven't met an art director or a production designer like Bansi Chandragupta ever again in my entire career. He was simply extraordinary. He never came and said, 'What kind of sets are you looking for?' He would study the script, look at everything and discuss it with you, trying to understand what your vision is—and then make his suggestions. You could have long, enriching discussions with him. And he would do it exactly the way you wanted. Subrata, too, was equally talented. He would ask whether it was morning, afternoon, evening or night. He would ask, 'What's the atmosphere like? Where are we? Why are we doing this?' I don't think we will have such people again in the industry. I have very fond memories of working with them.

The real fun used to be when Bansi and Subrata fought! You see, Ray was this tall man who had such an imposing presence that they all used to behave like kittens in front of him. But when he moved out of the scene, they would all become tigers! But the fact remains that Ray had created all these artists, who were huge talents in their fields. He managed to get the best out of them. He would like everyone to get invested in the emotion of the scene. That was the way he shot his films. These were all thinking men. They used to invest a lot of time in thinking before being part of the unit making the film.

Do you think the availability of technology has affected the art of thinking?

I think so. Now it has become so much easier to do things. Back then, you had to do everything mechanically, with your hands. Naturally, you used to function like a craftsman. Nowadays, since most things are automated, we don't use our imagination enough. I don't blame anyone, though. These things happen. But once you get used to the technology, you are free to use your imagination again.

India's film-censorship rules have been the subject of significant debate lately. Do you think Ray would have been able to make and release such films as *Devi*, *Hirak Rajar Deshe* and *Ghare Baire* today? Films with heavy anti-religious-fanaticism and anti-nationalism commentaries?

Oh yes, he would! Don't forget that Ray not only received the Bharat Ratna, but had a towering presence in world cinema as well. People wouldn't have the courage to challenge him. If Satyajit Ray would have made a film today, the state wouldn't dare to interfere with it in any way.

Siddhartha Chatterjee

'Not a single Bengali parent in the 1980s or the 1990s named their child "Topshe"'

Siddhartha Chatterjee played Topshe in two Feluda films by Satyajit Ray—*Sonar Kella* and *Joy Baba Felunath*. From one film to the other, Topshe grew not only in age but also in maturity and intelligence. Chatterjee went on to act in several other films in his career but has self-admittedly stayed away from the industry for the better part of his life, focusing on being a restaurateur and a renowned financial investor and advisor instead—a far cry from the world of cinema. But spend a few minutes with the gentleman, and the fond old memories come tumbling out. In this interview, Chatterjee talks about his relationship with his 'Manik Jethu', his co-actors, the golden days of shooting in and around the golden fortress and, of course, his bond with his Feluda.

In literature, a man's intelligence is effectively conveyed to the reader only if there's someone to understand and relay that intelligence along. And it is in this sense that you played one of the most loved, most celebrated characters in the history of Bengali literature, not to mention one of the most important ones. Because there is no

Feluda without Topshe. How and when were you chosen to play this immortal character?

I was taken to Satyajit Ray through my school—Patha Bhavan. Whenever child artists were needed for Satyajit Ray's films, the first port of call was Patha Bhavan. And I was taken to him not by design but quite by accident. One of our teachers was helping Satyajit Ray edit an omnibus of his father Sukumar Ray's literary works. I sometimes used to go to this teacher's home to clear some doubts that may have stayed with me from class. These were times when teachers used to gladly welcome us into their homes and explain concepts to us, answer our questions—all without charging a penny. I remember I had some questions from our Bengali literature class, so I went to my teacher after school. There was a power cut, a candle was burning on the desk and perhaps in that half-light-half-dark mysterious environment, my teacher felt that I would be suitable for the role of a boy that Satyajit Ray was on the lookout for. So he said, 'Will you give me a lift?' My car was waiting outside, my teacher had made a request—his wish was my command. So we went. He took me to Bishop Lefroy Road. I had no idea who Satyajit Ray was. I was just amazed to see such a tall man, with such a deep voice. But now that I think back, I think he must have liked me for the role of Topshe at first glance.

Was there an audition?

None. One of the things I really liked about Manik Jethu was the simplicity of his entire process of filmmaking. It was all so simple! Nowadays, when I look around, I see unnecessary complications in the way films are made. Screen test, look test, voice test, this test, that test. All this is nothing but the director's lack of confidence showing through. None of this used to happen with Satyajit Ray. Much more powerful than the lens of the camera were his eyes! A quick glance from those keen, artistic eyes was good enough. Yes, he did spend time speaking to me, though, and that was not because he wanted to test me but because he wanted to study my mannerisms so that he could incorporate them in his script. So that he could write dialogues that would seem natural for me to speak. You have to understand that I did not have to play Topshe at all. My actual self became the projection of Topshe. Therefore, there was no element of acting, no impositions. He never asked me to use certain ways for the portrayal of Topshe. Ray's favourite thing to say to me after explaining a scene was, '*Thik ache toh? Kore nish!* (You got it, right? Good, just go ahead and do it then)!' I suppose giving confidence to the artist in this way gives a filmmaker the best looks, the best shots and the best performances.

It is said that child actors need what is known in filmmaking parlance as 'handling'. How was Ray with children?

Have you ever wondered why directors of this new generation can't make good films for children? They cannot do it because working with kids is not a matter of joke and one has to know the psychology of children to be able to work with them. Nowadays, whenever I see a child actor, the kid comes across as overmature—a bit too clever for his age. But the innocence of Mukul played by Kushal Chakraborty and my portrayal of Topshe worked only because of Ray's exemplary understanding of child psychology and his deftness at handling kids. One of his greatest qualities I have seen was the way he treated children. We are on our way to Rajasthan for the shoot—the entire cast and crew are having fun, chatting away—and here is this man, playing a memory game with us in the running train. He would play Ludo with us on the shooting floor. He was more interested in those two kids than in all the other senior actors, because he always knew that if the minds of the kids got disturbed or distracted, or if the kids felt lonely or homesick, it would be very difficult to get them back in the right mood. And, more importantly, I have never seen him doing anything with us kids by bribing us with chocolates or toys or gifts. We often make this mistake, but Ray would never do it. Instead, it was storytelling, participating in indoor games or just having an interesting chat. Basically, he used to do all these things to expand and explore the minds of the children. Which was why I was never intimidated by this man called 'Satyajit Ray', although I have seen all the adults maintain a reverential distance from him. But I was very happy being with him and around him, because something fun was always round the corner. And his presence was so comfortable for me because he had already established this bond of friendship with me. A director is not merely a person who looks into the camera and shoots a film. There is so much homework that needs to be done in the background.

In *Sonar Kella*, there is a scene in which Feluda tells you, 'Here's a boy who has left his parents and family behind, and is running around with a total stranger, far away from home, looking for the golden fortress.' I have always felt that in many ways, that particular line of dialogue could be aptly used in your case too. What do you have to say about that?

Satyajit Ray has basically tried to tell Bengali parents to give their children some scope for adventure to broaden their horizons. He has also tried to tell them that not everything can be taught within the confines of a classroom. Here's something interesting that I have observed. Not a single Bengali parent in the 1980s or the 1990s named their child 'Topshe'. Because none of them want their kids to be absent from school and trot around the country on these amazing adventures! No, all children must go to school every day, never miss their homework, go to private tuitions and mug up their lessons for good grades. What do you think the outcome of such a generation of children will be?

On the day I first met him, even I said to Manik Jethu, 'I cannot do the film because, first of all, my mother won't allow me. And the school won't give me the permission to be absent.' He said, 'I will take care of that.' At that time, I did not understand the power of Satyajit Ray and how he would manage to convince my school to grant me a long leave of absence. I did not realise that he happened to be one of the founding members of the school!

'Have you opened the mind's window, Felu?' Sidhu Jetha asks Feluda in *Sonar Kella*. But our windows are shut tight. In a world that has been taken over by smartphones and gadgets, we see something on social media and immediately forward it without even thinking about it for a second or verifying its authenticity. Copy and paste cannot be a replacement for originality, you know. And Satyajit Ray was all about originality and he kept his mind's window open. Otherwise, explain to me how someone can make a film such as *Jalsaghar* after making *Pather Panchali*. Then he did *Sonar Kella*, *Goopy Gyne Bagha Byne* and a film such as *Nayak*. And even after all these, he made *Aguntuk*.

It is because of his open mind that a film such as *Sonar Kella* changed the entire economy of a small town in Rajasthan. I don't think this has ever happened in the history of Indian cinema. Kashmir has always been a tourism place and got showcased in hundreds of films. But we went to a barren place where tourists never came. He shot the film there—and look at what Jaisalmer has become today! I went to Rajasthan three years back and saw a store named something like Mukul Stones. They have neither watched *Sonar Kella*, nor do they know who or what Mukul is. But over time, they have heard that all the Bengali tourists will come and ask about Mukul and Feluda. Another name was Sonar Kella Stores, and they run a booming business today.

I met a person named Ramesh Parekh who was from Calcutta and knows Bengali quite well. Once upon a time, his ancestors used to live in Jaisalmer but they sold their lands at throwaway prices due to drought and settled down in other parts of the country. One of them came to Calcutta and Ramesh is his descendant, who has been born and raised here, in Calcutta. When he watched *Sonar Kella*, he became so interested that he went back to Jaisalmer to buy back his ancestral land. He started one of the biggest stores of antique pieces and semi-precious stones there. And in that store, there are photos of his late parents, along with a photo of Satyajit Ray. I was shocked to see this and he said to me, 'Satyajit Ray is god to me. He has changed my life forever through just one film.' He added, 'Whenever a Bengali comes and asks me about this picture, I try to explain it to them. You have come and I am really blessed.' Ramesh has done a spectacular job. The GDP of Jaisalmer changed forever because of a film! From tourism to the bookings at the railway counters—everything changed.

Another immortal character that Ray created was Jatayu, and he has been immortalised by the actor who played him in the films. Please tell us something about Santosh Dutta.

Oh, he was an excellent gentleman. A perfect 'Bengali bhadralok'. He was not at all funny the way we are used to seeing him on screen. He was a serious criminal lawyer. During make-up or lunchtime, he would browse these legal journals. But as soon as he was in front of the camera, he would be a completely different person. He knew exactly what had to be done. Santosh Kaku was a very good human being. He came to my marriage with his wife. He was a criminally underutilised actor in Bengali films. An actor such as Tulsi Chakraborty had never been utilised in Bengali films, except in *Parash Pathar*. In most of the cases, he was given the roles of a buffoon. It was only after *Parash Pathar* that one could understand his true calibre. Even Santosh Kaku's role in *Ogo Bodhu Shundori* seemed quite buffoonish to me. He was an extremely intelligent actor. And a sharp criminal lawyer too. I believe that his intelligent acting was only showcased in Satyajit Ray's films—be it in *Goopy Gyne Bagha Byne*, *Hirak Rajar Deshe*, *Mahapurush* or *Samapti*. Ray used to understand Santosh Kaku's talent, which is why he refused to make a Feluda film after Santosh Kaku passed away.

But did Ray ever think of a third Feluda film?

Of course! He was ready with the third film. He was to do 'Joto Kando Kathmandute'. Talkhad already started and I was gearing up to play Topshe again. But then, tragedy struck. Santosh Kaku passed away.

After Santosh Kaku's demise, Ray said, 'cannot do a Feluda film without Santosh.' I remember the possibility of doing a film without Jatayu was also discussed. But Ray said, 'No! I have already given the taste of Jatayu to people and I cannot make a film without Jatayu.'

Please tell us something about Kamu Mukherjee. He seemed to be a rather interesting character, even in real life.

Kamu Kaku was like four or five films together! In the sense that one could make four–five films just about him. We were shooting in Jaisalmer, in the middle of the desert. The crew ran out of alcohol. Naturally, the technicians were frustrated. No one dared to discuss the matter with Satyajit Ray, because he was a teetotaler. We were in the middle of nowhere. It was a desolate border area; a military convoy came one day and the commanding officer happened to have spent three-four years in Fort William. So he knew about Satyajit Ray. He watched us shoot for some time and then the convoy left. The sun was setting, so we were busy packing up, when we suddenly realised that Kamu Mukherjee was nowhere to be seen. Nobody knew where he was or what had happened to him. We were staying at the Royal Guesthouse and after three or four hours, a Jeep rolled into the compound. And I could hear Kamu Kaku's voice as he jumped out of the Jeep. Everyone ran out to find him staggering awkwardly and saying, '*Sambhaalke! Ekdum sambhaalke* (Steady! Absolutely steady!).' Turned out, he had ridden off with the army officers and arranged a crate of rum from the garrison nearby and brought it back to the guest house! And he had evidently helped himself to a bottle or two on the way, and by the time he had reached the guest house, he was already drunk. When someone asked him what on earth he was thinking, he said that the army officers were supposed to save people from disasters and catastrophes, and what worse catastrophe could befall a shooting unit than the running out of alcohol? That was Kamu Mukherjee for you!

In *Sonar Kella*, there's a scene where Feluda is almost stung by a scorpion. We bought two scorpions from a Sunday-afternoon fair at Maidaan. It was a peculiar fair, and strange types of things such as lizards, cockroaches, scorpions, etc., were sold. We carried the two scorpions as members of our shooting unit to Rajasthan in a bottle of Horlicks. Kamu Kaku was a daredevil by nature. The bottle of Horlicks used to be in his possession. He would open the lid of the bottle to take the scorpions out and leave them on the corridor of the Jodhpur circuit house. Then he would run after them and eventually put them back into the bottle. It became his daily ritual. It was well known that Kamu Mukherjee was always present at Ray's outdoor shoots, even if he was not a part of the film, simply because he was so fun! Every once in a while, he would get a role here and there. For instance, in *Joy Baba Felunath*, there was a shot of a hand with a knife in the scene where the old artisan Shashi Babu is murdered. That was Kamu Kaku's hand!

We have heard that he was very good at crowd management too?

Oh yes! He was proficient at that because he had an imposing figure and great strength as well. He used to eat eight to ten eggs for breakfast every day. It was a sight to watch him eat. He had been invited for my sacred-thread ceremony. The caterer came running to my father and asked, 'Who is that man over there, sir? He has eaten twenty-three lobsters all by himself!' They don't make men like Kamu Mukherjee any more, you know. Fun, witty and with an unrestrained love for life!

How was your relationship with your Feluda—Soumitra Chattopadhyay?

First of all, he never considered himself a star. We used to think of him as a star but *he* never did that. He was an extremely friendly person— even with a co-actor like me, who was an inexperienced teen. I was his child's age, so it would have been natural for him to have father-like affection for me. But he broke that on the very first day. I was thinking of Soumitra Chattopadhyay as this great actor and, of course, a big star,

but he came and said to me, 'Hey, what did you have for breakfast?'
And thus began a warm chat that had nothing to do with work at all.
He used to repeatedly do these things to ease the relationship between
us. And after a few days, he simply became my Feluda, my elder
brother. And he remained my elder brother until the day he passed
away. I never had any problem sharing the screen with him. I never
thought he was a star in front of me. I always thought of him as my
Feluda. He never wanted to prove that he was a star. The food that used
to come for him from his home was just like ours—rice, dal and some
fried item. He never used to yell at anyone or send us away. Instead,
he used to tell us that there was some grown-up talk going on, so he
would come and see me in a bit. When you have a superstar such as
Soumitra Chattopadhyay behaving like this, the illusion of stardom
actually gets shattered, just like the illusive magnificence of Satyajit
Ray was revealed to me. And he became my Manik Jethu, and I could
ask him anything I wanted to.

After the Feluda films, I did another film with Soumitra
Chattopadhyay and, coincidentally, that was also shot in Benares. The
name of the film was *Ahoron*. Soumitra Kaku was playing the role of a
father, and the film was about a huge dispute between the father and
the son. We had to go to Benares for the shoot and after a few days, I
started looking after his health. Kakima (Soumitra Chattopadhyay's
wife) even said to me, 'If your uncle sleeps alone at night, he will
definitely be in trouble. He keeps forgetting things.' And I assured her
that I would sleep beside him. I went up to him in the evening and
said, 'Kaku, I will be with you at night.' He replied, 'Yeah. That would
be better. At night, I often make mistakes as I can't find the right door
for the washroom, and things like that.' I had brought a lovely bottle
of brandy for him from Calcutta. After drinking that, his mood was
fine. He recited poems and talked a lot about films and his co-actors,
up until midnight. And then he said, 'Keep all this to yourself, don't
tell anybody else. All these are my personal experiences.' When I asked
him about dinner, he expressed his childlike wish to have all kinds of

spicy and unhealthy stuff. I refused, and ordered soup for him. I said, 'This is your dinner, and you are going to have it. No complaints.' He was crestfallen, and said, 'How about you?' I told him I was going to have the same soup with him. That was the kind of relationship I used to share with my Feluda.

You had a warm bond with him, didn't you?

Oh, absolutely! One evening he called me and said, 'Come over, will you? I cannot understand anything about these mutual funds.' And I went over with kebabs and we had a long, lovely adda. We discussed everything under the sun, except mutual funds! These are not the kind of people who know or understand money, you see? They didn't do what they did for money. Their passion, their art, cannot have a monetary label attached. And that's what makes them so beautiful.

You have been a renowned name in the world of stock trading and financial investments. What would you say about Ray's financial condition?

If Ray would not have written the books, the family would have been in really bad shape. And that's remarkable when you think about it. Nowadays, when I see the houses of directors who have made only three films, I wonder where they get all the money from! Some of them drive expensive cars, others go on to become politicians. I think Satyajit Ray never asked for his price. Nor did he ever get his due—the financial part of it, that is. Had he been a little more cautious about money, he would have earned much, much more. The only attention that I have seen him pay to the notion of money was in trying to figure out how to reduce the cost of making his films. Nor did he even bother with owning a house. That rented house on Bishop Lefroy Road is perpetually theirs. I suppose if one plans for these things, one cannot write a good story or make a good film. That's the life of an artist. A true artist.

Srijit Mukherji

'To someone like me, Satyajit Ray is like a multistorey library'

Srijit Mukherji is a national award-winning filmmaker. Mukherji's love affair with the cinema of Satyajit Ray is evident from the fact that his debut film, *Autograph*, was a tribute to Ray's 1966 film *Nayak*. Even before he became a filmmaker, Mukherji had had brushes with the world of Ray. In 2006, for instance, he played an important role in Abhishek Majumdar's stage adaptation of Sunil Gangopadhyay's novel *Pratidwandi*. Ray had adapted the novel for the screen in 1970. Mukherji is a self-admitted fan of Ray's immortal literary creation, detective Prodosh Chandra Mitra, popularly known as Feluda. In 2008, he wrote, directed and produced *Feluda Pherot*, a non-canonical dramatisation of Feluda. In 2020, Mukherji directed a web series of the same name to bring Feluda back to the screen yet again.

What does the cinema of Satyajit Ray mean to present-day filmmakers such as you?

The cinema of Satyajit Ray is something of a bible for filmmakers such as us. If you look at filmmaking as a craft, he excelled in almost all departments. Let me give you an example. The fact that he composed his own music and scored his own films—that alone alludes to the polymath in him. But even if he hadn't scored his own films, the very way he used his scores—that in itself is a textbook. And he had emphasised this so many times that if the visuals are powerful enough, you won't need background scores at all. That is the hallmark of great cinema throughout the world.

Also consider the brevity, the economy of his dialogue-writing, which is sharp and precise. Though I wouldn't go to the extent of saying that it covered a huge range of social milieu, but the social environments that he did cover were impeccably captured through the nitty-gritty of his dialogue. Add to this the magnificent structuring of the screenplay—how to build a climax, how to create drama, how to underplay drama, how to write a pre-climax. There's so much to learn from his screenplays.

Then comes his handling of the actors. He has worked with both established actors, stars and non-actors—people who had never faced a camera in their lives. As we all know, he was much inspired by [Vittorio] De Sica, so he believed in the neo-realistic casting methods as well. I think both his choice and his use of actors was impeccable—another huge learning for filmmakers such as us.

Him being a polymath, if you look at his sketches of costume design and production design, you will see how everything came together in his mind like a jigsaw puzzle. That's a massive learning point for us—how to visualise a film in its totality and put it down on paper before going to the floor to shoot it. Ray is also a lesson in how to flourish and make world-class cinema while overcoming seemingly insurmountable hurdles and constraints. To someone like me, he is like a multistorey library, you know? You walk up one floor, you reach a department, you pull out a number of books from the shelves and everything you want to know about that department of filmmaking can be found in those books. You simply don't need to look elsewhere.

Ray has said that whodunits do not make for good cinema. For one, there's the long speech at the end, where the sleuth reveals who committed the crime and how. Moreover, there's the additional burden of keeping the identity of the perpetrator a mystery—not a very easy task, and often, one might argue, not 'fair game' in a visual medium. Ray made three detective films in his career, and two of these three cannot be called 'whodunits' in the strictest sense of the term. In making the Feluda films, how do you deal with the problems of making a cinematic whodunit?

I don't really agree with the generalised statement that whodunits do not make good cinema. I have seen great films that are whodunits, and also not-so-great thrillers that are not whodunits. I don't think it is the form that dictates the quality of the film—I would say it is the treatment that makes a film good or bad or passable or average, etc. Having said that, whodunits do pose a great challenge to filmmaking, because you need to keep giving these red herrings, and there's one perspective, one narrative, one timeline, which always demands manipulation. You can't show what actually happened. That exposition comes at the end. In certain cases, I love the whodunit structure. In others, I prefer the structure in which you make your revelations right at the beginning and the entire film then becomes about the chase. That's the more Hitchcockian style. As far as Feluda is concerned, I have tried to imbibe the spirit of the book in the structure. I know that that's a very difficult transformation—for instance, Ray himself changed the structure while making *Sonar Kella* and *Joy Baba Felunath*. But I am more classical in that sense. In terms of the treatment of Feluda, I adhered strictly to the books. Since the books are in a whodunit structure, I have tried to replicate that structure in the films as well. The reception to *Chinnomostar Obhishap* tells me that I have succeeded to a fair degree.

In bringing such iconic characters as Feluda, Topshe and Jatayu on screen, how does one balance the need to contemporise the story and

the setting (giving Feluda a cellphone, for instance) and the desire to keep it as close to the literary original as possible?

See, for me, the setting is a very cosmetic need—as long as it doesn't interfere with or intrude into the inner workings of the plot. In bringing these three characters to life, I have naturally chosen the stories that are my favourites. But even within these stories, I have decided to alternate between two different settings. Because I wanted to have the best of both worlds. I want to savour and sample Feluda in the period setting as well as in the contemporary setting. That's how I have decided to bring in the balance you speak of. I started with *Chinnomostar Obhishap*, which is set in a jungle. So it's relatively easier to execute a more period setting—the film was shot mostly in a jungle and a bungalow somewhere in the hinterlands. Whereas for *Joto Kando Kathmandute*, we stuck primarily to a contemporary setting, shooting in a city. More importantly, a city ravaged by an earthquake. It was impossible to recreate the tourist spots, the big landmarks, and the city in general to the pre-calamity visuals that one comes across in the book. And going forward, that is going to be our pattern for the subsequent films. And apart from some very superficial elements, such as having a cellphone or a certain cut, design or pattern of the costumes, or certain words and terms used in the dialogues, the spirit of Feluda remains the same across both settings. I would say it's an attempt to enjoy the best of both worlds while trying to honour the legacy of Feluda.

Do you think Ray's films can work outside the milieu and the period? For instance, will a Hindi Feluda film have the same charm as a Bengali one? Would *Mahanagar* be as widely accepted if it were set in today's Mumbai? With rampant corruption becoming more of a rule than an exception, will a *Shakha Proshakha* be able to deliver its message with the same impact today?

That's a pretty introspective question. I think my answer would be both yes and no. Because there are certain Ray films, certain stories, that are timeless. In the sense that the protagonists, the antagonists, their values and their principles are—how should I put it—time-agnostic, so to speak. Let's take the example of Maganlal, from *Joy Baba Felunath*. You may say that your chances of stumbling upon a man like Maganlal Meghraj have increased over the years. Or the conversation that happened at the dining table in *Shakha Proshakha* has become extinct, because nowadays everyone knows what is what, and black money and dishonesty is hardly a subject of discussion anymore. But having said that, I still see people around me refusing to budge from their principles and values, refusing to cower down under pressure, refusing to sell out. Resisting, protesting, standing up and fighting for what one feels is right, even going to the extent of avenging wrongdoings. These are human emotions and actions that are pretty universal, and in them we see the Feluda we know and love so much. And what's interesting is that we see these in a world that is far more polluted and corrupt than Ray's world. Perhaps Ray was witnessing a cusp, an inflection point, when things were just beginning to take a downward turn. A twilight— if one might call it that—to the sunset we are seeing now. This is perhaps why we see glimpses of that sunset in films such as *Seemabaddha* and *Shakha Proshakha*. But certain elements in his films are universal and timeless—mostly the ones that talk about the victory of good over evil, of right over wrong.

As for a Hindi Feluda, it is true that the linguistics, the ethical dilemmas, the milieu, the surroundings and so on and so forth may not be that effective, but if you set it in Bengal and make the film in Hindi, it might work. And if you make it in a period setting, obviously things become that much more effective. I mean, if we can have a period Byomkesh Bakshi for national television, why can't we have a period Feluda? Of course, making a Hindi Feluda in the contemporary setting could be a problem.

What are your two most favourite cinematic moments from *Sonar Kella* and *Joy Baba Felunath*?

For *Joy Baba Felunath*, undoubtedly it has to be the face-off between Feluda and Maganlal when they meet for the first time. The entire sequence is extremely cinematic—including the sequence that follows, in which Feluda sits on the ghats in a grave mood and vows to avenge Jatayu's harassment. For *Sonar Kella*, there are quite a few, but I would specifically mention the train sequence in which the trio makes a run through the desert on camelback, trying to catch the train. That one, leading to the entire Ramdeora sequence, leading to the antagonist's final retribution.

How important is it to get the 'look' of a character such as Feluda or Maganlal right?

Oh, for a book lover like me, it is of paramount importance. Even Satyajit Ray the filmmaker did not necessarily stick to the visuals of Satyajit Ray the illustrator and children's story writer, because the sketches that he made were tailored according to the actors that he cast and not the other way round. I, however, stuck to Satyajit Ray the illustrator. And if you look at the casting of Tota [Roy Chowdhury] and Kharaj [Mukherjee] as Feluda and Maganlal, respectively, you will find that they have a high degree of resemblance to the sketches of Ray. So, for me, at least, the look is of absolute importance, because the imagination, the detailing starts from that look. Once that is cracked, one starts thinking about the mannerisms, the way one talks, the athleticism (or, in the case of Maganlal, the lack of it), the persona, the charisma, so on and so forth. But to start off, if you are making a film about Feluda and Maganlal, then Feluda should look like Feluda and Maganlal should look like Maganlal.

What is your opinion of the quality of subtitles used in Satyajit Ray's films? Do you think non-Bengali viewers get as much of the essence of the films as they should? Or do you think that much is lost in translation?

A lot of it can be better. See, we have to understand that Satyajit Ray's hold over the Bengali ethos and fabric is so strong, his access and incision so deep, that it goes without saying that no matter how hard one tries, there will be some cultural allusions and references that will get lost in translation. It is very difficult to prevent that from happening. But at least to capture the spirit of a particular line of dialogue, or a particular word or a cultural reference, should be one's primary duty. And in that aspect, there are quite a few films where the subtitles could be much, much better. I think the non-Bengali viewers could have enjoyed these films even more than they already did.

Tinnu Anand

'Tinnu, I don't want you to feel like an outsider!'

Tinnu Anand assisted Satyajit Ray in five films—*Goopy Gyne Bagha Byne* (1969), *Aranyer Din Ratri* (1970), *Pratidwandi* (1970), *Seemabaddha* (1971) and *Ashani Sanket* (1973). In these five years, Anand—who had come from Bombay to learn the ropes from Ray—grew from being an 'outsider' to one of the most important members of Ray's unit. In this interview, he fondly reminisces the days he spent in the tutelage of his Manik-da.

Your father, Inder Raj Anand, was one of the most renowned writers in the Bombay film industry. And while there were a significant number of Bengalis in the industry at that time, Satyajit Ray himself chose to remain in Calcutta and make films there. You have mentioned that your father and Ray were good friends. How and where did they happen to meet? And how did you happen to become a protégé of Ray?

I think they met at an international film festival in Delhi, where Ray came as a jury member and my father was invited from Bombay. My father knew very renowned directors from all over the world. Federico Fellini was his close friend, and Arthur Knight, a famous film critic based in New York, was also a close friend of his. He had watched all of Ray's films and become fond of his work. On the other hand, Ray may have found my father very interesting, because when it came to the craft of filmmaking and the art of storytelling, my father was one of the most knowledgeable people around. And this helped them to be friends right from the very first meeting. He had an open invitation to our home for meals whenever he came to Bombay. In this way, not only Ray but his wife, too, had become very close with my father.

My father never talked about films at home, as he used to hate gossiping about the film industry. He never wanted his children to join the industry. One day, my brother—who used to study with the nephews and nieces of Nargis in a school in Colaba—came home, went prancing to my father, who was having a meeting with a journalist, and said, 'Do you know what happened today? Nargis got married to Sunil Dutt!'

As expected, the very next day, the news of Nargis marrying Sunil Dutt became the headline of the day, thanks to my brother's lack of discretion. That very day, my father packed his bags and flew to Jaipur to admit my brother into one of the schools there. He met the principal of that school, Mr Gibson, and said, 'I don't want my children to be in the film industry. I want them to study here and stay away from films, film studios and film gossip.' This is how our disconnection with the film industry began. But as you know, we finally ended up in the film industry—both my brother and I.

My father had realised quite early on that I was not interested in academics. So he called me one day and said, 'I've bought some prime land on the beach in Madras. Why don't you study food and catering for some time and then open a hotel there?' He promised to give me his fully convertible car if I agreed. So I took the car and went to study catering. On his way to work, he used to see the car parked in front of the college and feel happy with the way I had turned out—until one day, the principal of the college called my father to his office and complained to him that my attendance was almost zero.

After wasting my father's precious time and money on that food and catering college for several months, when I dropped out, my father asked me, 'What do you want to do, son?' I immediately replied, 'I want to join films as a director.' He was crestfallen, but when he recovered from the shock, he said, 'Whom should I contact? I have Satyajit Ray in Bengal and Raj Kapoor, with whom I have already worked and you know him very well.' I didn't want to join Raj Kapoor as he was very close to us and I said that I wanted to join Federico Fellini. So my father wrote a letter to Fellini. Though Fellini accepted my father's proposal, there was another problem, as Fellini didn't speak English and communicated with his cast and crew only in Italian. He asked me to learn Italian and then go to him. My father then took me to language classes, but I didn't want to study any further and eventually said, 'I want to learn from Satyajit Ray.' So that's how I joined Ray.

I'll share a great incident with Ray. When I landed up in Calcutta to assist him, my father called me back as he had got a letter from Ray while I was on the train journey, and the letter said, 'Please ask your son not to come to Calcutta for this film because my producer can't afford a seventh assistant. I have six assistants already. I have huge sets, I have planned shooting in Rajasthan. That's why please ask your son to wait for another eleven months; I will start a new film and will take him under my wing.' As *Goopy Gyne Bagha Byne* was the most expensive Bengali film of that time, the budget was Rs 5 lakh. My father asked me to buy a ticket and come back after paying a courtesy visit to Ray as I was already in Calcutta. When I called him to introduce myself, his first words were, '*Ore baba, tumi ki eshe gecho* (Have you come already)?' And I said, 'Yes, sir. The letter you sent to my father reached him late. And by the time it did, I was already on my way to Calcutta.' Then he asked me, 'What time do you wake up in the morning?' I said, 'Whatever time you will ask me to come, I will come.' It was winter and Calcutta in winter is extremely beautiful. He asked me to come at eight in the morning. I was there at the steps of his house by 7.30 a.m. but rang the bell only at 8 o'clock. He opened the door himself and I was shocked. Ray opening the door of his house himself! I looked up at the 6-foot-4 magnificent personality wearing a pristine starched kurta-pyjama and he asked me to come in and hollered in Bengali, '*Tinnu esheche, ektu cha ene dao* (Tinnu has come. Please bring him a cup of tea).' He asked me to wait for another twenty minutes and have my tea as he was in the middle of something. The tea came, I finished it and kept waiting. As I was waiting, I wondered, 'Mr Ray, why did you have to call me so early if you were so busy? I could have slept for another twenty minutes on this lovely cold morning.'

He was typing something on his typewriter and just after twenty or twenty-five minutes, he got up and gave me six sheets of stapled papers. I looked up and asked him, 'Manik-da?' He replied, 'Tinnu, I woke up at 4.30 a.m. and typed out the synopsis of my story *Goopy Gyne Bagha Byne* in English because I don't want you to feel like an outsider, not knowing what I am doing on the sets.' I said, 'But sir, you asked me to go back!' He again said, 'No, no, now that you are here, you hang on, join my unit. You can be an observer first, as there are already six assistants. And Inder has told me that you would be paying for all of your expenses. And I have decided to look after your food. Don't worry, you are joining the unit today.'

You know, even after all these years, whenever I am alone or feeling low, the thought of those six pages gives me the warmth that Ray exuded on that cold winter morning in Calcutta.

What was the experience of shooting with him like?

It was just fantastic. We went to Rajasthan for a shoot. My college was in Ajmer and all the sons of the maharajas had been my classmates. The Maharaja of Jaisalmer himself used to come on horseback to see the shooting, and he asked me to call him if anything was required. We were shooting this one scene on top of a hill, in which the camera was looking down on two hundred camels. We were to give them instructions to make the camels stand up and then make them sit down again. The megaphone was under the senior Bengali assistant and he was trying to give all the instructions in Bengali. Instead of standing up, the camels would sit down or vice versa, and it was all a big mess. This went on for a long time, and we were losing light, so Ray called me, gave me the megaphone and asked me to pass on the instructions to the camel riders in Hindi. And I became his right-hand man from that day onwards, because I became an important part of the unit instead of just being an observer. And whenever he used to go from his house in the car, be it to the studio or to any other place, I used to sit between the driver and Ray. By the time he announced *Ashani Sanket*, I had already decided to come back to Bombay and start my work independently as a director. It was then that he wrote a letter to my father saying, 'Inder, I am starting a film. Tinnu has told me that he wants to do something in Bombay. Just like five years ago you had requested me to take your son in my unit, I am now requesting you to give your son to me as he has become such an important member of my unit—I will feel lost if he leaves. So let him extend his stay in Calcutta by a few more months and do one last film with me.' I went back for *Ashani Sanket*. Till date, that one letter is the biggest feather I have in my cap.

In subsequent years, it was only you from Ray's regular unit who went on to became a successful filmmaker in Bombay. Why do you think that must have happened?

This question has been asked before. Maybe the other assistants didn't have the luck I did because I belonged to the Bombay film industry and my father was a well-known writer. We were very close to the Kapoor family. I knew Rishi Kapoor and Randhir Kapoor quite well. In this industry, they always say you need a lot of luck riding behind you. I would say I was plain and simple lucky.

You have done quite well for yourself in the acting department as well. Did you always have the ambition to become an actor?

Oh, I always wanted to feature somehow as an actor in Ray's films. I used to ask him if I could stand somewhere in the background of a shot.

And he always used to refuse, saying, 'No, you stand here.' I was even dying to give a passing shot. I wanted to be an actor or a passer-by or a junior artist—*anything*—in a Satyajit Ray film. But he never allowed me. Except this one time when he called me up in the morning and asked me to wear a kurta-pyjama and come to the set. When I asked why, he said he had cast me in *Seemabaddha*. And I started jumping in joy and said to the whole unit, 'See, he has finally recognised me as an actor and today I am acting.' And he told Soumendu [Roy, Ray's cinematographer], 'Let's see what he does today.'

I went there and Manik-da said, 'The sequence is this—we are shooting an ad film and the director of the film is introduced in the scene to Barun Chanda, the protagonist. You will get up and shake his hand.' I was very excited, but then I saw the camera being placed behind me. I assumed that he was taking a general long shot kind of a thing and the camera would also come at the front. But what was finally shot was my long, flowing hair from behind. Then he said, 'Cut and pack up.' And I went to ask him whether he would take the shot from the front, and he replied, 'No, no, I don't need it, as we will cut to another shot in the factory.' And from that day onwards, the whole unit used to pull my leg and tease me by saying, 'He came from Bombay to become an actor and Manik-da took his back shot!'

What was Ray's reaction to the films you directed?

I don't think he saw many of my films. I am sure he had seen *Duniya Meri Jeb Mein*, which he must have hated! But I think he saw *Kaalia* and he may have found it interesting. I have always believed that I went to a university to study, not to become a professor. I wanted to be a student and learn under the shade of a tree. Ray was the university and I was fortunate enough to be learning from him. I may not have made films like the ones he did, but I think *Main Azaad Hoon* is very close to a Ray film. I am extremely proud of this film and I can proudly say that everything I learnt from Satyajit Ray I tried to put in this film.

Those who have studied Ray's life and his works have come to realise that he never really made enough money from his films. As someone who knew him closely for so many years, had you ever seen him worry about money? Did the lack of funds ever affect his filmmaking or his choice of films in any way?

Speaking about the choice of films, let me tell you a very interesting story about *Goopy Gyne Bagha Byne*. Raj Kapoor wanted to launch his son Dabboo [Randhir Kapoor] as a hero, and he was keen that Manik-da make a film under the RK banner. The finances were unlimited and Manik-da was allowed to make any kind of film. Raj Kapoor sent tickets to Manik-da and Boudi [his wife, Bijoya Ray] and invited them to his daughter's wedding. And by that time, Manik-da had lost all hope of getting financing for *Goopy Gyne Bagha Byne*. It was a highly ambitious project and he had worked hard on it as he wanted to make the film for his son. But even his regular producer, R.D. Bansal, had turned him down. And that film could only have been made in Bengali, as it had Bengali songs and Bengali cultural references in it.

But my feeling was that he would have accepted Mr Kapoor's offer of financing *Goopy Gyne Bagha Byne*, which was why he attended the wedding. But as they say, when you lose all hope, Lady Luck comes to your rescue. In the middle of the wedding, Ray received an unexpected phone call from Asim Dutta, from Calcutta. Mr Dutta wanted to finance the film and asked Ray to contact him after reaching Calcutta. Ray disconnected the phone call, went back to the wedding and refused Mr Kapoor by saying, 'Let me think it over, Raj', and returned to Calcutta. And that's how *Goopy Gyne Bagha Byne* was made.

Vikramaditya Motwane

'Satyajit Ray was India's greatest complete filmmaker'

Vikramaditya Motwane began his career assisting filmmaker Sanjay Leela Bhansali and soon moved on to making his own films. His films bring in fresh ideas, innovative treatments and have a unique storytelling signature. The subjects in his filmography so far have been a commendable mix of strained relationships, solitude, vigilantism and the struggle for freedom and survival. In this interview, Motwane speaks about the lessons present-day filmmakers could learn from the cinema of Satyajit Ray.

How and when were you introduced to the cinema of Satyajit Ray? And how was your experience of watching a Ray film for the first time?

I think it was in 2000 when I watched my first Satyajit Ray film. I was assisting Sanjay Leela Bhansali on *Devdas* and we had gone to the National Film Archives for research and reference. The film that we watched was *Devi*. Although it didn't have any subtitles, I was bowled over by the power of the film. Perhaps one of the most enchanting things about Ray is that he shows so many things in a non-dialogic way and it still connects with you emotionally. Before that, I had gone through a phase in the 1990s when I had this angst about the Indian film industry as I hadn't found anything interesting to watch—nothing without the influence of Bollywood, at least. And nothing was even close to the level of the incredible work that was being done in other parts of the world. In the middle of all this cacophony, I found Ray refreshing and mature.

Your mother is from Bengal. Was there any introduction to Ray's films at home?

Getting a Ray film at that time wasn't as easy as it is now. There were no DVDs. As it usually happens, being a son to a Bengali mother and a Sindhi father, I used to converse in English. And Ray's films didn't have subtitles at that time. So I discovered the world of Ray as a movie buff all on my own. I went back to Calcutta to look at his immortal creations. Later, when I became a filmmaker myself, I went back to Ray's films in a completely different capacity. As I was shooting *Lootera* in Bengal and it was about the zamindars and the ambience of the Bengali rajbari (palace), the reference points automatically came from *Devi*, *Charulata* and *Jalsaghar*.

In an interview with Shyam Benegal, Ray once stated that he loved the visual aspects of opulence, and loved recreating opulence on screen as a filmmaker, as a storyteller. You have been an assistant to Sanjay Leela Bhansali, who also has this love for grandeur and opulence. Even in your films, specifically in *Lootera*, you have tried to show grandeur in various frames. What is it about opulence that attracts filmmakers?

Well, we are all fond of captivating visuals, aren't we? I think this fascination that filmmakers have is purely from a visual perspective. There is something about showing opulence, wonderful rich frames on the big screen. It looks very attractive and Sanjay likes this too. In *Lootera*, the opulence in the frames was used to show the lack of opulence in the characters—like a contrast. In *Jalsaghar*, for instance, Ray has used this crumbling opulence to juxtapose the mind of the film's protagonist and his inevitable doom against what was once a glorious past.

Most of Ray's films were adaptations. Your film *Lootera* can also be considered a partial adaptation of O. Henry's short story 'The Last Leaf'. Now, we hear so much talk and lament about the lack of good content for our films, while the truth is that we are sitting atop a treasure trove of stories from Indian literature. And why just Indian literature—we have stories from all over the world. If Ray could do it, if you are doing it, why can't others?

Ray himself was from Bengal and adapted various Bengali stories from that particular milieu to make Bengali films. But our generation is completely different, as we have grown up in the cities and gone to English-medium schools. We had a huge disconnect with these beautiful stories—our loss, really. Though we want to make those stories, we don't know how we will bring them to the popular culture from the villages, small towns of India. How do we read these books? How will we tell these stories? I don't even know whether these new stories are written or published properly. Today, things are different. Stories in non-English languages hardly reach the mainstream readership at a national level. I don't know how, but we need to be able to make that connection all over again. It's quite possible to do that in Bengal, as every Bengali knows the Bengali language. Even in a state such as Gujarat this is true—but not in Mumbai, as not everyone in Mumbai knows, speaks or reads Marathi. So I would say the culture of adaptation is very specific to Bengal, as there is a culture of reading literature in the local language. And although general levels of readership may have come down, they are still very well aware of Sharatchandra Chattopadhyay, Bankimchandra Chattopadhyay and Sunil Gangopadhyay.

If that is the true nature of the problem, can it not be remedied by something as simple as modern-day filmmakers reading more Indian literature?

It is absolutely possible. I want to read more English and, of course, vernacular literature. As a filmmaker on the lookout for a good story, what can be better than that? But, of course, it also depends on whether the story attracts you.

You and several other contemporary filmmakers have been in a long-standing and rather bitter battle with the gatekeepers of cinema censorship in India. Do you think films such as *Devi*, *Ghare Baire* and *Hirak Rajar Deshe* would have even seen the light of day in the current sociopolitical scenario in India?

Even a film such as *Mother India* would have faced a lot of trouble today. Nowadays, the climate has become so sensitive that you are being told what you can do and what you cannot. And more often than not, these things are being dictated to you by lawyers. They literally tell you— you can go here, you can't go there, as there will be trouble. You can say this but you can't say that. That is the sad state of affairs. The job of the certification board is to certify the film, to give it an age-specific rating and not to do moral-policing of the film and its audiences in the theatres. The same thing is happening with OTT. We are being told we can't make our films and shows in a certain way because families sit down to watch it together. Well, that's not our problem. It is the job of the parents to take care of what their children are watching. That is not the job of the certifying board. The classic films of the past, which have become the cultural milestones of our cinema, would have gone through a lot of hurdles to get past the censors of today.

Filmmakers such as you and Ray have both raised your voices against the system. You in films such as *Bhavesh Joshi Superhero*, and Ray in his City trilogy. While Ray ended all three films on a note of

hopelessness, you seem to be rather hopeful that times will change. What gives you this hope?

Hope springs eternal. Perhaps because of my upbringing and exposure to the cinema of the 1980s and the 1990s, I believe that the justice system must finally win. That justice has to prevail. We all know about the ruthlessness of the system but even in *Bhavesh Joshi*, a vigilante has to go through the system of justice. At the end of the Batman movies, we see the same thing. It may not even be hope grounded in reality, but a thematic hope on screen can also make you feel a little better. If the justice system works, there is hope for all of us. Otherwise, what are we all living for? It is very scary to confront the failure of the justice system and the subsequent consequences.

The truth is that Ray never quite earned much of a living by making films. It has been said that had it not been for his books, which became immensely popular, he would perhaps have been in financial straits. As a modern-day filmmaker, do you make films for a living or do you just want to vent your creativity, no matter what it takes? Do you ever feel the need to create something that can sell well?

You see, as I have grown up in a privileged background, I didn't even have to think about that. I got a lot of support from my parents, my wife. Though I struggled to pay rent and other things, I always had people who had my back. At all times, I had a plan A and a plan B. If things went wrong, I had my back-up ready, as I had learnt both photography and editing. So I could have become an editor or a photographer. Luckily, my filmmaking career has come to a state where I will get work. If I don't, I may retire and write books. As I am growing older, I am also realising that your film has to be able to bring at least the invested money back. No one should have to lose their money because of what you did. And I think none of my films have ever lost money. It took time, but even my first film, *Udaan*, is profitable now. *Lootera* was profitable and so was *Trapped*.

As a filmmaker, do you sometimes have to compromise on your creative output due to the interference of people who write the cheque?

No, I've never had to do that. And I have always considered myself lucky on that front, because I have always got the freedom from the producers to do whatever I wanted to. The inputs, if any, have always been cooperative. And as I have matured as a filmmaker and as a human being, I have come to realise that it isn't always true that interference is a bad thing. Or that a suggestion that questions your vision is necessarily counterproductive. Fifteen years ago, I would have fought for my vision tooth and nail, but I won't do it today. I will try to assess the suggestion on its merit. I have understood that it is not personal and that there's always room for a reasonable discussion.

What do you think present-day filmmakers can learn from the cinema of Ray?

Oh, he was the master of his game! He wrote, composed the score and directed his films. He even handled the camera. He was a complete filmmaker. In fact, he was India's greatest complete filmmaker. The economy of dialogue in his films was phenomenal, to say the least. The way he has used the craft of filmmaking, the sound, the cut in a shot—all of that should be looked up to. The other day, I was watching the opening scene of *Devi* and I was once again amazed by the way he established the zamindar and his family in that one single shot. He opened with the making of the idol, and then the fireworks, and then the family. You immediately understand who is who and what is what. Without any confusion whatsoever. And all of this has been done without the use of dialogue. The density of information in that cut of that ritual sacrifice without any utterance of dialogue was supremely artistic. And he did this throughout his life. [Francis Ford] Coppola once said that the talkies came into cinema too early. We never had the time to explore cinema as a medium without the spoken word. When the talkies came, we began to make the same kind of films over and over again. The plays that we used to stage, we started putting them on screen. And that has been the biggest tragedy—to lose the opportunity to explore cinema as a pure art form. Ray is the filmmaker who managed to subvert that by making cinema for the sake of making cinema, without having any dependence on dialogue. He was an extremely brave filmmaker. Also, if you think about it, he wasn't making any esoteric stuff at all. All his films were very accessible, very universal—they touch your heart. This is the one thing we should learn from him.

Acknowledgements

Abhishek Majumdar
Ajitha G.S.
Amish Mulmi
Aniket Chattopadhyay
Ankan Roy
Aparna Sen
Arjun Raj Gaind
Arup Kumar Dey
Asit Baran Chattopadhyay
Avik Chanda
Ayan Chatterjee
Bappadittya Jana
Baradwaj Rangan
Barun Chanda
Basav Biradar
Chandak Sengoopta
Devansh Sharma
Dhritiman Chaterji
Emon Chattopadhyay
Ishaan Chattopadhyay

Jai Arjun Singh
Kanwal Kohli
Karthika V.K.
M.K. Raghavendra
Madhabi Mukherjee
Mamata Shankar
Nardeep Singh Dahiya
Nasreen Munni Kabir
Neeraj Ghaywan
Oliver Craske
Pinaki De
Pradip Mukherjee
Pritsikha Anil
R. Ajith Kumar
Riddhi Goswami
Rohini Nair
Sandip Ray
Satyaki Ghosh
Saugata Bhattacharya
Saurabh Garge

Shamya Dasgupta
Sharmila Tagore
Shatrughan Pandey
Shyam Benegal
Siddhartha Chatterjee
Sikha Chattopadhyay
Sonia Madan
Srijit Mukherji
Srinanda Mukherjee
Sweta Padma Gantayat
Swetha Ramakrishnan
Syamantak Chattopadhyay
Tinnu Anand
Turni Dhar
Ujjaini Dasgupta
Vikramaditya Motwane
Vipin Vijay
Vish Dhamija

www.ingramcontent.com/pod-product-compliance
Lightning Source LLC
Chambersburg PA
CBHW070503160726
48003CB00004B/1403